METHODS OF TEACHING RURAL SOCIOLOGY

METHODS OF TEACHING RURAL SOCIOLOGY

By

L. Venkateswara Reddy
M.A., M.Ed., (Ph.D.)
Vice-Principal
Chaitanya College of Education
Markapur
Prakasam Distt., A.P.

M.Lakshmi Narayana
M.Sc., M.Ed.,
Lecturer
Vinukonda B.Ed., College
Vinukonda, Narasaraopet
Guntur, Distt. A.P.

General Editor

Dr. Digumarti Bhaskara Rao
M.Sc., M.A., M.A., M.Ed., Ph.D.
Reader
R.V.R. College of Education
Srinivasa Nagar Colony
Guntur–522 006
Andhra Pradesh
India

DISCOVERY PUBLISHING HOUSE
NEW DELHI-110002

First Published - 2004
Reprinted - 2015

ISBN: 978-81-7141-811-4

Methods of Teaching Rural Sociology

Published by:
DISCOVERY PUBLISHING HOUSE PVT. LTD.
4383/4B, Ansari Road, Darya Ganj
New Delhi-110 002 (India)
Phone: +91-11-23279245, 43596064-65
Fax: +91-11-23253475
E-mail: discoverypublishinghouse@gmail.com
sales@discoverypublishinggroup.com
web: www.discoverypublishinggroup.com

Printed at:
Infinity Imaging Systems
Delhi

Foreword

Teacher education is quantitatively marching ahead towards quality education. The central and state governments through the NCTE and the Directorates of School/Higher Education are rendering their legitimate service in improving the quality of teacher education by formulating and implementing various academic policies and educational programmes. Along with these policies and programmes, the teacher educators and the prospective teachers teaching and studying in teacher education institutions need good curriculum and quality books.

The methods of teaching each subject play a pivotal role in enhancing the efficiency of their practitioners. Identifying the very importance of the methods of teaching and the quality of books, a series of books on the methods of teaching different subjects have been developed by experienced teacher educators for the benefit of teachers in making in teacher education institutions. Thanks to the authors.

Valuable suggestions for the improvement of these books are welcome from fellow teacher educators, prospective teachers and other academicians involved in the arena of teacher education.

The authors and the editor dedicate this series of books on the methodology of teaching to Mr. Tilak Raj Wasan, Proprietor, Discovery Publishing House, New Delhi, for taking up this commendable task of publication to meet the felt needs of teacher education faculty and clientele.

Dr. Digumarti Bhaskara Rao

Research Director in Education

Nagarjuna University

br_digumarti@rediffmail.com

Preface

The movement of modern education in India is almost two century old. It has come of age now. Over the decades, great educationists have contributed towards the development and evolution of education, as a discipline. Thus, education in India has been enriched a lot.

As a result, the Indian education system can be placed at par with any advanced education system in the modern world. In fact, education is a vast sea and Teachers' Training is a stream in it. So, it makes it essential that the responsibilities of the faculty members are focused on the task of providing better training to the future teachers, for their better learning and proper development. And this responsible exercise can only be undertaken, if the trainers are equipped with all the needed skill and knowledge of the subject, they are supposed to teach. Hence, it becomes essential for making adequate provisions, for each course to the teacher-trainees. Methods of Teaching are very important for the successful training of teachers and for their career in future.

In order to provide all related material in one cover, here is this book, on this important subject. Of course there are several books on the subject in the market, but, every book has its own style and way of presentation. Similarly, the present one, too has its own merits and advantages.

During the course of the preparation of this book, the undersigned has done his best for the accomplishment of the job. He would be pleased and feel contented, if this book is acknowledged, as a textbook and a reference tool for the teachers and students, alike.

Author

Contents

Foreword

Preface

1. Introduction 1

2. History 8

The Old Setup
The Classification
Rural vs. Urban
Factors at Work
Adverse Situation
Glimpses of Life
Setup Infrastructure
Social Bonds
Caste Factors

3. Evolution and Development 34

The Beginning
Scope and Sphere
The Controversies
Basic Issues
Academic Aspects
Progressive Rural Society

4. People in Villages 45

Rural Population
Life Style
Family Life
Wave of Urbanisation
Trends of Social Change

5. **Life in Rural Belts** 57
Wave of Reforms
Wave of Change
The Settlements
Important Features

6. **The Infrastructure** 64
Landless People
Small Cultivators
Main Problems
Price Factor
The Livestock
The Habitation

7. **Rural Economy** 88
Agriculture Supreme
Techniques of Production
Cultivation Lands
The Have-nots
Political Factors
Basic Problems and Issues
Targets for Welfare
Role of Caste System

8. **Agricultural Economy** 110
Reform in Land System
Farms and Produces
Village Industry
In-house Industry

9. **Agricultural Products** 128
Fundamental Issues
Schemes and Plans
Progress at Fast Pace
Hard Facts

10. **Farm Sector** 150
Background
New Trends
Means of Cultivation
The Prosperity
Labour Problem
Sale of Produces

11. Role of Education **188**
Basic Issues
Fiscal Problems
Factors at Work
Cultural Factors

12. Teaching Methods **205**
Assignment Method
Project Method
Problem Method
Source Method
Unit Method
Laboratory Method
Dramatic Method

13. Teaching Approaches **239**
Different Approaches
Concentric Approach
Topical Approach
Unit Approach
Material for Reading
Other Areas

14. Teaching Techniques **257**
Devices and Maxims
Different Techniques
Question-answer Technique
Illustration Technique

15. Pace of Progress **275**
Factors at Work
The Development
Various Trends
Social Organisation

16. New Trends **297**
Main Issues
The Response
Social Setup
Structural Setup

17. Social Revolution **313**
Social Elements
The Background
Industrial Boom
Social Change in Effect
The Traditions
Style of Life
The Departure
True Culture

Additional Reading **333**

1 Introduction

For successful Civics teaching, it is essential to know how the pupil learns and by which methods he learns. The teaching methods or strategies are based on certain principles. Therefore it is essential for a Civics teacher to follow these general or basic principles while teaching:

Principle of motivation. Motivation is the method which creates pupils' interest in the content. The principle of motivation is to create interest in the pupils for acquiring knowledge. It is a psychological fact that the process of teaching and learning goes on smoothly when a teacher motivates the pupils to acquire knowledge. In the absence of proper motivation, the pupil takes no interest in memorizing the contents. Hence the Civics teacher should follow the principle of motivation. How are the pupils prepared to gain knowledge? For this, the civics teacher should use the pupils' innate tendencies, for example, as the pupil is very much curious to know about the new things regarding environment, the civics teacher should create such situations in which a curiosity is aroused in the pupils regarding the acquisition of the latest knowledge concerning the novel things and contents about the social environment.

Principle of activity of learning by doing. The principle of learning by doing means that the civics teacher should create activity in each type of lesson. This activity is of two types- (1) Physical, and (2) Mental. The physical activity means to activate in the body organs of the pupils, while the mental activity means to activate the sense organs of the pupils. Temperamentally each pupil is active. This activity should be in accordance with his nature. According to McDougall, every child has inborn instinct of construction due to which he remains busy all the time in doing some or the other activity. The more the activity of the pupil, more would be the teaching-learning process. Therefore, for a successful teaching of civics the teacher should make use of the pupil's instinct of construction. The maximum use of the pupils' basic instinct at the time of teaching will make the teaching effective to the maximum: Both, the physical activity and mental activity depend upon each other. As the pupil's mind and body work together, he shows more interest in learning something new. The eminent educationist Froebel has called this principle learning-by-doing. The principle of "learning by doing" does not mean that the pupil himself should only be active for learning by doing, but it also means that the teacher should also make the pupil active for learning the new things. For example, while teaching civics the pupils can learn the historical facts and incidents concerning citizenship very conveniently if these are shown in the form of Plays as compared to the learning from books. Good feelings arise in the pupils by keeping themselves active.

Thus, the principle of activity should be used in each class and in all the school activities, such as — school council, declamations contest, various societies, meetings, conferences, clubs and games, etc. This will develop social habits in the pupils and they will get proper and sufficient training of social service.

Principle of interest. The principle of interest means to create interest of the pupils in the subject-matter in order to make the teaching useful and effective. When the interest of the pupil is created in the subject-matter, he acquires knowledge very conveniently. He faces no difficulty while studying. There are various methods for creating interest of the pupil for example— (1) Curiosity of the pupil should be aroused and the objective of the, lesson should be made clear. The clarity of the objective to both the pupil and the teacher creates the interest of the pupil for the lesson, (2) The civics teacher should establish a relationship of contents with the pupils' activities and objectives, (3) The principle of learning by doing should be followed, (4) The teaching should be linked with the active life of the pupil.

Principle of linking with life. The pupil at each level has his own world. As he grows, he begins to imagine his world in his own way. He shows his interest in those subjects or activities which are linked to his personal world. Keeping in view this thing, the activity and the subject should be linked with the learner's life. The principle of linking with life means relating the subject-matter with the life of the pupils. The pupils show interest in learning those things only which are expected to be used in their future life. They learn rapidly and conveniently those things which get related to their life. According to Ryburn, "Life is a continuous experience. Everything we do is linked up with what has gone before and with what comes afterwards." Out of childs daily experiences, only those get stabilized which have some relationship with his or her previous experiences. Therefore, it is necessary to relate the new experiences with previous experiences. After a relationship between new and old experiences, the new experiences or knowledge become a part of the pupil's life.

Principle of definite aim. Every lesson must have some definite aim or objective. In the absence of an objective, the teacher is like a boatman who has no knowledge of his aim and the pupil is like an oarless boat which is sailing in the sea-waves blindly. Therefore, there must be some definite, clear and completely defined objectives in order to make the lesson interesting and impressive. The objectives and the teaching methods are closely related. Every teaching method is based on some objective. The teaching method should be used according to the objective. For example, if our objective is the creation of the traits of good citizen, then its method would be entirely different from that method which has an objective of teaching a poem to the pupils. Full knowledge about the objective provides success to the teacher in his teaching task and the interest of the pupils is created in the lesson.

Principle of recognizing individual differences. Psychological researches have proved that the pupils are not alike in intelligence, nature, ability, interest, potentialities and needs. Each pupil is not at the same level. In order to develop all the pupils for equal opportunities, the teacher should impart proper guidance to the pupils, sympathy should be shared with the abnormal pupils, and in order to bring the mentally retarded and backward pupils to the Formal level, affectionate behaviour should be exhibited. Thus the teacher should maximize the development of all the pupils on the basis of individual differences.

Principle of selection. There is a close relationship between the contents and the objectives of education. The contents are selected according to the objectives. Since the human being appeared on this Earth, he has collected huge and complex knowledge. If a teacher wishes to impart the knowledge to the pupils without considering any definite objective of education, it would be a serious mistake. Some things are essential and some are non-essential. The non-essential things confuse the pupils. Hence, the teacher should select only those facts which the pupils can understand in order to achieve some definite objective. He should select what and how much is to be taught to the class. He should select the content according to the definite, clear and predefined objective. This benefits both the teacher and the pupils. The teacher develops the lesson successfully and the pupils acquire knowledge conveniently.

Principle of planning. The teacher should ascertain the teaching sequence and the lesson-plan should be prepared after proper planning. This enables him to solve every problem concerning teaching. He should decide how much cooperation of the pupils he can seek in order to solve a problem with the help of which method and at what stage before preparing a lesson plan. A problem may arise at the time of teaching which had never been imagined. In such a situation, a teacher should solve the problem immediately in accordance with his ability.

9. ***Principle of division.*** The subject-matter should be divided into some units for presenting it in certain order. The division of the content should be followed by the presentation in such a manner that each unit should seem to be complete in itself. One unit should create curiosity for other unit. By presenting the contents after dividing it into units, the lesson becomes very easy for the pupils. They acquire knowledge easily without any difficulty. By not doing so, the lesson becomes complicated and the pupils fail to understand anything. Hence, for a successful

teaching of civics the division of the lesson into an order of units or steps is necessary.

Principle of revision. Whatever subject-matter is taught to the pupils, it should be revised by them. Revision is very much essential in learning. Without experiments and revision, everything is forgotten. Therefore, the acquired knowledge should be revised by the pupils not only immediately, but also it should be used repeatedly. The frequency of the revisions depends upon the nature of the lesson. Hence, the more difficult, the lesson is more its revisions should occur.

Principle of creation and recreation. Activities are carried over by the pupils which are recreational and which can develop the creative power of the pupils. This will create interest in the pupils regarding the teaching activity without any fear of the teacher and the school. They will try for new innovations. They will have an opportunity of expressing creative activities. The principle of recreation is very essential for successful teaching. In civics so many teaching methods have been developed which are based on the principles of creation and recreation or learning by play-way.

Principle of democratic dealing. While teaching civics the teacher should adopt democratic attitude with the pupils. He should not be dictatorial. Dictatorship instigates the pupil's for revolt. In a democratic set-up, every pupil is considered as a holy and valuable member of the society. He gets maximum opportunities for developing his self-thinking and independent expression in order to develop his personality. As the modern age is democratic the teacher should adopt democratic attitudes for the pupils. It means the development of the lesson with the help and the cooperation of the pupils. The teacher should ask maximum questions and the pupils should be allowed to remove their doubts. This creates the habit of thinking independently and the pupils develop self-confidence, self-esteem and self-respect, etc.

These psychological principles are used for making the learning process effective. These principles are as follows :

Principle of motivation and interest. The motivation and the interest have been considered most important in the teaching-learning process. Both the teacher and the learner should work with interest and motivation.

Principle of recreation. If the pupil feels fatigue in the class it creates boredom in the pupil and he shows disinterest in the task. Hence, the principle of recreation should be followed in the class.

Principle of repetition and exercise. The process of forgetting starts due to the disuse of the acquired knowledge. Hence, repetition and exercise should be followed in the class daily.

Principle of encouraging creativity & self-expression. To encourage the creativity and self-expression is the duty of the teacher. He should develop the habit of innovations in the pupils. The pupils should be capable of presenting their views and attitudes.

Principle of remedial teaching. If there are errors in the pupils and the teaching activities, the teacher should identify these errors and provide remedy to his erroneous teaching activities. This task is not so easy. The teacher has to overcome many obstructions.

Principle of sympathy and cooperation. If a teacher exhibits sufficient sympathy for pupils and contributes in overcoming their difficulties, he can be a good guide to the pupils.

Principle of reinforcement. The term 'reinforcement' is concerned with making the learning process effective. In teaching process, the reinforcement is the utilization or presentation or removal of such stimuli that the possibilities of recurrence of any response increases. For example, if a teacher gives some reward to the pupils for correct answers, the possibilities of the similar behaviour from the pupils increase.

1. Describe the general principles of civics teaching.
2. 'In teaching, interest is the main word.' Throw light on the principles of creating interest in the pupils while teaching civics.
3. What is the importance of activity in civics teaching?

4. What do you mean by the principles of teaching? Describe general and psychological principles of teaching civics.

5. How are the general principles of teaching helpful in teaching civics? Support your answer with proper examples.

6. What do you mean by the psychological principles of teaching? Explain briefly various principles useful in teaching-learning in civics.

7. What is meant by psychological principles of teaching? Explain the implications of such principles in civics.

2

History

After having surveyed the chief characteristic differences between the rural and urban segments of social life, we will now proceed to analyse the structural pattern of the rural society since it provides the matrix within which the whole drama of rural life is unfolded.

The village is the unit of the rural society. It is the theatre wherein the quantum of rural life unfolds itself and functions.

Like every social phenomenon the village is an historical category. The emergence of the village at a certain stage in the evolution of the life of man, its further growth and development in subsequent periods of human history, the varied structural changes it experienced during thousands of years of its existence, the rapid and basic transformation it has undergone during the last hundred and fifty years since the Industrial Revolution—all these constitute a very fascinating and challenging study.

The rise of the village is bound up with the rise of agricultural economy in history. The emergence of the village signified that man passed from the nomadic mode of collective life to the settled one. This was basically due to the improvement of tools of production which made agriculture and hence settled life on a fixed territorial zone possible and necessary.

How humanity, in different parts of the world, passed from the nomadic hunting and food gathering stage to that based on *roving hoe* agriculture and thereafter, on settled plough agriculture carried on by means of draft animals, has been one of the most difficult and complex problems in the field of social research.

With the invention of the plough, man could develop stable agriculture, the basic source of assured food supply. Man's nomadic mode of life ceased. No longer men roamed in herds from place to place in search of means of subsistence. They settled on a definite territory and organized villages based on agricultural economy. Agrarian communities with villages as their fixed habitation and agriculture as their main occupation came into existence. This event marked a landmark in the history of mankind, inaugurating a higher phase of social existence. Agriculture assured the community, for the first time, a relatively stable food supply in contrast to previous stages of social life. While food supply derived from, such sources as hunting, fishing, fruit gathering and migratory hoe agriculture had always been insufficient and precarious, grain and other types of food products derived from plough agriculture could be counted upon and also be stored for use in periods of emergencies, thereby assuring relative food security for the future.

In the agricultural phase the struggle for existence became relatively less acute for man. Further, at a certain stage of the development of agricultural economy, due to the greater productivity of agriculture, a section of the community could be liberated from the necessity of participating in food production and could therefore concentrate on secondary industrial or ideological activity. This gave momentum to the growth of technology, arts, sciences and philosophy. It also brought about, though slowly, the significant transition in the social organization of humanity, from an organization founded on kinship and clan to that based on territorial ties. With the development of agriculture at a certain level, mankind took a leap from totemistic collectivist clan society to territorial civil society with its distinct multi-class social structure and the resultant institution of the state.

Civilization thus began with the development of agriculture. The village — the first settled form of collective human habitation and the product of the growth of agricultural economy—thus historically gave birth to rural society, and from the surplus of its food resources, nourished the town which subsequently came into existence.

The Old Setup

In the history of different peoples living in different parts of the world, different types of villages emerged with the rise and spread of agriculture. This was mainly due to differences in geographical environments in which those peoples lived. Further, the early village of a people also underwent changes in time due to its subsequent technical, economic, and social evolution as well as due to the impact of other societies on it.

The history of the village, in time and space, reveals such diverse village types as the Saxon village, the German Mark, the Russian Mir, the self-sufficient Indian Gram, the village of the feudal Europe which was an integral part of the manor; and finally the modern village, which is an integral part of national and world economic systems, with its variants such as the U.S.A. village, the typical West European village, the village of the backward modern countries of Asia, the village of the Soviet Union based on collectivized agricultural economy and others.

Hence the student of rural society should study the village, the basic unit of rural society as it originated and underwent a constant state of development and change due to the action of its own developing internal forces as also due to its interaction with other societies.

The Classification

Eminent sociologists have advanced a number of criteria to classify village communities.

(1) According to one criterion the village aggregates have been classified according to the types which evolved during the period of the transition from man's nomadic existence to settled village life. Thus villages have been divided into three groups: (i) the Migratory agricultural villages where the people live in fixed abodes only for a few months; (ii) the Semi-permanent agricultural villages where the population resides for a few years and then migrates due to the exhaustion of the soil; and (iii) the Permanent agricultural villages where the settled human aggregates live for generations and even centuries.

(2) According to the second criterion villages have been classified into grouped (or nucleated) villages and dispersed villages. In grouped villages the farmers dwell in the village proper in a cluster. They work on the fields which lie outside the village site. Since they dwell together in a single habitat, they develop a compact life. In the case of the non-nucleated dispersed village type, the farmers live separately on their respective farms. Their habitats being thus dispersed, their social life assumes a different form.

(3) Village aggregates have been also classified according to a third criterion, that of social differentiation, stratification, mobility and land ownership.

According to this criterion, village aggregates have been grouped into six broad types viz. (1) that composed of peasant joint owners; (2) that composed of peasant joint tenants; (3) that composed of farmers who are mostly individual owners, but also include some tenants and labourers; (4) that composed of individual farmer tenants; (5) that composed of employees of a great private landowner; and finally (6) that composed of labourers and employees of the state, the church, the city or the public landowner.

A systematic classification of Indian village aggregates on the basis of the above criteria and a study of their history will provide valuable information about village communities in India, about varied types of social institutions which have come into being in rural India, and also on the complex cultural patterns which have influenced and been influencing life processes of the Indian rural people.

An exhaustive survey of Indian villages co-relating the village types classified according to three principles will help to disclose the laws of the rise and development of Indian village communities. It will also help historians and sociologists to locate the laws of the peculiar development of Indian society and, further, will assist rural workers to evolve scientific programmes of rural reconstruction.

Rural vs. Urban

Social life in the countryside moves and develops in a rural setting just as social life in the urban area moves and develops in an urban setting. Their respective settings considerably determine rural and urban social life.

A correct comprehension of the specific characteristics of the rural framework is, therefore, indispensable for a proper grasp of the distinct features of rural social life. Such a study constitutes the first task of the rural sociologist and can be accomplished by studying in contrast the distinctive features of rural and urban settings. A brief outline of the principal points of contrast between the rural and urban settings will show how the different structures and life-processes of rural and urban societies are to a great extent the consequence of the difference between those different settings.

Outstanding sociologists have laid down a number of significant criteria for distinguishing the rural social world from the urban social world, such as the social composition of population, "the cultural heritage," the magnitude of material wealth, social stratification of the population, the degree of the complexity of social structure and social life, the intensity and variety of social contact and others. They have finally attempted to trace the sharp differences and contrasts between the two types of social phenomena, rural and urban, largely to the basic differences between the rural and urban settings.

The following are the most important criteria for distinguishing the rural social world from the urban social world

(1) Occupational differences.

(2) Environmental differences.

(3) Differences in the sizes of the communities.

(4) Differences in the density of the population.

(5) Differences in the homogeneity and heterogeneity of the population.

(6) Differences in the social mobility.

(7) Differences in the direction of migration.

(8) Differences in the social differentiation and stratification.

(9) Differences in the system of social interaction.

The following table reproduced from "Principles of Rural-Urban Sociology" reveals the decisive differences between the rural and the urban worlds.

	Rural World	Urban World
Occupation	Totality of cultivators and their families. In the community are usually a few representatives of several non- agricultural pursuits.	Totality of people engaged principally in manufacturing, mechanical pursuits, trade, commerce, professions, governing, and other non-agricultural occupations.
Environment	Predominance of nature over anthropo-logical environment. Direct relationship to nature.	Greater isolation from nature. Predominance of man-made environment over nature, stone and iron.
Size of community	Open farms or small communities, " agriculturalism" and size of community are negatively correlated.	As a rule in the same country and at the same period, the size of urban community is much larger than the rural community. In other words, urbanity and size of community are positively correlated.
Density of population	In the same country and at the same period the density is lower than in urban community. Generally density and rurality are negatively correlated.	Greater than in rural communities. Urbanity and density are positively correlated.
Heterogeneity and homogeneity of the population	Compared with urban populations, rural communities are more homogeneous in racial and psychological traits (Negative correlation with heterogeneity).	More heterogeneous than rural communities (in the same country and at the same time). Urbanity and heterogeneity are positively correlated.
Social differentiation and stratification	Rural differentiation and stratification less than urban	Differentiation and stratification show positive correlation with urbanity.

Mobility	Territorial, occupational and other forms of social mobility of the population are comparatively less intensive. Normally the migration current carries more individuals from the country to the city.	More intensive. Urbanity and mobility are positively correlated. Only in the periods of social catastrophy is the migration from the city to the country greater than from the country to the city.
System of interaction	Less numerous contacts per man. Narrower area of the interaction system of its members and the whole aggregate. More prominent part is occupied by primary contacts. Predominance of personal and relatively durable relations. Comparative simplicity and sincerity of relations. "Man is interacted as a human person."	More numerous contacts. Wider area of interaction system per man and per aggregate. Predominance of secondary contacts. Predominance of impersonal casual and short-lived relations. Greater complexity, manifoldedness, superficiality and standardized formality of relations. Man is interacted as a "number" and "address."

One of the important aspects from which rural social life is increasingly being analysed is the aspect of its spatial organization.

What factors determine the growth of varied types of villages, what factors operate to combine a cluster of villages into an agrarian region, what factors tend to transform an agrarian region into a cultural, linguistic or political region, and how do regions evolve into a province-these problems are of considerable significance in the study of rural society.

Factors at Work

Sociologists have attempted to locate the factors explaining this process. According to them, some of the important factors, which have determined the structural pattern of the village, the formation of regional and other bigger units and the interrelations of the village with those units, are as follows:

(1) Natural conditions like relief, configurations, soil, water resources and others; (2) the stage of agrarian economy, whether it is the nomadic stage, the stage of fixed subsistence agriculture or that commercial agriculture; and (3) the nature of social conditions such as needs of defence, forms of property and others.

The first great division which has been made of village communities from the ecological angle is that of nucleated or grouped villages and dispersed habitats. This distinction is vital from the point of view of the study of the entire social life of the rural community. The members of a rural community who dwell in villages have generally stronger social urges, exhibit a stronger feeling of social cohesion, and possess greater ability for co-operation than those who are dispersed and live on their respective farms. Each type of habitat furnishes a different framework for social life. The nucleated village is marked by "proximity, contact, community of ideas and sentiments" while in dispersed habitats "everything bespeaks separation, everything marks the fact of dwelling apart."

The study of the emergence of a larger rural area is one of the most baffling problems confronting the student of rural society. The factors which have combined to evolve homogeneous rural regions demand a very careful examination. Again we find that the larger rural regions change their characteristics with the change in the techno-economic, socio-economic and socio-political forces. The epoch of self-sufficiency evolved one category of regions. Under the impact of Industrial Revolution and production for market, a totally new type of rural areas came into being. The change from market economy to planned economy, where the agrarian sector is consciously developed as a part of the total life of the community, is creating in some countries and will create in other countries a new type of regional units. And, above all, the gigantic development of productive forces which is evolving an international economic and cultural community in the modern epoch is forcing the students of human society and especially of rural society to discover the appropriate variety of rural regions which will be in consonance with this development.

Efforts are being made to define economic, linguistic, administrative, religious and cultural regions in various countries. Efforts are also being made to find out where these regions coincide and also to study the laws which bring about this concurrence.

The works of Sanderson, Kolb, Taylor and others which embody an intensive study of rural economic and cultural zones in the U.S.A. have thrown considerable light on the phenomenon of the development of such zones. Various studies of primitive tribes— their geographical milieu, technical equipment, economic organization, social institutional structure, religion, arts and culture and, further, their transformation under the impact of communities belonging to various stages of civilized life—also furnish rich material for discovering the laws of rural development. Works dealing with the role of geographical factors—such as mountain, river, desert, sea, rainfall, various species of trees and animals—in indirectly or directly influencing the nature of economic organization, social institutions, styles of architecture, and beliefs and other ideological elements of man's life, also provide valuable clues for a correct understanding of the emergence of varied rural cultures.

The environmental and regional approach will help to distinguish chief village types and village social structures. It will also assist in scientifically classifying principal regional, district and provincial units. It will also aid in locating the underlying factors which have operated to create distinct culture-areas. And finally it will help to evolve a systematic account of the evolution of Indian society as a whole.

A detailed map of India indicating various natural and economic regions; indicating the areas inhabited by populations living in various stages of economic development; showing linguistic regions including regions based on different dialects as well as different variations of the main language; and showing, further, religious regions based on different, religious beliefs prevailing among the people; will throw great light on some of the most burning problems of Indian society and will also assist those engaged in the difficult task of reforming rural society to locate some of the fundamental causes of the present crisis of that society.

Adverse Situation

The Great majority of the country folk live in small or large nucleated settlements, and areas of dispersed habitations are few :the Himalayan zone is perhaps the only extensive area of true dispersal, of the type found in European highlands, elsewhere, even in the hills, the normal unit is the small hamlet rather than the homestead. This is enforced partly by the paucity of water-points, partly by the needs of defence—still visibly attested by the watch-towers of Pathan villages. In the Assam-Burma Ranges defence is also an important factor: villages are on hilltops or spurs, often stockeded; it must be remembered that in these jungly hills the valleys are extremely malarial, and that communication is easiest along relatively open ridgeways. Bengal — especially the En delta — is *sui generis*: there is indeed much settlement that is not nucleated, but "dispersal" appears an exceedingly inappropriate term for the dense stipple of separate homesteads, hardly isolated except in the most literal sense of the word when, during the rains, each is an island on its little earthen plinth. Other more or less dispersed zones are found in the Assam jungles, or in the great floodplains by farmers using the rick khadar for high-value crops after the rains. But in both groups the very small hamlet — say 6 to 12 huts — is the rule, rather than true dispersal: and in the latter case the huts are often only temporary, inhabited during the dry weather by people normally resident in big villages on the bluffs above.

These are anomalies: in the great homogeneous plains nucleation is almost invariable. In the past defence played its part, and in areas open to constant disturbance (e.g. the Sutlej/Jumna and Jumna/Ganges Doabs, Rohilkhand, the fringes in Central India, Khandesh, the Raichur Doab) villages are often grouped around a petty fort; and even today the close-packed houses, with blank outer walls and low doorways, massed into a ring with few entrances, present a defensive aspect. Often there is not much in the way of site selection; one place is as good as another, and the village rises are as often as not their own creation, the rubbish of generations. But any discontinuity, any break in the almost imperceptible slope produces linear settlement patterns: especially notable are the bluffs above flood-plains and the margins of abandoned river courses. The bluff villages tend to be larger than those on the drier interfluves; they have the advantage of two types of terrain, the upland doab and the valley-bottom with its tamarisk brakes and the excellent soil of its chars or diaras — the floodplain islands — submerged in the rains and liable to disappear completely in floods, but cropping up again sooner or later. These alluviated areas are often given over to cash crops of high value; near large towns they are often used for market gardens, easily irrigated by wells taking advantage of the high water-table.

Settlement lines tend to occur also at the marked break of slope where steep residual hills grade into a fan, which has usually a fairly high water-table. Lateritic shelves along deltaic margins are also important building sites, poor in themselves but offering rough grazing, scrubby woodland (the source of a great range of minor necessities from tiber to illicit alcohol), and providing space for dry crops, the flats below being entirely given over to paddy. They form as it were neutral ground between the jungly hills and the waterlogged paddy-plain. Here not only the general arrangement of settlements but also the village itself is often linear; islands of lateritic and older alluvium in the deltas are often completely ringed with houses. Linear settlement is also, of course, prominent in the deltas and wider floodplains themselves, strung out along levees or artificial embankments, and in places (e.g., Kerala and the Contai area of SW Bengal) along old beach ridges. Very often such sites are the only dry points in the rains and the only water-points in the hot weather.

There is in general very little that looks like a "Plan," other than that dictated by such site factors as alignment along bluffs or levees, grouping round a fort or a tank; but within the seemingly chaotic agglomeration there is, as a rule, a strong internal differentiation, that of the separate quarters for various castes.

These points are best brought out by a close view of a specific village, not indeed 'typical' (no single village could be that) but certainly the most random of samples. Our example is in the Deccan, more precisely in the Bombay-Karnatak.

Aminbhavi lies seven miles away from Dharwar; an old settlement, going back at least thirteen centuries, originally walled and moated. Essentially its site is governed by the junction of the Dharwar rocks, forming poor red soils around the mosque-crowned hill to the W, with the crystallines which have weathered into deep black cotton soils in the E. It is a typical black soil agricultural village, with a rainfall of about 24 ins. devoted mainly to dry crops (cotton, jowar, wheat, pulses, safflower, in that order), tending to become a satellite of Dharwar, the market of its dairy and agricultural produce. On the poorer land to the W is rough grazing, supporting a few shepherds, and immediately W of the village the common or gauthana, an essential part of its economy, the centre of all harvesting.

Caste and community largely govern the layout. Of its 4,106 inhabitants, Lingayats, the sturdy agricultural caste of the Karnatak, number some 2,650. Next come 550 Muslims, an unusually high proportion, but the place was of some importance in the days of the Bijapur Kingdom, and the first element in its name is indeed that of some forgotten Muslim (Aminbhavi roughly – Amin's Well). But the culturally dominant groups are the Jains (250) and the Brahmins (75); this is an Inam(landlord) village, most of it belonging to the Desai (Jain) and Deshpande (Brahmin) families, whose wadas (more or less equivalent to manor houses) stand on the best sites, within large compounds. The Desai provide the village patel or headman. For the rest, each caste tends to occupy a solid block of contiguous houses in a lane named from the caste; where, as with the leading family residing in it. Besides those mentioned, there are 300 Talwars (domestic servants and agricultural labourers), 200 Harijans ("untouchables"), and smaller groups of other low castes – Wadars (quarrymen), and so on. These groups live on the circumference of the village, or even beyond the old moat.

Occupations likewise are still mainly on a caste basis: the Lingayats provide the bulk of the tenant-farmers, Talwars and Harijans, landless agricultural labour; carpenters, smiths, cobblers, washermen, barbers are all separate castes. Apart from these crafts and agriculture, there is some handloom cotton weaving, a subsidiary occupation of the Lingayats.

Houses are generally built on to each other, or at least the mud walls of the compounds are continuous. The house layout is as standard as in any English working class street. In front is a porch (katte), used for drying agricultural produce, as a formal reception room, as "a place of female gossip when the master of the house is out," and above all as a sleeping-room in the stifling summer nights. Behind this is the main room, some 25 ft. square, part of which is a cattle pen, at threshold level; the remainder, raised some 2 or 3 ft. is the general living-room, for sleeping, eating, more intimate entertainment of guests, and perhaps handicrafts. The most prominent object is the pile of grain stored in gunny bags and sadly depleted towards the end of the agricultural year. Behind is a separate kitchen (with a corner for the bath) and the backyard with manure-pit and haystacks. This is the standard pattern; construction is similar in all groups (except the lowest), differences in economic status being reflected merely in size, except that the well-to-do have more separate single-purpose rooms. Jains and Brahmins do not live so tightly packed as the rest, either in the spacing of the houses or within them.

The poorest castes live in wretched one-room wattle huts with thatched roofs. Apart from these all houses have walls 1 or 2 ft. thick of mudbrick, with few (and high) or more likely no windows: Indians in general have a doubtless well-founded burglar-phobia. The flat roof is supported by wooden posts and made of mud on a framework of crude beams and babul (acacia) branches; they have rounded mud parapets and clay rain water pipes.

As for services, these are mostly grouped around the main village lane: market-place for the weekly bazar, eight shops (four grocery, two cloth, one tailor, one miscellaneous) and a number of booths selling tea and bidis, the cheap crude cigarettes of the Indian masses. Near the market-place is the room of the village panchayat or caste council, an ancient institution generally fallen into dustbin but now being fostered as the first step in local government. Associated with this tiny 'urban core' are the government establishments — Police Station, Post Office, grain warehouse. There are three mosques, one giving its name to the Idgah hill in the W, and eight temples, including that of the Deshpandes, as well as the Lingayat math, a centre of religious and charitable fellowship. The professions are represented by an Ayurvedic (indigenous) dispensary, a Urdu school for the Muslims, and separate schools for boys and girls. The boys' school is the most modern building in Aminbhavi, its stone walls and red-tiled roof standing in sharp contrast to the monotony of mud walls.

Finally we may note the large masonry-lined public well, sunk in what was once the moat; it is no mean excavation, an apt reminder of the all importance of water-supply in Indian life.

Once more, no one village can be typical of the whole sub-continent; but many of the features detailed above can be parallelled over and over again in most parts of India. Our random sample is at least very representative.

Glimpses of Life

The aspect of the village varies not only with the general regional setting, with building materials and house-types, but with social factors. The generally greater emphasis on caste in the S takes social fragmentation allied with spatial separation to the extreme, segregating the untouchables in outlying cherish or sub-villages, sometimes located several hundred yards from the main villages of which they are service-components. This is indeed the climax of geographical differentiation; apartheid. A typical cheri may consist of two rows of huts with a narrow central "street" in the middle this widens to make room for a tiny temple. The huts have thick mud walls, roofed with palmyra thatch, and low mud porches scrupulously swept. To enter one must bend double; the only light comes from the door and from under the leaves and the furniture consists of a few pots and pans, a couple of wooden chests, and the essential paddybin, 4 to 6 ft. high and 3 to 4 in diameter, raised from the ground to escape the rats, and built up of hoops of mud. Poor as they are, these dwellings are yet homes, and obviously loved as such: their cleanliness, the surrounding mangoes, coconut and palmyra palms, redeem them from utter squalor. The nadir is reached in the bustees of Calcutta and the revolting camps of casual tribal labour found on the outskirts of the larger towns: shelters (they cannot be called even huts) of matting, of rags, of petrol tins beaten flat, on waste spaces open to the sun and reeking with filth.

A geographical study of Indian house-types would be a work vast in scope and rich in instruction; a few of the more striking instances are mentioned in the regional chapters. Social factors are no less important than environmental, at least once we go beyond the fundamental antithesis of the NW (or SW Asia) type and the thatched gable of the more humid areas. Not only the site and layout of the village, but the "geography of the house" often reflects age-old religious and magical traditions; the round huts of some lower castes in Telengana, with bold vertical stripes of white and rusty red, are clearly culturally rather than geographically influenced. At the other extreme from the rude massive huts of Bundelkhand we have the elaborate courtyard house of the richer U. P. farmer, with some pretensions to elegance — the survival of decayed traditions — in doorways and arcading.

Some Indian domestic building indeed reaches a high standard of artistry: the carved timber of Kumaon or of the small towns of the Konkan, the restrained but excellent brick details and the very pleasant white bungalow-style houses, with low gables of semi-cylindrical tiles, found in small Maharashtra towns. Environmental influence is well seen in the flat-roofed blank-walled box standard in the Punjab and Wn U. P. — so strongly reminiscent of arid SW Asia, and fitting so well into the four-square planned villages of the Canal Colonies. Against these may be set the Bengal house, matting-walled, with thatched gables pitched high to shed the rain and ingeniously designed to take the strain of cyclonic gales. In Madras " We see flat-roofed stone houses in the Ceded District (Deccan), so constructed as to protect the dwellers from the severe heat of the sun, the rocks and slabs locally available being used. In contrast we find in Malabar timber entering into the construction. Here the buildings are on high ground and have sloping roofs, both necessitated by the high rainfall..... In the Tamilnadu we have brick houses with open courtyards, reflecting an equable climate and moderate rainfall."

As for what life in the Indian village is really like, who knows save the Indian villager? A few officials like M. L. Darling, whose Punjab rural rides compare with Cobbett's, a few devoted social workers, Indian and European, Christian and otherwise. But even then there is the difference between living in the village from cradle to grave (or burning-ghat), and living in the village with a territorial-and social and psychological — base outside. The alien may perhaps glean something from that rich harvest of salty rural proverbs (a comparative anthology of them would be fascinating) which are as vital a part of India's cultural heritage as the lyrical and metaphysical visions of her sages. Not that this latter strain of culture is absent from the village; the great epics Ramayana and Mahabharata pass from lip to lip in folk-versions, to some extent at least every man is his own poet, and not a few of the noblest figures in India's predominantly devotional literature sprang from the village rather than the schools: Kabir the weaver and Tukaram. The things that strike the outsider, then, are not perhaps ultimately the most important: the flies and the sores, the shrill clamour of gaunt pi-dogs, the primitive implements, the utter lack of sanitation.

At its worst the Indian village is infinitely depressing: in the plains where so much ground is cultivated that the scanty village site cannot grow with its growing population, or where a few miserable huts cling to shadeless stony rises in the drier parts of central India or the Archaean Deccan. Yet cheerfulness keeps breaking in, in the most unfavourable circumstances; fatalist as he is and must be, the peasant often displays an astonishing resilience and refuses to be broken by his often bitterly hard geographical and social environment. And over much of the land the villages have their amenities, even their beauties: in the plains and deltas they rise out of the sea of cultivation, emerald or gold or drab grey in the stubble season, like dark green islands, shaded in mango or orange trees, tamarinds, bamboos, palms. The tank or the well, the shade of the great banyan or the porch of the headman's hut, are essentially free clubs for the women and the men-folk respectively. Though the substratum of life — the gruelling round of the seasons — remains and will ever remain the same, though a miserable livelihood exacts an exorbitant price in endless toil, there have been great changes, material and psychological, since Edwin Montagu, Secretary of State for India spoke in 1918 of the "pathetic contentment" of the Indian village. Pathetic it still too often is; contented, less and less; which is as it should be. "These idyllic village communities confined the human mind within the narrowest possible compass." This is overstated: there were the epics and the proverbs; but the horizons were far too narrow for a full life. Now new motifs are changing the tempo of life in the large villages: perhaps a radio, perhaps a mobile film unit, more and more frequently a school. The mass movements launched by Congress have not always been amenable to a thus-far-and-no-farther policy: the peasant has other enemies than British imperialism, and Congress taught him organisation. All are helping to break down the isolation and lack of information which rendered the villager so helpless a prey to the money-lender, the retailer, and the grain broker — often all three being one and the same person. Perhaps the most powerful agent of change is the battered, ramshackle motorbus, packed to the running-board and coughing its way through clouds of dust along the unmetalled roads to the nearest town. There may be loss as well as gain in all this; but it is idle to bewail the break-up of integrated codes of life — too often integrated by religious, social, and economic sanctions which were a complete denial of human dignity. In any case the disintegration set in long ago with the impact of world market; and it is high time that new horizons should be opened, that the villager should see whence the forces that have subverted his old life have their origins and what of good they may bring.

Setup Infrastructure

A structure is something concrete and visual as also something abstract and conceptual. It is objective and subjective and the grades of objectivity and subjectivity differ from people to people depending on their social conditioning. A structure has a form or gestalt which may be sharply defined and simple or indistinct and vague. For a casual observer the habitation area called a village has a gross form in most cases. This form gets disturbed and becomes indistinct in certain ways and still something called "a village" remains with its objective boundaries and its subjective feelings for those who live in a village as also for those who are its neighbours. In some recent field work in certain areas of Maharashtra (the region where Marathi is spoken) I felt forcibly the gestalt aspect of the entity we call a village. The question presented itself to me in a negative way. As I viewed certain villages and walked through them I found myself asking why the area was called a village at all.

It would be very difficult to experiment about the gestalt of a village but one can define certain types of villages. For a casual observer the habitation area called a village has a gross discernible form in some cases. This form tends to be obliterated in certain ways and yet a village remains a felt entity for one who lives in it. In Maharashtra there appear to be three types of villages which are differently constituted as regards their gestalt.

One type is the tightly nucleated village with the habitation clearly defined from the surrounding cultivated fields. These villages are situated on high plateau of the Deccan.

In such villages, while the habitation area is well marked, the boundaries of the village together with its fields are never perceived. The fields owned by one village merge into those owned by another except where a hillock or a stream or a highway forms the boundary.

The second type of village is found on the west-coast (the Konkan) near the coast. The villages are generally strung along length-wise on the two sides of a road. The houses stand in their own compounds with their fruit and cocoanut gardens and are fenced on all sides. One walks or drives through fences on both sides of the road all the time. There are numerous tiny streams joining the Arabian sea and there are also spurs of the western mountains (the Sahyadri) coming right into the ocean where the streams join the sea they widen considerably, are forbidable at low tide and have on both sides strips of the salt marshes called Khajana. These natural obstacles divide one village from the other. Where these are absent one village merges into the other and a casual traveller does not become aware of having crossed from one habitatic area into another. The gestalt has changed not merely as regards form but also as regards the inter-relation of the background and the gestalt.

In such villages the exploitation of land is of two types—horticulture and agriculture. The gardens of cocoanut and arecanut palms and plantain, jack fruits and cashewnuts are planted near the house and fenced in, while the rice fields may lie a little away from the houses though in some areas they come right to the steps of the houses. There is no sharp distinction between the habitation area and the cultivated area.

The third type of the village was found in the Satpura mountains on the north-western boundary of the Marathi-speaking region. The Satpura mountains are made up of seven main east-west folds with undulating high valleys in between.

The houses are situated in their own fields in clusters of two or three huts, all belonging to a single close kinship group. They are either the huts of a father and grown-up sons or brothers and their wives. Sometimes a woman and her husband may have a hut in the same cluster as that of the father and brothers of the woman.

The next cluster of huts may be as far as a furlong or two away depending on how big the holding of each cluster is. The village boundaries are many times not defined by streams or hillocks because the houses belonging to one village are situated on separate hillocks or divided by streamlets. Added to this scattering is the habit of the Bhils to change the location of habitation on the smallest pretext ranging from a mishap to just wish to be near a friend or even just wanting a change.

In this area the village loses its gestalt completely, on all four sides. The habitation area is not distinguished from the cultivated area and the widely scattered houses of such villages are many times nearer to the houses in the next village than to the houses of its own village.

The clusters of habitation illustrated above may belong to two or three villages and but for the stone heaps erected by the revenue department to mark the boundaries it would be difficult to separate one village from the other.

The function of the roads is different in these three types. In the first type (the tightly nucleated villages) there are two types of roads.

(a) The roads connecting different villages meant for inter village communications ;

(b) Internal streets or narrow alleys connecting housing areas; sometimes a main arterial road may pass through or near a village and owing to modern ribbon development may become the main street of the village but such cases are very few. One can generally distinguish between roads connecting, villages and streets connecting internal habitation areas.

In the case of the villages of the second type, the main road in the village is generally also the main arterial road joining the villages of the coast for miles and miles in one linear direction. Such roads are seen in most villages of the west-coast from Bombay to Cape Comorin. The road from Cape Comorin to Trivandrum in the extreme south-west of India is a typical example of such a road.

In the third type of village there are no village streets because no houses are aligned along streets. There are only footpaths leading from one house cluster to another and the continuation of these leads to houses in the next village.

As a consequence of these different ways of grouping houses in habitatic areas, the individual dwelling or a cluster of dwellings gain individuality—are seen as a gestalt—to the same degree that the village or the whole habitation area loses its individuality or distinctness. In the tightly packed Deccan villages one loses sight of the individual houses which are but vaguely felt as parts of a big conglomerate. In the linear coastal village a house being situated in its own compound and separated from the next house, has a greater individuality is however blurred to a certain extent as a single house in the Deccan villages. This individuality is however blurred to a certain extent as a single house is but one in a long row of similar houses. It is the row which impresses itself on the observer rather than the individual house. In the Bhil area the individual house or houses cluster is a gestalt whose individuality is not disturbed by the proximity of the other houses. On the other hand, the widely spaced houses or cluster are not experienced as a unity making one village separating itself from a similar unity called another village.

The first type of village is the one found all over the Maharashtra plateau as also in other parts of India like Uttar Pradesh, Gujarat, Andhra, Mysore and Orissa.

The second type of village is found as already stated all along the west coast. Whether the same type is found also on the eastern coast I do not know.

The third type of village is found in parts of the Satpura region as also along the coast slightly in the interior. There are villages of scattered homesteads in the coastal area where sometimes the only way of internal communication is walking over the narrow bunds of the tiny rice fields, a very tricky business for strangers especially when all the fields are full of water. Though this type is found in some hilly regions as also in some parts of the coast it cannot be called a jungle type or a primitive type either, as there are a number of jungle people who live in villages where the houses are clustered together in a nucleus but are not as tightly packed as in some of the Deccan villages. The Gonds and the Kolams in Maharashtra and Andhra and the Katkaris in Maharashtra, the Bette Kuruba, the Jenu Kuruba, the

Erawa and the Sholega of Mysore also live in villages made up of many huts. The Warli of the west coast and the Chenchus living in the Nallamalai hills live sometimes either in an individual family house apart from others or in a cluster of a few houses which cannot rightly be called a village.

The nucleated Deccan villages show a clear distinction between communications within one village and communications with other villages. In modern Marathi there are words which are used exclusively for roads within a habitation area. There are also words as in Sanskrit which are used for both internal and external communication arteries but there is a whole series of words which denote various types of roads inside a habitation area. Ali, Galli, Bol are some of these words. Ali is a row of houses of one caste, or one profession; Brahmin Ali means a road both sides of which there are Brahmin houses, Tambat Ali means a road both sides of which have the workshops of the makers of brass and copper pots. Galli is a narrow street. " Galli Kuchchi " is an expression used for narrow roads full of mean houses. "Kuchchi " might have relation with word `Kancho' used for a certain type of communication in Gujarat.

We find that an explanation of the various words used for an internal system of communication involves reference to social structures like the family and the caste. It would appear that these words have primarily reference to a type of habitation area with the larger habitation area called a village and secondarily mean communication arteries with a village. They reflect a differentiated society, leading to a separate area for houses leading to sub-areas and hence to internal communication channels. The differentiation with an inhabited village may be based on lineage or caste and we will describe it presently.

Whatever the place name suffixes, the most common word for an habitation area in Marathi is 'Gaon' and in Telugu it is "Oor."

Social Bonds

In Maharashtra each 'Gaon' has habitation clusters a little away from the main habitation area. These clusters are called

'Wadi' and are said to belong to a 'Gaon.' In the same way in the Andhra Pradesh there are clusters of huts a little away from the main village which are called 'Palli' or 'Guda' which are said to belong to an 'Oor.' The interrelation of the Wadi and Gaon is manifold. The Wadi people sometimes call the Gaon to which they belong 'Kasaba' or 'Pethi' words which mean an area where various types of craftsmen (Kasabi) live or where there is shopping and market centre. The hereditary village servants and village craftsmen live in the Gaon. The village headman, the Patil, also must live in the Gaon, the revenue records and office are situated in a Gaon. A Wadi is generally a cluster of agnatically connected households. It may sometimes have just one big family with its farm servants and livestock. Sometimes people live in temporary huts in Wadis and have more permanent houses in the Gaon. Sometimes a Wadi is a settlement of a particular caste which by the nature of its occupation may need a larger space than is available in a Gaon. In the eastern parts of the Satara district many villages have Banagar Wadis a few furlongs away from the main village. The Banagars are shepherds who need large compounds near their houses for their mixed heards of sheep and goats. It also seems probable that this is an immigrant element which has made a separate settlement near a village with the consent of the villagers. In the same way there are Ramoshiwadis, i.e., hamlets where only the Ramoshi live.

They were counted among criminal tribes. Wadis are called generally after clan name or after a tribe or a caste. Vagh Wadi, Shinde Wadi, Kamat Wadi are names of the first type. Banagar Wadi, Ramoshi Wadi, Brahman Wadi are of the second type.

The Wadi originally is a cluster of hutments belonging to one family or belonging to two or three families whose fields lie in the immediate neighbourhood. Sometimes these are temporarily inhabited during the sowing and the harvesting season for facility of work in the field and the necessity to guard the crop.

Sometimes when the population is growing and there is available land for new settlement and the habits of the people are semi-nomadic, an originally compact village splits into different habitation areas. Recently, I came across such a village in the jungle tract of the Shrikakulam district of the Andhra Pradesh. The village is called Devanpuram. The original village was a settlement of two tribes, the Jatapu and the Savara. The Savara went a few furlongs away and had their own settlement. The Sávara settlement split and one part has gone about a mile away over the hills and has a settlement there. Devanpuram is thus an Oor with three Pallis-(1) A Jatapu palli, (2) a small Savara palli called China Savara palli and (3) a bigger Savara palli called Pedda Savara palli. This split has occurred since the last survey. If they remain in their present situations, the three parts may be acknowledged as three separate villages with the same name but separate headmen; for example, the villages called 'Gondi.' The two villages are within a mile of each other. The one near the road is as usual Jatapu-Gondi and the one nearer the hills and a little more inaccessible is the Savara Gondi. Generally, the most important and the most independent of these Wadis or Wada is that of the fisher folk and in a recent study we found that in one village the Koli or Bhoi are successfully defying the authority of the main village.

A village is thus an ever-changing nucleus of habitations from which tiny clusters separate and remain attached or separate completely to form a new nucleus. The quality of being a 'gestalt' objectively and subjectively is thus a dynamic quality which makes it difficult to give a definition of a village which would apply to all villages. This difficulty will be more apparent when we look closer into the internal structure of a village.

Among many semi-nomadic primitive agriculturists a village may endure for as few as three years. When the soil round about is exhausted the whole village moves off to somewhere else. Villages which were registered as existing at a particular place during the last elections are no longer there.

In the plains the villages are generally permanent and of long standing and hundreds of epigraphic records have shown that villages with the same boundaries have existed for over a thousand years.

In Maharashtra, there is a great variation as regards villages and the families they contain. For a particular caste there may be only one family (with one clan-name), for other castes there may be several families so that for one caste there is village exogamy while for the other castes there may be marriage within a village.

In the South, multi-clan village is the rule. In the North, where there are no clans, villages are supposed to be peopled by descendants of one ancestor for each caste and there is strict exogamy. This exogamy applies even when people of separate ancestries and Gotras come and live in the village.

Caste Factors

Generally, a village in India is, however, socially a far more complicated structure and the complexity is reflected in the way houses are built and roads existed. A village generally has more than one caste. In the North and sometimes even in Maharashtra there may be only one lineage of a caste, but generally in the North and almost as a rule in the Dravidian South, each caste in a village is made up of more than one lineage and clan. A map of a village will show almost invariably that the habitation area of each caste is separated from that of the other by a greater or a lesser distance. A few castes may live in houses situated side by side but others live apart. The castes which are always separated from the others are those whose touch was supposed to pollute the rest—the so-called untouchables. Their habitation area has generally a distinct name. In Maharashtra there is a Maharwada in almost every village. Mang is another untouchable caste which has its dwelling cluster separate from the rest of the village and also from the Mahars. The same is the case in Andhra Pradesh where the Mala live apart from the rest of the village. The Madiga live near the Mala but have a separate cluster of houses. The Maharwada or the Mala and Madiga Wadi are generally at the end of a village, hence the Sanskrit name Ante-Vasi (living at the end) and the Marathi name Vesakar (living near or outside the wall of a village. The Kumbhars (potters) also live a little away from the rest of the village and their part of the village is called Kumbhar Wada. Villages which have weavers in their population also have a separate area where weavers live. If there are a number of Brahmin houses they, have an area for themselves. The shepherds live so far away that their habitation area is termed a Wadi of the village.'

This tendency to have separate sub-areas for habitation within a larger unit called a village can be explained in various ways and on different grounds like caste-hierarchy, ideas of impurity and pollution, the need for certain occupations to have room for carrying out the different processes needed for their craft. The first reason applies to the house complexes generally, the second applies to the distance found between the untouchable quarters and the rest, the third applies to castes like potters, brick-makers, weavers and dyers, shepherds, wool carders and blanket makers, etc. To me it appears that there is an inherent tendency in the Indian culture to form separate groups and remain separate. The arguments listed above all strengthen this tendency and the phenomenon called 'caste,' apart from its hierarchical structure, is the direct outcome of this tendency. The primary group is the large family, sometimes unilateral sometimes bilateral. This group extends into the caste. The family as well as the caste are based on territory. The smallest territorial unit is the area in which the house and the family land are situated, the largest territorial unit in that part of linguistic area through which a caste has spread. Rarely is any area, small or big, in sole possession and occupation of a single family or a single caste so that we find in each such area a check-pattern of sub-areas belonging to families, clans, and castes. I have not seen anywhere either castes or tribes living inter-mingled. However tightly nucleated and crowded a village, the check-pattern sub-areas were always there.

This tendency is seen even among the primitives. The Bhils are divided into endogamous sub-divisions. They have villages of mixed population where sometimes allied tribes like Dhanak and untouchables live. Each of these has a separate habitation area and within each area there are house-clusters belonging to different lineages.

This is but a preliminary study of habitation areas and their structure. The way people build their houses, the way they group them, the way arteries of internal and external communication are formed would lend itself to ecological and anthropological analysis and may help to establish environmental-geographical as well as cultural zones and by linking with social institutions like the family and the caste will help to understand the meaning of the social institutions. It will perhaps reveal the fact that the unity or uniformity of Indian culture is based on tiny check-patterns fitted one into the other rather than a unicolour homogeneity.

3

Evolution and Development

Rural Sociology or the science of the laws of development of rural society in general has come into being only in recent times.

The Beginning

Reflections on rural society, indeed, are as old as the rural society itself. In the past, social thinkers had made attempts to comprehend the life processes of the rural world and to advance solutions of the problems arising therefrom. A comprehensive survey of the views of eminent thinkers belonging to various countries in the past epochs regarding rural life and its problems as they emerged in the changing rural society in various stages of development has been made in the "Systematic Source Book in Rural Sociology" Vol. I, edited by Sorokin, Zimmerman and Galpin. It reveals how some of the basic features of rural society and urgent problems of changing rural life had commanded the interest and attention of earnest social thinkers of ancient, medieval and early modern periods and impelled them to make sociological reflections, though they would betray to the well-equipped modern rural sociologists a lack of scientific methodology.

It was since about the middle of the nineteenth century that more systematic observations on the history of the origin and transformation of rural society have been advanced. The impact of the capitalist industrial civilization upon the rural economy and social structure, in various parts of the world, forced the attention of scholars to the study of the trends of rural social development. Research in the subject of the origin and the nature of village communities which were undergoing transformation was launched.

Olufsen, Maurer, Maine, Hexthausen, Gierke, Elton, Stemann, Innes, Coulanges, Nasse, Laveleye, Baden Powell, Ashley, Pollock, Maitland, Lewinski, Seebohm, Gomme, Guiraud, Jubainville, Slater, Vinogradoff, Meitzon and others are some of the outstanding scholars who have thrown light on rural society from various angles.

Subsequently eminent scholars, professors and others interested in the phenomena of the rural life have published in various countries enormous material dealing with its various aspects.

However, rural sociology as an organized discipline consciously developed, is of very recent origin. Due to historical reasons it has originated in the U.S.A. and slowly tends to draw attention elsewhere as its importance is being realized. During what is called "Exploiter Period" of American society (1890-1920), a period when the American rural society witnessed allround decay, a considerable literature, describing and analysing the problems arising out of its growing crisis, came into existence. This literature, however, did not explore, locate, and formulate the fundamental laws governing the development of rural society. It created the prerequisites for the birth of the science of rural society but did not still create that science. However, the beginnings of rural sociology may be traced to those " streams " of publications.

The first valuable work on the subject was the Report on the Country-life Commission appointed by President Theodore Roosevelt in 1907. A number of Doctorate theses based on the study of the rural community comprised further significant literature dealing with problems of rural life and providing, revealing information thereon. Finally a group of rural church and school studies made by individuals interested in an investigation of maladjustments in rural life constituted the third "stream" of publications. This literature served as the basis for creating the science of rural sociology in the U.S.A.

The Countrylife Commission, under the chairmanship of Dean Bailey, the eminent scholar of rural problems, circulated 5,00,000 questionnaires to farmers and leaders of rural life and received nearly 1,00,000 replies. The Commission, on the basis of this investigation, published a report in which they attempt to analyse and diagnose the defects and deformities of rural society. "This report actually provided what might be called a charter for Rural Sociology."

"An American Town," "Quaker Hill" and "A Hoosier Village," of which James Michel Williams, Warren H. Wilson and Newell L. Sims were respectively authors, represented further studies of the American rural community. These studies were based on statistical and historical data and field-interview techniques and were submitted as research documents at the Columbia University between 1906 and 1912. Dr. Warren Wilson, along with others interested in the processes of rural life, carried on a number of rural church studies. These studies, together with some rural school studies and "The Social Anatomy of an Agricultural Community" by Dr. C. J. Galpin based on an investigation into rural life made by him at the Agricultural Experiment Station of the University of Wisconsin in 1915, comprised additional literature germane to rural sociology until 1916.

"Rural Sociology" by Prof. John M. Gillettee published in 1916 served as the first college text book on the subject. Subsequently, a number of writers devoted themselves to the study of rural life and published valuable works which also enriched the literature on the subject. The publication of "A Systematic Source Book in Rural Sociology" in 1930 recognised as an "Epoch-making" work contributed decisively to accelerate the advance of rural sociology.

Later on, other intellectuals also focussed their attention on the subject and helped its further development.

Sorokin, Zimmerman, Galpin, Taylor, Kolb, Brunner, Sims, Dwight Sanderson, Landis, Redfield and Smith are some of the outstanding social thinkers in the U.S.A. whose intellectual labour resulted in a phenomenal advance of the new science of rural sociology.

The founding of the journal "Rural Sociology" in 1935 (at present a monthly) and the establishment of "Rural Sociological Society of America" in 1937 were further landmarks in the history of its growth.

In the U.S.A., rural sociology, though a new science and still in a state of immaturity, is commanding wider and wider interest among social thinkers today. More than eight hundred professors and research workers are engaged in developing that science in that country.

In other countries also, increasing attention is being paid to study and systematise this branch of study.

The various studies organized by the League of Nations and embodied in a number of monographs, together with the recent studies made by such organizations as UNO, UNESCO, FAO and others, have also contributed to the rapid advance of rural sociology.

Such is the history of the genesis and growth of rural sociology, the youngest amongst all sciences. It has started taking roots and is slowly but securely spreading itself in various parts of the world including India which needs it the most in view of its very large rural population with innumerable complex problems.

Scope and Sphere

As in the case of every young science, especially of a young social science, a great controversy has taken place over the question of the definition and scope of rural sociology among scholars engaged in the endeavour to develop it.

The Controversies

Is rural sociology a distinct science or is it merely an application of the general principles of sociology (or the science of society as a whole) to the sphere of rural social phenomena? Should rural sociology restrict its scope merely to the life processes of rural society or should it also include as an integral part, a study of rural and urban social life, comparative as well as in their mutual inter-connection and interaction and, further, have as its central concept what Zimmerman describes as "The mechanism and effects of urbanization and ruralization upon a population"

Further, should rural sociology only provide scientific knowledge about rural society and laws governing its development or should it also serve as a guide and suggest practical programmes of reform or reconstruction of that society in the economic, social or cultural fields? In short, should rural sociology merely give an objective authentic composite picture of the changing rural life in all its multifold and multiform aspects or also function as an ideological instrument to remould it according to a social purpose and a practical plan?

These are some of the principal problems over which extensive controversy is at present raging among sociologists. Such a disagreement among social scientists is not a characteristic peculiar to the field of rural sociology. Even regarding sociology in general, neither a clear, universally accepted definition nor a unanimous view of the scope of its study have as yet emerged among sociologists. The sub-domains of the single concretely whole domain of social life are so intermingled, interacting and even overlapping, that it is difficult to isolate one of them, study it and evolve a distinct science disclosing the laws of its structure and its evolution. Hence it is that disputes take place among social thinkers regarding the method and approach to be adopted to evolve a social science.

Basic Issues

In spite of a wide divergence of views among rural sociologists regarding the definition, scope, and objective of rural sociology and also about the emphasis to be laid on this or that factor of the rural society as the point of departure of its study, there also exists a number of basic agreements among them.

All rural sociologists recognize that the social life of the community is divided into two distinct segments, rural and urban. Though these segments interact among themselves, each is sufficiently distinct from the other.

All of them hold the view that social life in rural setting exhibits characteristics and tendencies which are peculiar to it, which constitute its specificness and which, therefore, sharply distinguish it from social life in urban setting.

All of them unanimously declare that the prime objective of rural sociology should be to make a scientific, systematic and comprehensive study of the rural social organization, of its structure, functions and objective tendencies of development, and on the basis of such a study, to discover the law of its development. Since every science, social or natural, has for its aim the discovery of the hitherto hidden law of development of a domain of nature or society, the basic task of rural sociology, they unanimously declare, is to discover the law of development of rural society.

A Systematic study of the rural social organization, its structure, function and evolution has not only become necessary but also urgent after the advent of Independence. The very process of achieving national freedom and transfer of power from the British to the Indians as also the colossal and very significant consequences which have followed this achievement, have revealed the signal importance of a careful, all-comprehensive, and methodical study of the rural society in our country.

The extensive participation of the rural masses in the long drawn out national liberation struggle; the devastating communal frenzy which swept over the rural social world and resulted in the uprooting of a great section of the village population in a number of provinces; the deep ferment which is, at present, seething in the agrarian area and which frequently bursts out in varied forms of struggles between different strata of the people; the numerous prejudices which are corroding the life of the rural people and which manifest themselves in various caste, linguistic, provincial and other forms of tension, antagonism and conflict; and similar other phenomena reveal that rural India is not so inert and quiescent as it was once assumed to be.

The grave problems pertaining to rural society outlined above have been brought to the forefront in the post-independence period. The Constitution of the independent India has already fixed the goal towards which Indian society is to develop. A secular state, based on universal franchise and with the welfare of its citizens as its prime objective as provided for in the directive principles of the Constitution, is the national ideal which has emerged after the transfer of power. The realization of such an ideal, however, is a most complex and stupendous task which a people can set to itself.

To evolve a truly secular state in a country which is a citadel of the most stubborn religious prejudices rampant among its people; to create a social and cultural atmosphere for the intelligent exercise of universal adult franchise by the citizens who are living within the traditional, authoritarian, joint family, caste and semi-feudal social framework and the overwhelming majority of whom are illiterate; to develop a welfare economy in a country where the entire productive system is increasingly deteriorating; to implement such directive principles of the Constitution which accept the need to provide such rights as the right to work, the right to social security, and the right to education to citizens when even the task of providing primary necessities to them is increasingly becoming more and more difficult; – to fulfil such a programme it is vitally necessary to have a precise and thorough understanding of the Indian social structure and its developmental tendencies.

Those who desire to strive for such a creative social transformation have to bear in mind that India is overwhelmingly an agrarian country; that not less than three-fourths of her population is engaged in agriculture; and that the agricultural economy, which forms the material basis of the life of this vast mass of the population, determines their social organization (the institutional matrix within which their life processes flow) as well as moulds their psychological and ideological life. Further, since the rural society forms the major sector of the Indian society, the specific programme of the re-casting of the former must inevitably play a decisive role in any scheme of transformation of the latter on a higher economic and cultural basis.

Academic Aspects

Statisticians, economists, sociologists, social workers and government agencies have, hitherto, overwhelmingly focussed their attention on the study of the phenomena of the problem of the urban society, though by far the greater portion of the Indian humanity lives in the rural area amidst conditions of immense material and cultural poverty. Even the literature dealing with the factual data about the life of the rural people is very meager. It is true that there has grown a literature, though insufficient, devoted to the study of different kinds of soil, manure, seeds, techniques of agriculture, land holdings, land tenures, processes of marketing of crops and other matters pertaining to agrarian economy. There are even some fragmentary studies delineating the life history of some castes and tribes and indicative studies of some villages. However, uptil now, neither the problems of the rural society have been formulated in all their bewildering complexity and variety, nor have scientific diagnosis and solutions to these problems been offered.

The study of the Indian rural society, which varies from state to state, from even district to district, due to their extreme geographical, economic, historical, ethnic and other peculiarities, hitherto made has been spasmodic, insufficient and often superficial. Such a study cannot give an authentic, composite picture of the variegated landscape of the rural life, nor can it serve as a guide for evolving a scientific programme of reconstruction of the rural society, so essential for the renovation of the entire Indian society.

In fact, a concrete and comprehensive study of the rural society in all its aspects, ecological, morphological, institutional and cultural, has hardly begun.

Progressive Rural Society

It is, however, urgently necessary to make a scientific and systematic study of the rural society, of its economic foundation and social and cultural superstructure, of its institutions and their functions, of the problems arising from the rapid process of disintegration which is undergoing and which even threatens its breakdown.

(1) India is a classic land of agriculture. Its long past history, its complex social organization and religious life, its varied cultural pattern, can hence be understood only if a proper study is made of the rise, growth crystallisation and

subsequent fossilisation and break up of the self-sufficient village community, the principal pivot of the Indian society only till recently.

(2) Due to historical reasons, the existing Indian rural society has become a veritable mosaic of various types of rural societies and hence reveals a diversified cultural pattern. The culture of the hunting and food gathering tribes; the culture of the primitive hoe-agriculturists; further, all the varied cultures of peoples engaged in agrarian production with the plough and the bullock, as also the modern culture of a rural people influenced by new technical and economic forces – all these cultures are juxtaposed in the contemporary rural India. Further, the Indian rural humanity is also being influenced by the ideological currents of the modern era. Consequently we find in the Indian rural world today, the persistence of primitive cults of magic and animism, polytheism, pantheism of the ancient world, monotheism and other idealistic philosophic world outlooks inherited from the ancient medieval periods as also a minor current of modern rationalist world view. This has transformed it into a veritable museum of different and even conflicting cults and ideologies.

(3) The unique agrarian socio-economic structure of India experienced a decisive transformation as a result of the impact of the British conquest and rule. On the eve of the British conquest of India the Indian rural society was composed of a multitude of villages. Each village lived almost an independent, atomistic, self-sufficient social and economic existence. The village represented a closed society based on economic autarchy and social life governed by caste and community rules.

In the economic sphere, the village experienced a steady transformation during the British period. Its economic self-sufficiency was dissolved. It slowly began to produce for the Indian and the foreign market and, not as before, for meeting the needs of the village population. The village economy became increasingly an integral part of the national and even world economy. The influx of cheap foreign and, subsequently, of indigenous industrial goods into the village, progressively undermined the village artisan industries. The old self-sufficient economy based on an equilibrium between the village agriculture and the village artisan industry was thus disrupted.

In the social field, the rule of custom enforced by the joint family, the caste and the village panchayat, was gradually replaced by the reign of laws made by the centralized British state in India and administered by its own revenue, executive and judicial officials posted in the village. This considerably undermined the powers of the joint family, the caste and the village panchayat.

The introduction of the modern means of transport and communication accelerated the processes mentioned above.

Every aspect of the village life, social, economic, political and cultural, experienced a steady transformation. The old pattern of village life, the old structure of village society, became appreciably changed.

Since the transformation was mainly brought about by a foreign power to serve its own political and economic interests, it resulted in the destruction of the old type of the rural society without its being replaced by a socially healthy, economically progressive and culturally more advanced new type. The transformation culminated in the emergence of the present impoverished and culturally backward village which, moreover, lacked stability and a definite structural design.

The Indian agrarian economy is at present in a state of acute crisis. This has resulted in the unbearable economic misery of the rural people. The agrarian situation has consequently become almost explosive.

It is, therefore, vitally necessary to focus attention on the crisis of the rural economy. The solution of the crisis is the essential pre-condition not only for eliminating poverty of the rural population but also for building a prosperous national economy which can guarantee a higher material standard of life to all citizens.

It should be noted that the role of social institutions in accelerating or retarding the fulfilment of an advanced programme of agrarian re-construction is greater in India than in any other country. Programmes and policies of rural renovation based on pure economic factors have not, therefore, met with appreciable success. The role of such institutions as the caste and the joint family organization in thwarting such programmes and policies has not been hitherto properly grasped. The necessity of Rural Sociology becomes all the more important in India.

To reconstruct such a rural society on a higher basis, it is urgently necessary to study not only the economic forces, but also the social, the ideological and other forces operating in that society. It is a complex and colossal task.

As referred to above, only stray, spasmodic efforts have been hitherto made to study the life processes of the Indian rural society. No systematic study has still been launched to study that society in all its aspects, to study its life processes in their movement and, further, in their interconnections.

In fact, Indian Rural Sociology or the science of the laws governing the specific Indian rural social organism has still to be created. Such a science is, however, the basic premise for the renovation of the Indian rural society, so indispensable for the renovation of the Indian society as a whole.

4
People in Villages

The first task confronting the rural sociologist is to define the rural people and distinguish them from the urban population. Various approaches have been suggested for that purpose by eminent thinkers. Classification adopted by Government Census Departments in various countries is, however, generally accepted as the most convenient, though it may vary from one country to another.

The next task before the student of the rural people is to determine the ratio of rural and urban populations. In many countries, this ratio in a great measure indicates the level of living of the people as a whole since it shows the relative proportion of industry, and agriculture and hence the total wealth of the people. The ratio, further, considerably influences the apportionment of social amenities within the country. It thereby serves as a guide for evolving a correct programme for social advance. One of the great mistakes committed by a number of reformers and social engineers is to transplant mechanically the techniques adopted for reform in a country inhabited by a small agrarian population and with a vast area of land to a country inhabited by an overwhelmingly agrarian population and with scarce land resources. The recent effort to introduce measures adopted to improve the agrarian sector of the U.S.A. which is overwhelmingly industrial to predominantly agrarian backward countries of Asia is an instance of such an error. Even within the same country a detailed study of the ratios of rural-urban population in different regions is essential because these differences considerably alter the nature of problems relating to those regions. For instance, the problems of Gujarat and those of Bihar are different as there is a difference in the proportion of rural-urban population of these states.

Rural Population

The next important problem is that of the density of the people living on land. Sociologists, after adequate investigation, have reached the conclusion that the average density beyond a particular limit indicates an undesirable over-concentration of the people in that area. This is because the density of the population affects production and distribution and also generates various social reactions which greatly influence the total life of a society. The density of the population further affects the level of the standard of living of the people.

A systematic study of the density of the population in different regions and districts in India and also of the proportion of various groups belonging to diverse castes, religions, and vocations which comprises the population, will unfold the variegated picture of the complex social life of the Indian people with all its multiple tensions, antagonisms as well as mutual adjustments among these groups.

The study of birth rates, death rates, rates of suicides, specific bodily diseases and such other matters regarding the rural population is another important aspect of a demographic study of the rural society as it reveals the quantitative and qualitative growth or decline of the rural people. Further, when this study is correlated to that of the social, economic and religious life processes of various social groups, it provides intelligent and correct criteria of evaluating the norms of those groups.

Apart from a study of the death and survival rates prevailing among the rural people, there are also other means to determine their vitality such as a study of their general health and longevity. Further, estimates of mortality prevailing among separate groups such as infants, females and old people; upper, lower and middle social strata; and land labourers, farmers, artisans, and other social categories, will give a detailed picture of the vitality of various sections of the rural people.

Another aspect of the life of a population which requires a close study is their distribution in age and sex groups. The analysis of age groups gives us a correct understanding of the proportion of the people who are of productive age and those who are to be sustained by the society. The preponderance of children and the aged over the working section of the people would considerably influence their economic and social life.

Similarly the analysis of the sex composition is also essential, since it is generally recognized by sociologists that "sex mores, social codes, social rituals, and social institutions are all likely to be affected where extremely unbalanced sex ratios are found."

Life Style

Caste, race, nationality and religious composition of the people has a great social significance. It gives rise to a rich, complex, diversified social life and varied patterns of culture. More often it breeds animosities, antagonisms and conflicts. We know how in India in recent years the multi-religious composition of the Indian people engendered ghastly communal Hindu-Muslim riots. We know how nationality conflicts are steadily corroding the body politic of India.

A very peculiar type of social grouping which is found in India is the caste grouping. A student of the Indian society who fails to study closely and carefully this variety of social grouping will miss the very essence of that society. Looking to its important role in India a separate chapter has been devoted to the sociological significance of caste elsewhere.

A systematic, co-ordinated and inter-related study of the rural people from various angles is an urgent need.

Among the institutions that compose rural society, the family is the most important. It has been its very foundation. It plays a decisive role in the material and cultural life of the rural aggregate and in moulding the psychological characteristics of the rural individual as well as the rural collectivity. In fact, according to some thinkers, family and familism impress their stamp on the entire rural structure. Familism permeates it from top to bottom.

A systematic study of rural family, of its structure, functions, evolution, and interrelations with other institutions of the rural society is vitally necessary for the rural sociologist.

The Indian rural society provides a classic field for the study of the institution of rural family. Within it are found many types and patterns of family organization which humanity has hitherto evolved.

Family Life

Prof. Rivers has distinguished four types of institutions which have been designated by the term family, viz., the clan, the matrilocal joint family, the patrilocal joint family and the individual family composed of only parents and minor children.

According to one group of sociologists, these four types reveal four main stages of the evolution of the family form corresponding to four stages in the evolution of society. The first type corresponds to the hunting and food gathering stage of social evolution; the second to the phase of hoe agriculture and the beginnings of domestication of animals; the third – a classic type – to the phase of agricultural economy based on the plough and domestication of animals, and, finally, the fourth type to the modern industrial capitalist phase of human existence. As a result of the growth of market economy in the agrarian area and of the impact of urban socio-economic forces on the rural society, the last type is increasingly becoming predominant today.

The Indian rural society provides a great laboratory to test this view, since it includes within its fold the relics of the clan as well as matrilocal and patrilocal family types and the recent individual family group also. A methodical study of the structure and functions of these various family types and their correlation with the stages of civilization to which they correspond will throw a floodlight on the history of Indian humanity and will enable Indian historians to evolve a correct sequence of the developmental phases of the Indian society.

In almost all fully developed agrarian societies depending on plough agriculture, patriarchial joint family has been found to be the predominant family form in rural areas. Outstanding rural sociologists have made a close study of the characteristics of this type of family. They have observed the basic structural, psycho-social, and functional features of this type of the rural family which distinguish it sharply from the urban family. They are as under:

Greater Homogeneity: The rural family is far more homogeneous, stable, integrated and organically functioning than the urban family. The ties binding the members of the former, for instance the husband and the wife, parents and children, are stronger and last longer than those in the case of the urban family. A glance at the Indian countryside will corroborate this view. The Indian village still remains a cluster of joint families though, due to a number of historico-economic causes, the joint family has been exhibiting a tendency of slow but steady disintegration. The rural family is composed not only of the members of the family but also frequently includes distant relations which hardly happens in the dovecotes of the urban society.

Based on Peasant Household: Another essential characteristic of the rural family is that it is generally based on the peasant household. All its members are engaged in the agricultural occupation. Work is distributed among them mainly on lines of age and sex distinctions. "The Community house, common land and common economic functions along with the common kinship bond create the peasant household." Since the members of the rural family form a single economic unit and constantly co-operate with one another in agricultural operations, since they hold property in common usually managed by the eldest member of the family, since also they spend most of their time together, the psychological traits they develop are very similar.

Greater Discipline and Interdependence: The rural family is characterised by greater discipline among its members than the urban family. Further, since there is considerably less state or public provision for meeting the educational, cultural, or social needs of the people in the rural area than in the urban, the rural family attempts also to satisfy these needs of its members. It thus serves as a school, a recreation centre, as well as a maternity or a non-maternity hospital.

Dominance of Family Ego: The interdependence of the members of the rural family and the dependence of its individual member on it are, therefore, far greater than in the case of the urban family. This welds its members into a homogeneous, compact, egoistic unit, strengthens emotions of solidarity and co-operation among them and fills them with family pride. They develop more collectivist family consciousness and less individualistic emotion. In a rural society, a family is discredited if any of its individual members perpetrates an infamous act. Similarly the glory of his or her achievement also accrues to the family from which he or she springs. The urban family in contrast to the rural family, is less authoritarian of the family even at the cost of their lives.

Authority of the Father: Since the rural family is a more integrated and disciplined unit than the urban family, the head of the rural family exercises almost absolute power over its members. It is he who distributes the work of the peasant household among the family members on lines of sex and age differences; arranges marriages of sons, daughters, nephews and nieces; administers the joint family property according to his wisdom; and trains the youngsters for future agricultural work and social life. All initiative and final authority are vested in him. In fact "the head of the family has had the rights and authority to be the ruler, the priest, the teacher, the educator and the manager of the family." Thus, the family, through its head, subordinates its individual members to itself. The latter are completely submerged in the family; hence they hardly develop any individuality or personality. Such a family type can only be a nursery for the growth of family collectivism but not of individuality. The urban family in contrast to the rural family, is less authoritarian but also less co-operative. This is due to a variety of reasons. First, it is not a single productive unit administered by the family head since its adult members are mostly engaged in occupations unconnected with, and outside the home. Further, educational, recreational and a number of other needs of its members are satisfied by extra-family institutions like school, club, and others. Property of its earning members, too, tends to be individual, ,since it is derived out of extra-family occupations. In the sphere of marriage also, its members are increasingly exhibiting independence and marry persons of their own choice.

Closer Participation in Various Activities: One striking feature of the rural family lies in the fact that its members, being engaged in work connected with the peasant household, spend practically the whole day together. In contrast to this, the members of the urban family engaged in different occupations or being educated outside home, spend only a small portion of the day together. Even their recreational centres such as clubs and others lie outside the home. Hence the home becomes only a temporary nightshed for the members of the urban family.

Wave of Urbanisation

Rural society has been increasingly urbanised in modern times. In proportion to its urbanization it exhibits the characteristics of urban society. The rural family more and more develops centrifugal tendencies. Its economic homogeneity based upon a single cumulative economic activity of its members declines. Joint family property tends to be disrupted since its individual adult members begin to demand its partitioning. Being increasingly engaged in different occupations, they earn independent separate incomes which they retain as their own. They live less and less together and spend only a fraction of the day in association. They begin to seek extra-familial centres like clubs, hotels, unions, associations, cafeteria, which are also slowly growing in and around rural areas. All this results in the growth of individualistic psychology among them which weakens family emotion and egoism so vital for the vigorous functioning of a homogeneous family.

The individual hitherto submerged in, and subordinated to, the family tends to become atomistic. He more and more breaks away from the family restrictions. He develops his own initiative and independence. This inevitably results in the weakening of the family authority, family ties, and the family itself.

According to the views of such eminent sociologists as Sorokin,

Zimmerman and others, the social and political organization of all agrarian societies during their subsistence stages bears the fundamental traits of rural family, the basic unit of rural society. These traits they characterise as familism.

"Since the family has been the basic social institution of the rural social world, it is natural to expect that the whole social organization of agricultural aggregates has been stamped by the characteristics of the rural family. In other words, all the other social institutions and fundamental social relationships have been permeated by, and modelled according to, the patterns of rural family relationships. Familism is the term used to designate this type of social organization ..... Familism is the outstanding and fundamental trait in the gestalt of such a society."

These sociologists enumerate a number of important characteristics of such societies bearing the stamp of familism. They are as under :

Marriage Earlier and its Higher Rate: The members of these rural societies marry at an earlier age than those of urban societies. Further, the rate of marriage in the former is higher than that in the latter.

Family, Unit of Social Responsibility: Since family is the unit of rural society, it is the family collective that pays the taxes and discharges social responsibilities. The individual is also appraised according to the status of the family to which he or she belongs.

Family, Basis of Norms of Society: Further, ethical codes, religious doctrines, social conceptions and legal norms governing rural societies have always condemned anything which would weaken the stability of the family. They have preached implicit obedience to parents on the part of sons and daughters and to husband on the part of wife.

Family, its Impress in Political Form: The political organizations of those rural societies have been also based on the conception on which rural family rests. Their political ideology has conceived the relation between the ruler and the ruled as that between the head of the family and its members, i.e., paternalistic. "King, monarch, ruler, lord have been viewed as an enlarged type of family patriarch the predominant type of political organization in the rural community is represented by the institution of the village elder, the head, elected by the peasants as the family elder is either openly or tacitly elected by the family members. The whole character of the village chief's authority and administration is a mere replica of the paterfamilia's authority and administration."

Co-operative rather than Contractual Relations: The relations between the members of the rural society are basically co-operative in contrast to those between the members of the urban society which are preponderatingly contractual. This difference, according to the view of the outstanding sociologists, is the result of the difference between the rural and urban families. "In a rural family the solidarity of its members is organic and spontaneous. It springs up of itself-Naturally as a result of close co-living, co-working, co-acting, co-feeling and co-believing. Any contractual relationship between its members would be out of place and contradictory to the whole tone of family ….. it is no surprising, then, that purely contractual relationships have been but little developed in familistic societies." The members of the urban family on the other hand have separate interests as well as individualistic 'psychologies. They have more or less lost collective family feeling. The urban society bears this characteristic of the urban family. Spontaneous cooperation and solidarity-feeling are found to be appreciably less among the urban people than among the rural people.

Family, Unit of Production, Consumption and Exchange: The economic structure of the rural society also bears the traits of the rural family. It is based on family ownership. The production and consumption are familistic. The market is less developed. Exchange has more the characteristics of simple barter than of full-fledged monetary transactions. The entire code of laws regulating the economic relationships within such a society bears the stamp of familism. In contrast to this, the urban economy is predominantly a commodity economy and therefore the economic and hence the general social relations between the members of the urban society are competitive and contractual.

Dominance of Family Cult and Ancestor Worship: The ideology and the culture of rural society also exhibit traits of familism. The cult of family dominates. Religious and other ceremonies have for their object the security and property of the family. Ancestor worship is almost universally prevalent. Even the relationships between its gods and goddesses are familistic, they being related to one another as father, mother, brother, sister, etc.

Dominance of Tradition: As a result of all these factors rural society is marked with much less mobility than urban society. Tradition severely governs its life processes. It undergoes change with extreme slowness.

Trends of Social Change

To sum up, until the impact of the Industrial Revolution and the competitive market economy, familism was the heart of village communities. Subsistence agrarian economies and rural societies based on them were familistic through and through. However, the rise and development of modern industries steadily undermined subsistence agrarian economy and brought the rural economy within the orbit of capitalist market economy. This transformation together with the growing pressure of various urban forces brought about the increasing disintegration of the old rural family. The rural society, too, more and more lost its familistic traits.

In India, due to lack of sufficient industrial development, the forces of urban society have not penetrated rural society to the same extent as in the U.S.A., Great Britain and other industrially advanced countries. The rural family consequently retains its specific traits to a far greater extent in India. Urban industrial development affects the rural family in many ways. It creates new occupations such as those of factory and workshop workers, of clerks, typists, and others. The members of the rural family develop a desire to take to those occupations, demand their share in the joint family property and migrate to towns and cities. This process undermines the joint family based on a common occupation of its members and joint family property, income and expenditure.

Modern industries produce a number of articles cheaply and on a mass scale. They reach out to the village population who purchase them. Thus the peasant family which was formerly producing cloth and other necessities with primitive techniques more and more ceases to produce them now. Thus it loses a number of its economic functions with the result that the scope of the collective labour of its members narrows down.

Capitalist economic development transforms the social and political environments of a people also. In India, British capitalism transformed the socio-economic structure of the Indian society and, further, established a centralized State. This resulted in a number of consequences. Private and State agencies increasingly established schools, dispensaries and administrative and judicial machinery in the village. The rural family which served as the school for its members no longer functioned as such, since its members now began to receive education outside the family. Also not the grandfather or the grandmother, the embodiment of traditional medical knowledge, but the doctor appointed by an agency unconnected with family, now increasingly treated the members of the family. Caste and panchayat councils were deprived of their functions as guardians of law and dispensers of justice. The customary law was replaced by the new law of the centralized state which operated through its administrative and judicial organs. The process progressed in proportion as the urbanization of the country advanced.

The historical tendency of the rural family is towards its increasing disintegration and loss of functions. The more this tendency grows, the more the family ego and solidarity feeling cradled in and nourished by the collective labour and life of its members weaken and atomistic individualistic psychological traits develop among them.

During the last hundred and fifty years, the traditional joint family and the familistic rural framework have been undergoing a qualitative transformation. The basis of rural family relationships is shifting from that of status to that of contract. The rule of custom is being replaced by the rule of law. The family is being transformed from a unit of production to a unit of consumption. The cementing bond of the family is being changed from consanguinity to conjugality. Further, the family is ceasing to become an omnibus social agency, it being shorn of most of its economic, political, educational, medical, religious and other social and cultural functions. Instead, it is becoming a specialized and affectional small association. From a massive joint family composed of members belonging to a number of generations, the family is increasingly shaping as a tiny unit composed of husband, wife and unmarried children. Familism, too, is gradually dropping off. The rural society is acquiring quite a new gestalt.

A systematic study of the rural family from many angles has never been so necessary as at present in India. Its methodical, intensive and extensive study will provide proper direction for evolving a programme of appropriate measures to realise grand objectives that are embodied in the Constitution of the Indian Union. Rural sociologists in India require to launch a very comprehensive campaign of study to locate the laws of the transformation of one of the most classic familistic civilizations that has emerged in the history of humanity.

5

Life in Rural Belts

There are numerous individuals and groups who desire and strive for improvement of the material and cultural life of the rural people.

They can be broadly divided into the following three categories (i) The Philanthropic group; (ii) The Reformist group; and (iii) The Revolutionary group.

The Philanthropic group does not view the problem of the material and cultural poverty of the rural people in the context of the institutions and the basic structure of the rural society. It holds the conviction that it is possible to ameliorate the position of the rural people through direct humanitarian effort, without changing those institutions and structure. It evolves economic, educational and other programmes of village uplift which embody such items as creation of charity funds to help the village needy, moral appeals to landlords and such other groups to relax their pressure on peasants, establishment of hospitals and schools, and others.

The basic feature of the standpoint and the programmatic approach of this group to the problem lies in the fact that it attempts to improve the conditions of the rural population within the matrix of the existing institutions and structure of the rural society, by means of purely humanitarian endeavour.

Wave of Reforms

The Reformist group subscribes to the view that it is the malfunctioning of the existing rural social system and its institutions (and not the social system and its institutions in their basic essence), which is the social-genetic cause of the economic misery and social and cultural backwardness of the rural people. They therefore, work for a healthy functioning of the social system and its institutions, or, at most, for reforming them. They assert that once this institutional reform is accomplished, it will result in the all-sided betterment of the life of the rural population.

The distinguishing characteristic of the standpoint and the programmatic approach of this group to the problem lies in the fact that for elevating the conditions of the rural people at present it does not regard it necessary to replace the existing social system and its institutions by new ones but strives only to reform them.

Wave of Change

Finally, there is a third group whose standpoint and programmatic approach to the problem are based on a revolutionary conception. They think that the abysmal poverty, crass ignorance, and cultural backwardness of the mass of the rural people are fundamentally due to the existing social system and the institutions which are its organs to sustain that system. The social system and its institutions, they feel, cannot but breed these evils. They declare, therefore, that both the programme of individual aid and relief and that of institutional reform will be unable to achieve the desired end. They contend that no reform can appreciably liberate the rural people from want, disease, illiteracy, and lack of culture. They argue that new wine cannot be filled into the old bottles.

Thus, according to this group, the evils of the rural society are not the result of any malfunctioning of the rural social system or its institutions but are inherent in this system and institutions themselves, are the inevitable product of the natural functioning of the present social order. This group, therefore, evolves and attempts to carry out a programme of a revolutionary transformation of the rural social structure from its economic base upward.

While laying decisive emphasis on its social revolutionary objective, this group includes in its programme a number of items of the first two programmes. It however, links its struggle to implement those items with the struggle for the change of the entire social system.

These three groups with their diverse and even conflicting programmes are at present struggling for hegemony in the agrarian area.

The Settlements

Various individual groups, associations and parties, each according to its own light, are thus engaged in the movement of rural uplift and reconstruction. Among them are individual philanthropists and philanthropic bodies; social, political, religious, economic and educational organizations including welfare associations; missionary groups; Governmental institutions and others.

We will make a few observations regarding the work of these groups and organizations.

Exclusive Concentration on One Aspect of the Rural Life

Some of them exclusively concentrate on one single aspect of the rural life like education, economic welfare, sanitation, crusade against reactionary social customs and practices, religious superstition, ethical uplift or fight against disease. They isolate one aspect of the rural life from its other aspects. The, organic unity of the rural life and the interrelations and interdependence of its many aspects are thus lost sight of.

This results either in the abortion or limited success of their programme even when dealing with one single aspect of the rural life.

Most of these groups and organizations, while inspired by ethical and humanitarian motives, lack scientific training for the work they undertake. They forget that an objective study of the rural society and its conditions is vital for evolving a correct programme and methodology of work and that merely good intentions are no guarantee of successful social work. They forget that a patient gathering of factual data pertaining to the life of the rural people and a detailed concrete study of their specific prerequisites for formulating a correct programme of rural work.

A study of the psychological traits, ethnic and communal composition, customs and beliefs of the rural aggregate, is also indispensable for the purpose. Further, these groups and organizations require to have a concrete knowledge of the economic structure of the rural society, the specific system of land tenure prevailing in it, the various socio-economic groups bound up with its economy and with different and even conflicting interests, the religious and other ideologies which have a hold over their mind, the particular types of family and other social institutions existing there and many other things. Such knowledge is necessary because the task before them is not the renovation of a vague and vast rural society, in general, but of a specific type of rural society; not the amelioration of the abstract rural people but of a particular rural people with local limits, defined past and crystallized present conditions. It is, therefore, essential to study the particular rural society and its people in concrete details. Then alone, it is possible to evolve an appropriate programme of rural work for the recuperation of a particular rural society and the advance of the specific rural aggregate living in that society. Then alone, also, it is possible to locate the specific social, economic, psychological, ideological and other obstacles in the way of the fulfilment of that programme. A rural aggregate in Gujarat is different from that in Saurashtra, Bihar or Maharashtra.

Many individuals and organizations oriented to the work of rural reconstruction and uplift lack this understanding. They evolve naive programmes of rural work which, not being based on concrete detailed knowledge of the specific rural society and its people, fail or meet with partial success. This breeds the sentiment of defeatism among them and results sometimes in their abandoning of the rural work altogether.

Lack of Co-ordination of work

Lack of co-ordination of activities in various spheres marks the work of some organizations and groups. Further, their activities are often based on conflicting value systems.

This, too, is detrimental to the success of the programme. It is obvious that all activities should be co-ordinated and should constitute a single organic stream of total work. Also it is evident that a single principle must determine and permeate the diverse activities in diverse fields. Otherwise there will ensue mutual negating of activities.

Some groups and organizations exhibit insufficient ability for a proper assessment of the results of their efforts in various domains of rural work. Since they have, therefore, no adequate conception of the cumulative result of their activities, they get a hazy notion regarding their advance towards their objective. Inability to properly evaluate their work in terms of productivity also denies them that power of self-criticism which is also vital for a correct planning of next stages of work.

When work is not properly planned and correctly assessed, there is also the danger of deviating from the correct road to the goal.

Sporadic and unplanned forms of rural welfare work are also sometimes launched. In a number of instances, they degenerate into mere fads. This reveals unconscious lack of earnestness or absence of scientific understanding of the problem on the part of their sponsors. We find a mushroom growth of such efforts embarked upon by individuals and even institutions in the rural area. This tends to make the picture of the rural reconstruction work chaotic to some extent, and often leads the rural people to become victims rather than beneficiaries of such endeavours since they yield unstable and distorted results.

The principal weakness characterizing these organizations however, generally lies in their lack of proper sociological understanding of the problem of rural reconstruction. To evolve a successful programme of rural reconstruction at a higher level, it is quite necessary to know the law governing the development of the rural society. The structure, the functioning and the objective tendencies of development of the existing rural society, the interconnectedness and the interdependence of various elements of that society (technical, economic, social, political, ideological), and the relative significance of those elements in determining the life of the rural society and their respective role in the total social change, require to be comprehended.

To change society consciously, we must have a science of society. Rural sociology is the science of rural society. The laws of the structure and development of rural society in general can aid us in discovering the special laws governing a particular rural society. Without the science of rural society, it is not, therefore, possible to get an authentic picture of a particular rural society. Rural sociology alone can provide a correct, organic, synthetic and multi-sided knowledge of a specific rural society and the tendency of its further evolution.

Important Features

Rural sociology will help the rural worker to make a correct diagnosis of its ills and will, further, enable him to evolve a correct prescription or programme to overcome those ills. If the diagnosis of the ills is erroneous or imperfect, the prescription itself will be unscientific and therefore futile. The uniformed rural worker will adopt unhistorical and inappropriate means to cure the defects and deficiencies of the rural social organisms. The social ills may have a deep-seated cause in the very social system itself and may be merely symptoms proclaiming the general disease of the social organism. Not knowing this, the rural worker will engage himself in a symptomatic treatment of the social ills which, as all physicians know, gives no relief or gives only a partial and temporary relief.

There is another grave danger for a rural worker who is ignorant of rural sociology. The present social evils are the features of the present society and therefore cannot be overcome by methods adopted to cure the social evils of bygone societies. For instance, solutions of the evils of self-sufficient society would not be adequate for the solution of the maladies of the present competitive commodity society. If the rural worker is unaware of this fact, he will attempt to graft the former on the present society. He will recommend the resuscitation of the techniques, political systems or ethical concepts of the past societies to overcome the crisis of the present one. Such a view is unscientific. The evils of the present rural society arise out of its own inner structure and can be cured by means determined by its own trend of development.

The programme of rural reconstruction should be derived from a strict sociological analysis of the actual conditions and tendencies of the actually existing rural society and evaluation of the actual forces at work within it.

Here comes the decisive creative role of rural sociology which is as indispensable for the purpose of rural reconstruction as the science of medicine is to a medical practitioner.

6 The Infrastructure

In a clear, interesting and systematically developed study, under the title of "Social Structure and Change in Indian Peasant Communities" has been presented a general panorama of the Indian population in this century.

The population of an Indian village is united by three different bonds of solidarity: (a) family ties, (b) the caste system, and (c) territorial affinities.

The caste system is the most important and over-rules family and territorial ties; in order to understand the extent and depth of its influence, it is only necessary to know that internal relationships within the castes are subject to rules governing matrimony, meals, physical contact and occupations and that these rules are obeyed because they are considered to be of divine origin.

Castes have remained as exclusive groups throughout the ages, since strict endogamy is observed.

The influence of the castes in social relationships is, accordingly, very great in India, although sometimes of a negative character. "The taboos of the Indian caste system," asserts Max Weber, "inhibit social intercourse much more than the system of Chinese belief in spirits hindered trade." Nevertheless, according to this same author, "the railways will gradually render caste taboos illusory."

The interesting paper by Dr. S. C. Dube on present day India confirms the study made by the great German sociologist at the end of the last century. In effect, according to S. C. Dube, the social structure of India is subject to considerable changes under the impact of Western culture and civilization. Modern systems of transport and communications, modern technology, industrialization and Western type education during the last 10 years have combined to produce the following obvious changes:

(1) The social position of the individual in India is dependent upon his caste; but at present that system of class distinction is being superseded by another rival system by which the individual's position in society is determined on his own personal merit.

(2) This change in class distinction is more apparent when a person moves from country to town since on esta-blishing himself in the city, he has to accustom himself to urban customs.

(3) There is a noticeable weakening in the authority of the individual castes in rural India.

(4) A certain individualism has developed within the family.

(5) Western forms of life and modern technology have been accepted by the upper strata of society as they have the opportunity of acquiring them.

(6) On the other hand the lower strata are, in a way, conservative because of their lack of education and poverty.

(7) Notwithstanding the relative conservatism of the lower classes, it appears that the social structure of the village is in a state of dissolution and disintegration.

The work of Dr. Tarlok Singh of the New Delhi Planning Commission complements the information given by Dr. Dube.

Dr. Tarlok Singh discusses the "Landless Labourer and the Pattern of Social and Economic Change" and explains in detail in this valuable work the effect upon India of what is known as "the impact of the West". This impact is particularly noticeable in the villages and has developed slowly and indirectly.

(a) The products of Western industry introduced into the

villages of India by pedlars diminished the demand for home-produced goods. Many craftsmen who used to make such local products became redundant and turned into farm workers without land of their own.

(b) Western ideas on ownership and finance changed the self-sufficient spirit in the village for an acquisitive, profit-seeking spirit, with the exploitation of the weak by the strong under the guise of legality. Wealth and self-seeking replaced the community spirit in the scale of values.

(c) These conditions created an internal capitalism represented by foreigners and by Indian traders and landowners who promoted the feudal conditions by means of latifundism and monetary loans.

(d) New techniques diminished the opportunities for work in a growing population, thus accentuating the effect of Western economic influence and Indian capitalism.

(e) As a result of all this, in the last 60 years, the population dependent upon agriculture has increased. It is calculated that it increased from 193 to 250 million between 1931 and 1951.

(f) Under Western influence, the bonds created by the social castes are tending to decrease, and some castes have disappeared altogether; but this has created the problem of providing work for men who were formerly employed within the strict caste system.

Landless People

The increase in the number of agricultural workers in India without land of their own is a problem which requires early solution. For this reason a democratic planning scheme is being put into practice and is founded on various definite points which tend to explain what should be done. Dr. Tarlok Singh is working on this. But can a Sociological Congress embark upon the study of these questions which properly belong to politics? We think not; the role of sociology should be defined as the study of prevailing social conditions for the purpose of obtaining scientific theories capable of serving as a basis for action; but sociology cannot indicate the precise terms for this action since they are dependent upon political conditions and the economic and social potentialities of each individual country.

Dr. A. R. Desai, of the Department of Sociology of the University of Bombay, with his work on "The Impact of the Measures Adopted by the Government of the Indian Union on the Life of the Rural People", confirms the concepts we have just put before you. He describes firstly the changes which took place in Indian society under the influence of Western culture and civilization during the period of British rule and the effects mostly negative of the measures adopted by the present Government of the Indian Union to reconstruct the country on new social and economic bases. The study of the effects of these measures certainly comes within the scope of sociology since they form part of the social structure of India and the failure of many of them shows how daring and dangerous it is to prescribe them.

The study now being made by Dr. Desai of the results of the contact between Western culture and civilisation and Indian culture, under British rule, to a large extent confirms and also complements the information given by Doctors S. C. Dube and Tarlok Singh

(a) Western culture dealt a mortal blow to the rural organization of India, based on an autarchical village community, with common ownership of land.

(b) It destroyed the collectivistic spirit and introduced individualism and competition.

(c) It introduced private ownership, letting out of land and individual cash taxation.

(d) In this way, agrarian economy based on the satisfaction of the needs of the family changed to an economy based on satisfaction of the demands of the market.

(e) It destroyed the self-sufficiency of rural life, at the same time ruining the small village industries by the introduction of machine-made products.

(f) The mass of craftsmen-deprived of their crafts by the articles imported from modern British factories-turned to agriculture, thus increasing the volume of labourers without land and accentuating the pressure of the rural population on the land. The size of small holdings diminished, and uneconomic properties increased in number.

(g) It increased the power of moneylenders, tradesmen and landowners over the poverty-stricken farmers.

(h) It increased the number of tenants and intermediaries (farmer-tenants, sub-tenant, sub-sub-tenants, etc.) supported by those who actually cultivated the ground.

(i) It decreased the power of the caste and reduced the size of the family.

(j) All this produced considerable impoverishment of the masses and internal lack of balance in the rural structure of India. To remedy this situation the Government of the Indian Union has put various measures into practice: (a) measures of a political nature establishing universal suffrage which gave rise "to considerable social and political quickening in rural India"; (b) measures of an economic nature such as irrigation projects, the introduction of better seed and fertilizers, reforms in letting arrangements to protect the tenant and cut out intermediaries, protection of the peasants against abuse by creditors, economic development of rural zones and the creation of co-operative societies and assistance to the small rural industries.

But these and other measures have failed because they only benefit those farmers who are in a sound economic position. No measures have been taken to allocate land to rural workers who have none, or to provide them with employment. The protective measures are easily circumvented; the co-operative societies only favour the clever farmers.

The plans for rural economic development do not favour those who have nothing and, on the other hand, the subscriptions required to put them into operation overburden them.

To sum up, according to Dr. Desai, the governmental measures adopted in India have produced changes in the rural community which tend to intensify the opposition between classes in the rural communities and also between castes, thus causing tension, antagonism and clashes.

What sociological conclusions can be obtained from the three studies we have mentioned? What can the sociologist advise in regard to the changes which are taking place in the rural community of India?

The experience of the Indian people, like that of other peoples as history shows, supports the following generalization: whenever peoples of different culture and civilization come into contact, the most advanced tends to dominate and exploit the least developed. When these latter gain their independence, their upper classes who succeed in assimilating the civilization of their rulers, replace them in ruling and exploiting the masses.

The failure of the measures adopted by the Government of India to help the rural working class in the face of the changes in agrarian economic structure brought about by British rule and Western culture and civilization, in the same way as similar failures suffered by other peoples, serves as a basis for this further generalization: the upper classes of a country, who hold the economic power, tend to circumvent all the protective measures devised by the Government to help the working classes or to turn these same measures to their own profit.

From a strictly scientific point of view this is what, in our opinion, the Third World Sociological Congress can prove by way of general conclusions on the interesting studies submitted by Doctor Dube Singh and Desai with regard to the changes in agrarian economic structure in India.

Although it is certain that sociology must study prevailing

conditions, it does not follow from this, arms the talented French sociologist, Emile Durkheim, " that we should give up trying to improve them: we would feel that our speculations were not worth the trouble if they had no more than a speculative interest." " Science, " he adds, " can help us to find the road we should follow and to determine the goal towards which we blindly struggle."

With the support of the above mentioned theories the sociologist can recommend, also in a general way, that in all those countries where peoples of different civilizations come into contact with each other, the Governments should not adopt empirical action in favour of the economically and politically weaker rural classes, but action planned on the basis of investigations and research carried out by scientists experienced in the social sciences so that the political action guides the changes in agrarian economic structure efficiently, preventing abuses, social inequalities and injustices.

Small Cultivators

The agricultural reconstruction has proved an achilles hill of planning in India. The official policy of 'betting on rich' in rural areas has only aggravated agrarian crisis in India. One of the basic prerequisites for the revitalization of agriculture is the effective resolution of problems of marginal farmers in rural India. The overwhelming majority of Indian cultivators operate on sub-marginal or marginal units of cultivation. The inadequate appreciation of this vital phenomenon has undermined official endeavours for rural reconstruction. An attempt is made here to unfold the deeper implications of the problems of marginal farmers within the profit-oriented matrix of Indian economy. A proper appraisal of their problems assumes greater significance in the light of the emerging trend among the experts, advocating inherent superiority of marginal farms compared to bigger units of cultivation.

Distribution of ownership holdings amongst rural households according to size groups crop season

	Household ownerships holdings			
Size-Group	P.c. of holdings to the total	Cumulative p.c. of holdings	P.c. of area to total area owned	Cumulative p.c. of area
1	2	3	4	5
0.00** 23.09	-	-	-	
0.01- 0.99	24.17	47.26	1.37	-
1.00-2.49	13.98	61.24	4.86	-
2.50- 4.99	13.49	74.73	10.09	16.32
5.00- 9.99	12.50	87.23	18.40	34.72
10.00-24.99	9.17	96.40	29.11	68.83
25.00-49.99	2.66	99.06	18.63	82.46
50.00 or above	0.94	100.00	17.54	100.00
Total	100.00	-	100.00	-

Main Problems

It is generally accepted that the cultivators whose holdings are below 5 acres, can be placed in the category of marginal farmers in the present state of agriculture in India. The vast bulk of these farmers are deficit cultivators as the farming has ceased to be a gainful occupation for them. The Table reveals the proportion of these farmers in the total cultivating population.

It can be seen from the above Table that nearly three-fourths of all rural households operate on holdings which are below 5 acres, and together own only one-sixth of the total area. In sharp contrast to this, the top one-fourth of households hold 83.68 per cent of the total area in size group, above 5 acres. It can be also further observed from the above figures that, 12.77 per cent of the rural households hold as much as 65.28 per cent of the total owned area in size-groups of more than 10.00 acres. Even after implementation of land reforms the land distribution pattern has not altered in favour of marginal farmers. This fact is also confirmed by the Mahalanobis Committee Report.

We shall now examine how the laws of market economy remorselessly operate against marginal farmers and gradually worsen their plight.

Price Factor

The last decade witnessed unprecedented rise in the prices of manufactured articles as well as agricultural products. The recent sharp rise in the prices of foodgrains transcended all past records. This inflation of prices caused primarily by deficit financing, erodes the standard of living of masses and leads to further concentration of wealth in the hands of the richer sections. According to Prof. Gyanchznd, "Rise of the prices in the Second Five Year Plan period has been of the order of 25 per cent and since 1956 the rise has been maintained and even accelerated. This has happened in spite of the increase of 33 per cent in agricultural and 66 per cent in industrial production..... The premise that in a developing economy rise of prices is inevitable is being made a cover for all errors and failings in respect of price policies..... The fact that in spite of the peak of agricultural production of 76 million tons and increase of industrial production of 11.7 per cent during the course of 1960, the average level of prices has risen during the year by 6.5 per cent, of raw materials by 16 per cent. The index number of general price level at the end of war with 1939 as base was 260, the average at 1952-53, when the new base for the revised index number was adopted, was 380, and in January 1961 it was 475. In everyone of these indices are congealed unwanted and iniquitious changes in economic relativities of different income groups, which have been known to exist but have been deliberately left unredressed owing to the extreme difficulties of righting the wrongs created by inflationary upsurge from time to time. The result has been that these inequities have accumulated and their incidence has been severe on agricultural labourers and even industrial labourers, small peasants, small traders and lower middle classes with fixed and relatively in elastic incomes. The whole income structure of the country has been gravely distorted on this account and the increasing national income has not accrued to the benefit of these classes i.e. the vast majority of our people, and they are as a matter of fact distinctly worse off than they were before the war. Any price policy which leaves this cardinal fact of the economic situation out of account follows the line of least resistance and is escapist in the worst sense of the word."

Though it may sound paradoxical, it is still true that high agricultural prices hit the marginal farmers as much as the urban population. The rise in agricultural prices benefits only the rich farmers with marketable surplus. They profit from higher prices and strengthen their economic position, at the expense of the deficit cultivators and agricultural labourers. Nearly 40 per cent of the Indian cultivators have to buy a part of their food requirements from the market and they suffer heavily from the high prices of essential commodities. Thus rise in prices only depresses the already depressed consumption standard of vast bulk of our deficit farmers. Even the exchange equivalents in the countryside are also more unfavourable to the marginal farmers than suggested by the wholesale price indices. The overwhelming proportions of small farmers are still under the firm grip of the village Shaukars, most of whom perform the combined functions of moneylending as well as trading. It is estimated that the 'moneylender-cum-traders' profit over the prices paid to the growers ranges from 30 to 200 per cent whereas in other countries it seldom goes beyond 15 to 20 per cent. Thus the market mechanism within the frame-work of underdeveloped economy intensifies the process of impoverishment of the marginal farmers. The following Table distinctly reveals the worsening plight of the marginal farmers in terms of the quantity of sales per acre.

Distribution of sales of paddy by farmers in selected villages

Size group of holdings (acre)	Percentage sales of each group to total		Quantity of sales per acre of holdings (in mds)	
	1942-43 1944-45	1955-56 1956-57	1942-43 1944-45	1955-56 1956-57
upto 2.5	3.29	1.94	1.76	0.82
2.5 to 5	12.92	10.91	1.90	1.94
5 to 10	37.99	30.32	3.60	4.57
10 to 20	33.15	28.58	6.22	6.46
Above 20	12.65	28.25	5.14	10.69
Total	100	100	3.94	4.61

It is evident from the above Table that the quantity of sale by small farm registered a fall while that of the big farms relatively increased during the periods under review. Similarly eminent scholars like Prof. Khusro, Dharam Narain and others have also pointed out that marketable produce as a proposition of total produce increases generally with increase in farm size.

It can be seen that the marginal farms possess much less capital and labour compared to the larger farms. In contrast to this they exhibit too much capital and labour per acre in com-parison to larger units. "This aspect of farm structure has an important bearing upon the costs of production, input output coefficients, and profit ability or remunerativeness of the farming business in different size-groups. As a result of this farm assets structure, the inputs of labour and capital per unit of land decline and the costs of production per acre go down with an increase in the size of farm. In fact, the inputs per acre even of other resources such as seeds, fertilizers, manures and irrigation decline with an increase in the size of farms, leading to a considerable decline in total inputs per acre. Evidently, the output input coefficient is more favourable on large farms and the profitability or remunerativeness of farming increases with an increase in farm size, despite a somewhat larger gross output per acre on small farms".

Unremunerative and uneconomic character of marginal units of cultivation can be further elucidated from the following Table.

Per acre resources of land, capital and labour on 400 holdings

Size-groups acres cattle (units) stock	No. of draught cattle (units)	No. of milch vest- ment on live- stock Rs.	Value of in- imple- ments Rs.	Invest- ment on farm build- ings Rs.	Invest- ment on ment on fixed assets exclud- ing land Rs.	Total invest- (units)	No. of workers
1	2	3	4	5	6	7	8
Below 2.5	0.70	0.53	233	77	178	523	1.1
2.5- 5.0	0.47	0.26	150	66	87	305	0.6
5.0-7.5	0.35	0.22	129	57	83	282	0.4
7.5-10.0	0.26	0.19	116	47	83	272	0.3
10.0-15.0	0.25	0.14	100	42	74	236	0.2
15.0-20.0	0.23	0.11	96	40	62	231	0.2
20.0-25.0	0.19	0.09	80	25	56	199	0.2
25.0 & above	0.18	0.10	76	32	76	208	0.1
Average	0.27	0.16	107	44	76	215	0.4

Under the circumstances, it is no wonder that the under-utilization of available resources is a chronic problem faced by the marginal farms. This can be better illustrated from the under-utilization of the working capacity of bullocks on small farms. A pair of healthy bullocks is presumed to be capable of work for 8 hours each day for 350 days in a year. On this basis, it can be seen from the following figures that, the utilization of bullocks varies from 13.1 to 43.30 per cent of their available labour on holdings of different sizes.

Below 2 acres	13.14%	5 to 10 acres	36.79
2 to 5 acres	34.12 %	10 to 15 acres	43.35

It is evident from the above figures that the considerable amount of the working capacity of the bullocks remains unutilized on smaller farms. Dr. C. H. Shah has further highlighted this phenomenon. He observes, 'The field survey in the Kodinar taluka reveals that the central problem of the small farmers is relatively greater imbalance of factors of production. This affects on the one hand farm production and land productivity and on the other affects his income, savings, credit and investment and through them his economic betterment. Since two aspects are interlinked they set into motion a vicious circle which with passage of time brings about deterioration of his economy. Imbalance in factor combination takes two forms. Firstly, since the quantum of family labour is given and the size of holding is inadequate to provide full employment to all working members of the family, his economy has surplus of labour, only a part of which is employed outside. Unemployed labour is a heavy drag on his small income. Secondly, a certain minimum of equipment and housing facilities is necessary but his investment is rather heavy for his size of holding. On the other hand, his equipment is inadequate for efficient farming. Further the low income leaves very little for investment in working capital, with his small holdings, he commands low credit which is inadequate to meet the requirement of working capital." The above observations of Dr. Shah distinctly reveal the paucity of resources and resultant helplessness of the small farmers in a relatively prosperous tract of Gujarat. He also prognosticates decay of small farming with the passage of time.

Distribution of Cultivators' Holdings According to Size-groups

	Under one acre		1 acre to 2-5 acres		2.5 acres to 5 acres		5 acres to 10 acres		10 acres to 25 acres		Above 25 acres		
Census Zones	Number	Area	Number	Area	Number	Area	Number	Area	Number	Area	Number	Area	Average size of holdings (acres)
1	2	3	4	5	6	7	8	9	10	11	12	13	14
North India	14.8	1.4	26.2	8.3	25.1	16.7	20.6	26.4	11.4	30.6	1.9	16.6	5.3
East India	21.4	2.1	24.4	9.1	26.4	20.8	18.4	27.6	8.0	25.1	1.4	15.3	4.5
South India	28.0	2.7	27.1	9.5	20.9	16.3	14.0	21.1	7.9	25.4	2.1	25.0	4.5
West India	11.2	0.5	15.6	2.1	13.9	4.1	20.4	11.9	25.4	32.6	13.5	48.8	12.3
Central India	7.4	0.3	12.3	1.5	16.4	4.5	22.1	12.0	28.4	33.7	13.4	48.0	12.2
North-West India	5.4	0.2	14.4	2.0	16.9	5.1	22.5	13.4	31.0	39.3	9.8	40.0	12.6

We shall conclude this paper, by referring to the extent of underemployment that prevails in marginal units of cultivation in the absence of opportunities for gainful employment.

The number of labour days put in per acre is more on the marginal farms. Even if it is assumed that the intensity of cultivation and reliance on mixed farming is greater on marginal units that by itself cannot explain such a wide range of difference in the number of days put in per acre which vary from 133 for the size group of 2.5 acres and below, to 31 for 25 acres and above. Therefore, it can be safely concluded that the labour input on marginal units of cultivation has very low returns. This precisely indicates that there is considerable amount of underemployment of small farms. The unremunerative character of marginal farms becomes evident from the fact that family labour income per acre increases with the increase in the size of farm though the family labour input is much smaller.

The following Table provides some pertinent facts with regard to labour days and family labour income per acre for different size groups of farms in U. P. in the year 1954-55.

Size group (acres)	Labour days (per acre)	Family labour income (per acre)
Below 2.5	133	83.72
2.5 to 5	114	
5 to 7.5	96	119.87
7.5 to 10	67	
10 to 15	52	91.81
15 to 20	49	111.84
20 to 25	40	124.47
25 & above	31	

From the foregoing discussions the conclusion remains irresistable that economically, farming is a unremunerative occupation for the large bulk of marginal farmers. These farms also suffer from under-utilization of available resources and man-power. The input-output coefficient too works unfavourably against marginal farmers. Further the prevailing price structure also affects them adversely. This phenomenon viewed in context of our competitive economy, spells their disintegration, perhaps a rapid one from the Indian agriculture.

The inequality of cultivators' holdings is considerable in India. While the average size of the holdings was about 7-5 acres, about 70 per cent of the holdings were below this average. Holdings below one acre formed about 17 per cent, those between one and 2½ acres about 21 per cent and those between 2½ and 5 acres another 21 per cent. These accounted respectively for 1.0, 4.6 and 9.9 per cent of the total area. At the other end of the scale, 16 per cent were in the group 10 to 25 acres accounting for 32.5 per cent of the area and another 5.6 per cent above 25 acres covering about 34 per cent of the area.

The overall average size of holdings was 5.3 acres in North India (Uttar Pradesh) but the number of holdings upto 2.5 acres in size formed about 40 per cent of the total number of holdings and cover 9.7 per cent of the total area. The largest concentration of holdings, viz., 25 per cent was in the group 2.5 to 5 acres covering 16.7 per cent of the total area; 20.6 per cent were in the group 5 to 10 acres and covered 26.4 per cent of the area, while 11.4 per cent were in the group 10 to 25 acres covering 30.6 per cent of the area.

In East India zone, the overall average size was 4.5 acres. Here also, the largest concentration of holdings, namely 26.4 per cent covering 20.8 per cent of the total area was in the group 2.5 to 5 acres. However, 45.8 per cent were below 2.5 acres and covered 11.2 per cent of the area. The rest were above 5 acres.

In South India zone, as much as 55 per cent of the holdings covering 12.2 per cent of the area were below 2.5 acres, the overall average size being 4.5 acres. About 21 per cent of the holdings occupying 16.3 per cent of the area were in the size group 2.5 to 5 acres, while the rest were above 5 acres.

In West India zone, the overall average size was high, namely 12.3 acres, but 61 per cent of the holdings were below 10 acres and occupied 18.6 per cent of the area. A little above 25 per cent of the holdings covering 32.6 per cent of the area were in the group 10 to 25 acres, while 13.5 per cent covering 48.8 per cent of the area was above 25 acres.

The overall average size of holdings in Central India zone was 12.2 acres but 58 per cent of the holdings covering 18 per cent of the total area were below 10 acres. About 28 per cent were in the size group 10 to 25 acres and accounted for 34 per cent of the area, while 13.4 per cent occupying 48 per cent of the area were above 25 acres in size.

The average size of holdings was the highest, viz., 12.6 acres in North-West India zone. However, 59 per cent of the holdings occupying 20.7 per cent of the area were below 10 acres. About 31 per cent of the holdings was in the size group 10 to 25 acres and occupied 39.3 per cent of the area, while 9.8 per cent covering 40 per cent of the area were above 25 acres.

The above statement gives the percentage distribution of cultivator's holdings according to size groups in the different Census Zones.

The enquiry revealed that besides the cultivating owner families and tenant families the agricultural labour families as also the non-agricultural families were also cultivating holdings, smaller though, as a subsidiary occupation. Of the total number of holdings, about 35 per cent were cultivated by owners, another 35 per cent by tenants, 20 per cent by labourers and 10 per cent by non-agriculturists. The percentage distribution of the total area of the holdings as amongst these categories was 52.4 for landowners, 35.7 for tenants, 7.8 for agricultural labourers and 4.1 for non-agriculturists. While the average size of the holdings of owner families was larger, being 11.37 acres, that of the tenants 7.74 acres approximated the overall average. The average size of holdings of the agricultural workers was 2.86 acres and that of the non-agriculturists 3.10 acres. About 51 per cent of the area of the holdings were occupied by landowners and 37 per cent by tenants, while agricultural workers and non-agriculturists occupied 8 and 4 per cent respectively.

The Livestock

Small farming requires livestock, implements and considerable human labour since mechanisation is possible only on large farms. Livestock such as bullocks, buffaloes and horses and to a small extent camels, are used as draught animals for ploughing, irrigating and sometimes for threshing. Bullock labour is also used for transport of manure to the fields, agricultural produce to the market, etc. Operations such as preparatory work, sowing, weeding, irrigating and threshing require many implements such as crowbars, spades, hoes, seed-drills, charas and persian wheels, etc. In case the cultivator does not own suffi-cient livestock or implements, he either borrows them or engages workers who bring their own in return for higher wages.

The number of work animals and ploughs owned are thus closely related to the number of holdings and their size. It is possible to arrive at, broadly, the average work unit for a pair of work animals and a plough in a particular region by dividing the total cultivated area by the number of pairs of work animals and ploughs separately and obtain a mean of the two sets of figures relating to average area per plough and per pair of work animals. This concept of a work unit will have some value in attempting to estimate the labour surplus in agriculture.

During the General Family Survey, data on livestock and ploughs possessed by each family living in the sample villages were collected. The average number of cattle, sheep and goats, poultry and ploughs according to different categories of families.

The families of agricultural landowners had 44.8 per cent of the ploughs, while those of tenants, agricultural workers and non-agriculturists had 38.2, 11.7 and 5.3 per cent respectively. On an average, there were 0.7 plough per family. The zonal figures were almost the same. The following statement gives the zonal differences:

Average Number of Ploughs per Family

	Number of ploughs per family of Zones				
	Land-owners	Tenants	Agri-cultural labourers	Non-Agri-culturists	All families
North India ...	1.2	1.0	0.2	0.2	0.7
East India ...	1.4	0.8	0.2	0.2	0.6
South India ...	1.5	1.5	0.3	0.1	0.6
Western India ...	0.9	0.9	0.2	0.1	0.8
Central India ...	1.4	1.1	0.3	0.3	0.8
N. W. India ...	1.1	1.2	0.2	0.2	0.8
All India ...	1.2	1.0	0.3	0.2	0.7

On an average, a landowner's family had 1.2 ploughs, whereas a tenant's family had 1.1. The average number of ploughs per agricultural labour and non-agricultural family was extremely small, viz., 0.3 and 0.2 respectively. As stated already, about 50 percent of the agricultural labourers held land. If, therefore, adjustments are made keeping this point in mind, the average number of ploughs per family would come to about 0.6. Similarly, the average number of ploughs per family of non-agriculturists having land would come to 0.7. The average number of ploughs per landowner and tenant family in South India zone was higher than that in other zones. The average was the least in West India zone.

For purposes of the Agricultural Labour Enquiry, the term 'cattle' included oxen or bullocks, cows (over 3 years), he-buffaloes and she-buffaloes. There were, on an average, 2.2 head of cattle per family taking all rural families together. The families of agricultural landowners had 3.8, tenants 3.3, agricultural labourers 1.0 and non-agriculturists 0.9 head of cattle. The zonal details are given in the statement below:

Heads of Cattle per Family

Zones	Heads of cattle per family of				
	Land-owners	Tenants	Agri-cultural labourers	Non-Agri-culturists	All families
North India ...	3.0	3.1	1.2	0.9	2.4
East India ...	4.1	2.5	1.1	0.9	2.0
South India ...	3.8	3.8	1.0	0.6	1.7
West India ...	3.4	3.5	0.8	1.0	2.4
Central India ...	4.3	4.7	0.8	1.1	2.6
N. W. India ...	3.7	4.3	1.2	1.1	2.9
All India ...	3.8	3.3	1.9	0.9	2.2

The average head of cattle per family of landowners and tenants varied between 3 and 4 in all the zones. But the average for agricultural labour families was about 1 and even slightly less in some of the zones.

The average number of sheep and goats per family came to 1.3, the corresponding figures for families of landowners, tenants, agricultural labourers and non-agriculturists being 1.7, 1.1, 0.8 and 1.5 respectively. The statement below gives the zonal details:

Sheep and Goats per Family

Zones	Average number of sheep and goats per family of				
	Land-owners	Tenants	Agri-cultural labourers	Non-Agri-culturists	All families
North India ...	0.4	0.6	0.5	1.1	0.7
East India ...	1.1	0.9	0.7	0.6	0.8
South India ...	2.4	1.2	1.1	0.4	1.2
West India ...	1.4	0.9	0.7	3.7	1.6
Central India ...	2.0	1.2	1.1	3.9	1.8
N.W. India ...	1.9	2.7	1.0	2.2	2:1
All India ...	1.7	1.1	0.8	1.5	1.3

The average number of sheep and goats in each category of family was comparatively small in North India zone. The average for land-owners family was quite high in South and Central India zones. This was due to high averages for Mysore (5.2) and Hyderabad (3.6). The average for tenant families was also quite high (2.7) in North-West India zone. This was due to high average for Rajasthan, viz., 2. 8. The relatively high average for non-agricultural families in West and Central India was partly due to high figures for Saurashtra and Madhya Pradesh and Hyderabad respectively.

Average Number of Poultry per Family

Zones	Average number of poultry per family of				
	Land-owners	Tenants	Agri-cultural labourers	Non-Agri-culturists	All families
North India ...	0.2	0.1	0.1	0.2	0.1
East India ...	3.5	1.8	1.1	1.1	1.5
South India ...	2.1	3.2	1.0	1.0	1.4
West India ...	0.9	0.9	0.6	0.3	0.8
Central India ...	0.5	0.6	0.5	0.5	0.6
N. W. India ...	0.3	0.3	0.3	0.5	0.5
All India ...	1.2	0.9	0.8	0.7	0.9

The average for East and South India zones were much higher than that for any other zone.

The following statement gives the zonal differences:

The average number of poultry per family was 0.9. The average per family of tenants, agricultural labourers and non-agriculturists was almost the same, it being 0.9, 0.8 and 0.7 respectively. The figure for landowners families was, however, relatively high being 1.2. The above table gives the average area of cultivated land per plough and per pair of work animals in the sample villages. In working out the figures, however, it has been assumed that only the ploughs and the work animals owned by the families living in the same villages were utilised for the various agricultural operations, that no ploughs or work animals were brought from outside and that the ploughs and work animals owned by the families in the sample villages were not utilised by others outside the villages. The average area of cultivated land per plough and per pair of work animals in the sample villages worked out to 6.04 and 7.18. acres respectively. The relatively high figures for Saurashtra and Kutch have to be viewed in the context that the average size of holding was high and the soil sandy.

The Habitation

During the General Family Survey, information on housing was collected through a special rubric. The data collected have, however, considerable limitations. In the first place, it is very difficult to have standard definitions especially for purposes of place to place comparisons. Broadly, houses were classified into pucca houses and kacha houses. Pucca houses are those the walls and roofs of which are built of bricks and stones with lime and mortar. If the walls were made of bricks and stones but the roof was made of thatch, the house was called partly pucca and partly kacha. Others were classified as kacha houses. The nature and structure of the house differed from region to region and was determined primarily by the climatic conditions on the one hand and the building materials easily available on the other. Thus, in the hilly regions of Assam, U. P. and Himachal Pradesh the houses were mostly of wooden structure. In regions with hillocks around, the walls were usually built of stones as they were available in plenty. In villages which were situated near rivers, the reeds grown on these river banks were used as thatching material. It was also common for villagers to use dried stalks of maize, cocoanut leaves and palm leaves for making roofs.

Since the construction of pucca houses with bricks and mortar require substantial initial investment, only those who were relatively better off owned such houses. Thus, a few big landlords, merchants and moneylenders had pucca houses and the rest, working classes, the artisans and the marginal cultivators lived in kacha houses with mud wall and thatched roofs.

Data on the floor area of houses and the rent paid either for the house or for the ground on which it was erected were also collected. These are not, however, given here since these were not considered to be quite accurate in view of the difficulty in getting precise information from the villagers.

In the sample villages about 84 per cent of the houses were kacha houses. Amongst the major States, this percentage was more than 90 in U. P., the Eastern States of Assam, Bihar, West Bengal and Orissa and the Central States of Madhya Pradesh and Hyderabad. It ranged between 80 and 90 in Rajasthan and Madhya Bharat and between 70 and 80 in Punjab, Bombay, Madras and Travancore-Cochin. The position was comparatively better in Pepsu and Saurashtra, the percentage being about 60. This was so presumably due to availability of stones. The following statement shows the percentages in the different Census Zones:

Percentage of kacha houses occupied by important categories of families

Zones	Percentage of kacha houses occupied by families of	
	Agricultural workers	All families
North India	99.7	92.5
East India	97.2	98.5
South India	90.0	78.1
West India	68.5	63.5
Central India	95.6	92.1
North-West India	88.6	76.1
All Sample Villages ..	92.6	84.1

The percentage of partly pucca and partly kacha houses was only 2.1, taking the Indian Union as a whole. Thus the percentage of pucca houses came to 13.8. The percentage of partly pucca and partly kacha houses was, however, relatively high, viz., about 8 per cent in North-West Zone mainly due to existence of such houses in Punjab and Pepsu.

Ownership of houses: The houses were almost all self-owned. This meant that the plot on which the house was erected was also owned by the house owner. However, when ground rent was paid, it generally meant that only the house was owned but not the plot. Such cases were included in the owned houses. Taking all the sample villages, the percentage of rented houses was about 1.7 and varied up to 4 in the major States. In respect of the agricultural labour families in particular, this percentage was about 1.3.

Families per house: Generally there was only one family per house. In fact the percentage of houses accommodating a single family was 95.3; those with two families formed 3.2 per cent and those with three or more families only 1.5 percent. The same trend was observed in each of the six Census Zones. The percentage of houses having one family varied from 93.6 in North India to 96.6 in South and Central India, while the percentage of those having 2 families varied from 2.3 in South India to 4.2 in North India, and those having 3 or more families varied between 1 and 2.

Distribution of houses according to number of families living in them

Zones	Percentage of houses accommodation		
	One family	Two families	Three or more families
North India	93.6	4.2	2.2
East India	94.4	3.7	1.9
South India	96.6	2.3	1.1
West India	95.7	3.0	1.3
Central India	96.5	2.6	0.9
North-West India	94.8	3.6	1.6

Number of rooms per house: Houses with a single room formed the largest percentage, viz., 38. Two room houses formed 28 and those having three or more rooms 34 per cent. The average number of rooms per house was 2.3. The agricultural labour families had limited accommodation, the average number of rooms per house being 1.9 and houses with one room formed the largest percentage, viz., 55, while two room houses constituted 27 per cent. The following statement gives the frequency distribution of houses according to rooms in the different Census Zones.

Taking the major States, the average number of rooms per house was 1.3 in West Bengal, 1.8 in Madhya Pradesh, 1.8 in Bombay, 1.9 in Madras and varied between 2 and 3 in the remaining States. The position in important States is given in the statement below:

Percentage Distribution of Houses According to Number of Rooms

Zone	All families			Agricultural labour families		
	1 room	2 rooms	3 or more rooms	1 room	2 rooms	3 or more rooms
NorthIndia	17.7	24.6	57.7	27.5	32.3	40.2
East India	42.0	24.7	33.3	48.8	27.5	23.7
South India	47.9	27.5	24.6	60.6	25.6	13.8
West India	42.7	38.6	18.7	54.7	33.9	11.4
Central India	48.6	30.3	21.1	63.9	27.4	8.7
North-West India	25.9	32.3	41.8	46.0	34.1	19.9
All sample villages	37.7	28.2	34.1	54.8	27.7	17.5

Number of Persons per Room: The number of persons per room depended on the number of rooms per house and the size of the family. Taking all the sampled villages, the average was about 2.3. The average generally varied between 2 and 3 as among the different States and was the highest in West Bengal being 3.6.

Taking the agricultural labour families, the size of the family was generally less than that of other classes of families and still the congestion was higher in view of the limited accommodation. In most of the major States, the number of persons per room was 3 with the exception of U. P., Assam, Bihar, Orissa, Rajasthan and Travancore-Cochin where it was, 2, 1.8, 2.5, 2.2, 2.1, and 2.6

respectively. The following statement gives the average number of persons per room in the different zones:

Average Number of Persons per Room

Average number of persons per room in the houses occupied by families of		
Zone	Agricultural workers	All families
North India	2.1	1.7
East India	2.5	2.3
South India	3.0	2.4
Central India	2.6	3.2
West India	2.9	2.8
North-West India	2.7	2.6

Number of Persons per Room

Average number of rooms per house occupied by families of		
Zones	Agricultural workers	All families
North India	2.5	3.2
Uttar Pradesh	2.5	3.2
East India	2.1	2.4
Assam	1.9	2.6
Bihar	2.4	3.2
West Bengal	1.2	1.3
Orissa	2.2	2.9
South India	1.8	2.1
Madras	1.5	1.9
Mysore	1.8	2.1
Travancore-Cochin	2.0	2.0
West India	1.8	1.9
Bombay	1.6	1.8
Saurashtra	1.2	1.6
Central India	1.5	2.0
Madhya Pradesh	1.5	1.8
Madhya Bharat	1.5	2.3
Hyderabad	1.5	1.8
North-West India	1.9	2.8
Punjab	1.6	2.4
Pepsu	1.6	2.6
Rajasthan	2.3	2.9
All sample villages	2.0	2.3

7

Rural Economy

Since economic production is the basic activity of a human aggre-gate, the mode of production (productive forces and social relations of production) plays a determining role in shaping the social structure, the psychology and the ideology of that human aggregate.

Rural society is based predominantly on agriculture. Village agriculture is sharply distinguished from urban industry by the fact that it is based on direct extraction from Nature by man.

Agriculture Supreme

Land is the basic means of production in the countryside. Land is a part of Nature, though made arable by human labour. From land, the rural people produce, by means of technique and their labour power, such a variety of agrarian products as food, cotton, jute, tea, coffee, tobacco and others.

Urban industry only transforms the products of agriculture into industrial products. In city factories and mills, such agricultural products as cotton, jute and sugarcane are transformed into cotton and jute cloth and sugar respectively.

This basic difference between agriculture and industry plays a significant role in shaping the social institutions, the psychology and the ideology of the rural and urban populations.

Further, the level of production and the way in which the products are distributed among the different strata of a society, determine the level of the material prosperity of the society as a whole and of the various socio-economic groups comprising it. They also, to a very large extent, mould the institutional set up of that society as well as the cultural life of its people.

For instance, in India, the primitive nature of agriculture, the resultant low level of agricultural production and the specific types of land relations which determine the differing shares of agricultural products among the social groups composing the rural society, explain the general poverty of the rural people, their hierarchic gradation into a pyramidal system of socio-economic groups and, further, their distinct social institutions and cultural backwardness. They also largely fix their customs, conceptions, and social mores.

The rural sociologist should find out whether, in the given society agricultural production has for its objective the direct satisfaction of the subsistence needs of the rural aggregate or is carried on for the market and profit of the producers who do not themselves consume their products. This means whether the agricultural economy is a subsistence or a market economy.

For instance, in pre-British India, village agriculture mainly produced for meeting the needs of the village population. This subsistence village agricultural economy was transformed into a market economy during the British period. This was due to a variety of causes. The British Government created private property in land in the form of ryotwari and zamindari. In the ryotwari area, it introduced the system under which the peasant producer had to pay to the state land tax in cash instead of in kind. The land tax grew progressively heavy resulting into the increasing indebtedness of the agriculturist. In the zamindari area, the burden of increasing rent imposed on the tenant producer by the zamindar impoverished the tenant and saddled him also with the ever expanding burden of debt. Largely due to the necessity for cash for the payment of land tax, rent and debt, the agriculturist, the peasant proprietor or the tenant, was more and more constrained to produce for the market. Thus village agriculture increasingly ceased to produce for directly satisfying the needs of the village population and began to produce for the national and subsequently even world market.

There is a third and new conception of the objective of agricultural production. According to it, not only should agriculture produce to meet the needs of the community but also it should be adapted to the consciously assessed needs of the total community. The exponents of this view argue that this will not only eliminate the competitive market intervening between the producers and the consumers but will also transform agriculture into planned agriculture, a planned sector of the social economy conforming to the needs of the community. They further declare that planned agriculture together with planned industry will transform the entire social economy into a planned economy which alone would make the maximum use of the natural, the technical and human labour resources of the community possible with the result that the material wealth of society would enormously increase and hence the standard of life of the people would rise higher and higher. The rural sociologist needs to devote greater attention to this aspect of the study of agricultural production. This is because not only the technique of agriculture but also the motif of agricultural production determine the level of that production and the resultant wealth of the agrarian community and, therefore, its standard of life.

Techniques of Production

The history of agriculture reveals that a variety of implements have been employed by rural communities. Generally speaking, we can divide the rural technical cultures into the following three types:

(1) *Hoe culture*: During this phase of mankind's existence, even the plough had not been invented. It was the early stage of agriculture when it was carried on only through the hoe operated by the human hand.

(2) *Plough culture*: During the next historical phase, man invented the plough. Being technically superior to the hoe, the plough enabled the agricultural community to produce more with the expenditure of the same amount of human labour power. The plough culture implied the use of animals in agricultural operations. Though our country

has advanced beyond hoe culture centuries ago, the hoe still lingers in the existing phase of plough culture in some agrarian areas.

(3) *The higher technical cultural phase of tractors and fertilizers*: The invention of power-driven machinery in modern times resulted into the production of such amazing labour-saving agricultural machines as tractors and fertilizers. Though this new agricultural technique is used on a large-scale in a number of advanced countries at present, it has not yet displaced the plough to any appreciable extent in our country.

The productivity of the labour of the agriculturist and hence the volume of agricultural products have increased in proportion to the advance of agricultural technique. The extent of the material wealth of rural society, therefore, depends mainly upon the technical basis of agriculture.

It may be noted that the power basis of agriculture has also changed in history. As pointed above, the hoe excludes the use of draft animals or any kind of power. The plough is worked with the aid of draft animals. The tractor eliminates even the necessity of draft animals and is propelled by oil power.

The technique of production also determines the division of labour among the members of a society actually engaged in the production process. It gives rise to a definite number of functions in the production process. This results in the emergence of various working groups, each of them attending to a particular function in production.

Thus we have a greater division of labour where the technique employed in production is higher. Correspondingly, we have a greater number of working groups.

Where agriculture is based on the plough, the division of labour is limited. The whole process of agricultural production in various stages is carried on by a peasant family on the basis of the simple and restricted division of labour among its members. In contrast to this, where agriculture is carried on by means of tractors and fertilizers, we have not only a larger physical unit of agriculture (land) but also a greater technical division of labour. We have then such working groups as engineers, electricians, chemists, tractor drivers and others.

The rural sociologist requires to study the various working groups determined by the technique used in agriculture as a part of the study of the rural population.

Cultivation Lands

Next, in the course of the study of the economic life of the rural society, it is vital to understand the land or property relations within the framework of which agricultural production is carried on.

While technique strictly determines the techno-economic division of labour and the resultant number of specific working groups, it does not, as we find from our study, of history always lead to the rise of the same property relations. For instance, the plough was the technical basis of agriculture carried on within the framework of such different land relations as existing in slave and feudal societies. It has also remained the technical basis of agriculture, in modern times, in underdeveloped capitalist societies of countries like India, Burma, Indo-China, and others. Again we find that such advanced techniques as tractors and fertilizers are used in agriculture within the framework of such diametrically opposite types of land relations as capitalist and collectivist which exist in the U.S.A. and Soviet Union respectively.

Thus, while techno-economical relations based on functional division of labour correspond to the existing technique of agriculture, land relations or socio-economic relations of production do not always conform to the technique in the form of a single pattern. Hence even when agriculture is carried on with the same plough, we find such varied socio-economic groups as serfs and barons, zamindars and tenants, peasant proprietors, and labourers and others. And, further, when it is worked by tractors and other kinds of modern machinery, even then we observe such diverse groups as wage workers, capitalist landowners, agriculturists who are members of state-owned collective farms and others.

(1) The nature of land relations determines the share of various socio-economic groups associated with agriculture in the total agricultural wealth. For instance, in the zamindari area, the zamindar receives by far the larger share of agricultural income than the cultivating tenant. The staggering disparity between the colossal income of the former and the meager income of the latter is basically due to the zamindari type of land relations. Further, the agrarian economy based upon a specific type of land relations has its own logic, its own law of development. Hence we find that the general tendency of the agrarian economic development in the zamindari zone is to accentuate the economic contrast. The cultivating tenant, in spite of a series of reforms, is being increasingly impoverished.

To take another instance, where full-fledged capitalist agriculture exists, a wage worker gets from the capitalist owner of land a wage determined by the state of the labour market.

Thus land relations determine the mode of distribution of the agricultural wealth among the various sections of the rural population just as technique determines the volume of that wealth.

(2) As a consequence of the above, land relations determine the degree of enthusiasm and interest of various groups bound up with agriculture, in the process of pro-duction.

For instance, in zamindari area, the cultivating tenant has meagre incentive to work since he has to surrender a big share of the crop, the fruit of his labour, to the zamindar and his agents. This is in contrast to the peasant proprietor in the ryotwari area, who feels appreciable incentive since he retains the whole product of his labour. However, even in his case, if he feels the burden of land tax and debt too heavy, his enthusiasm for agricultural effort would decline.

(3) Land relations play a decisive role in determining the degree of homogeneity or heterogeneity of the rural population.

In the zamindari area, the rural society is mainly divided into such groups as zamindars, non-cultivating tenants and sub-tenants, and finally cultivating tenants. In the ryotwari area, there are generally peasant proprietors of various grades and landless workers. In the case of large-scale capitalist agriculture, there exist such groups as agrarian capitalists, farm managers, technicians, wage labourers and others.

(4) The nature of land relations which determines the share of material wealth of various sections engaged in agriculture thereby also determines the respective specific weight of those sections in the social, political and cultural life of rural society. The class of rich zamindars or capitalist landlords, by virtue of its wealth can have leisure and material means whereby it can establish its hegemony over the life of rural society in all spheres. The mass of poor cultivating tenants or land labourers can hardly have any say in shaping it.

(5) The nature of land relations will also decide the degree of stability and social harmony in the agrarian area. For instance, in the zamindari area, due to the extensive contrast between the wealth of the zamindars and utter poverty of the cultivating tenants, there will exist a permanent condition of bitter struggle between the two classes. If poverty becomes unbearable, the struggle may even take forms which would undermine the stability of the existing rural society. In fact, contemporary India is rapidly becoming an amphi-theatre of such struggles.

If we survey the past and the present history, we find that the rural society has been the arena of numerous struggles which had their genetic cause in the existing land relations. During the French Revolution the serfs wanted to abolish feudal land relations and become free peasant proprietors. The success of the commu-nists in China is also largely explained by their skilful solution of the land problem.

The question of land relations has become the crucial question in all backward countries of the world today.

Thus the degree of stability or instability of the rural society is largely determined by the nature of extant land relations.

(6) Wealth is the material means to get access to education and culture specially in modern commodity society. Land relations, by basically determining the share of various agrarian social groups in the total agricultural wealth, therefore, also decide how much scope each of these groups will have for education and culture. Land relations, thus, play a big role in determining the degree of the intellectual and cultural development of various strata of the rural people and their individual members since this development largely depends upon the education they have received and the culture they have assimilated.

The points mentioned above reveal and emphasize the great significance of land relations in moulding the economic and hence the social, the political, the intellectual, and the cultural life of the rural people.

The standard of life of a village community and its sections will indicate the amount of wealth at its disposal and the manner in which it is distributed among those sections. The volume of wealth of the rural community depends primarily on agriculture, and in final analysis, on the technique used in agriculture since the higher is the technique, the greater is the productivity of agriculture. Land relations determine, as we saw above, the share of various groups comprising rural society in the total agrarian wealth. Yet even where they engender sharp contrasts of wealth among these groups, the absolute share of even the lowest group will be at a high level if the total wealth of the rural aggregate, due to advanced technique of agricultural production, is considerable. For instance, in the U.S.A. where agriculture is mechanised and, therefore, creates great agrarian wealth, in spite of the fact that agrarian capitalists make millions, the income of the wage workers on land is on a much higher level than that of the agriculturist in India.

The problem of the standard of life of the rural population has been keenly studied by eminent sociologists like Sorokin,

Zimmerman, Sims, Kirpatrick and others. The criteria and methods laid down by them for such a study can serve as a useful guide to the students of rural society in India.

It is observed by these scholars that the standard of life of the rural people on an average is lower than that of the urban people. This is because the income of the rural people on the average is lower than that of the urban people. "Further, the standards of living of the rural population and its various groups (owners, tenants, croppers and labourers) are more homogeneous than those of the urban classes."

It has also been noted that the standard of life of the farmers approximates more to that of the lower strata of the city population.

Though income is the primary factor determining the standard of life of a social aggregate, there are other factors also which influence it. "To be sure, income may be chiefly responsible for the existence of classes; but wholly apart from material possessions, there are class norms and values dictated by tradition." For instance, in India, the Middle class strives to adopt a standard of life according to its own specific conception of life. This is reflected in their choice of food, dress, recreations, cultural amenities and other things. Their standard of life is thus determined not merely by their economic position but also by their specific group outlook, temperament and taste. The role of caste in India as a determinant of the group standard of living demands special study.

It has been further observed that the degree of civilization existing in a society also influences the standard of life of the people. For instance, such institutions as well-furnished libraries, cultural and sport clubs, radio, telephone, cinema and theatre, swimming pools, restaurants and others, do not generally exist in the rural zone of India. Hence the standard of life of the rural people is not affected by them unlike that of the urban people.

However, due to the interaction of the rural and urban societies and the resultant growth of mutual contacts, the rural people are slowly but inevitably influenced by the urban. They begin to develop a predilection and craving for such amenities. They also tend to adopt the food and dress habits of the urban population.

Bicycles, modern footwear, games like cricket and football, school's libraries, cinema, and other things associated with urban life, begin to penetrate the village. This results in gradually modifying the mode of life of the rural people.

In his study of the economic life of the rural people, the rural sociologist needs to study the impact of the more powerful influences of urban life on the rural society and hence on the standard of life of the rural people. Further, he should not take a static view of their standard of life. Human needs are not an immutable entity. They grow from phase to phase.

The Have-nots

A very big section of the rural population has been living in varying states of poverty in all countries. Even in the U.S.A., the most prosperous country of the world today, the poverty of a large stratum of rural society has become a crying problem. As Sims remarks, "Although students of rural conditions have long been aware of the existence of country slums and of disadvantaged or submerged classes, such as the share croppers of the south (U.S.A.) no one fully realised how precarious the lot of a large part of the country population was and how quickly millions could be plunged into a state of destitution until the industrial depression revealed the true situation," and further, "all in all, it is estimated that more than one-third of the rural families of the nation have suffered poverty."

When, as seen above, a large section of the rural population of even such an economically advanced country like the U.S.A. suffers from poverty, it is no wonder that chronic poverty is rampant among the agrarian population in India, an economically much less developed country.

The immense poverty of the Indian agriculturist is proverbial and presents the fundamental problem of the programme of national economic reconstruction.

The principal causes of the rural poverty in India have been, in general, laid bare by eminent Indian economists and sociologists. Primitive agricultural technique, insufficient irrigation system, land fragmentation, uneconomic holdings, overpressure on agriculture, alarming rural indebtedness and, above all, the existing land relations are some of its principal causes.

It is necessary to study the problem of poverty not merely of the rural people as a whole but also of its different strata and, that too, in detail.

Poverty adversely affects not only the health and vitality of the rural people but also explains their backward social and cultural conditions. If the rural people are ignorant, superstitious, uncultured, it is mostly because they are abysmally poor and cannot afford to pay for education. They, thereby, remain excluded from any access to scientific knowledge of the natural and social worlds imparted by educational and cultural institutions.

Economic prosperity is the basic pre-requisite for a flourishing social and cultural life. Hence the problem of rural reconstruction at a high social and cultural level is organically bound up with the problem of the eradication of rural poverty.

Political Factors

One of the vital problems which requires to be intelligently studied by the rural sociologist is the political life of the rural people. Writers on rural problems as well as social workers in the rural area have generally paid insufficient attention to this aspect of the rural life. They have often presumed that the agrarian population is politically almost an inert mass and have attempted to evolve and work out schemes of better villages on that premise. However, nothing is more unreal in modern times than the hypothesis of the political inertness of the rural people. When we study modern history, we find that the agrarian masses, predominantly composed of farmers, have participated in mighty political movement in a number of countries. For instance, in India, large sections of peasants and artisans supported and joined the great National Revolt of the Indian people against the British rule in 1857. Subsequently peasant struggles like the Deccan Peasant Riots and others directed both against the moneylenders and the government broke out in some parts of the country. In more recent times, increasing sections of the peasantry participated in a series of national political movements like the Non-cooperation

Movement of 1919-24, Civil Disobedience Movement of 1930-34, a number of political satyagraha campaigns in different districts, Quit India Movement and others. After 1934 the peasant masses even started building their own class organizations like kisan sabhas and launched a number of struggles against the government and landlords. During and immediately after the partition of India, the peasant discontent and restlessness found a distorted political expression in bloody communal clashes which occurred in a number of provinces.

Recent history also records such peasant struggles as took place in Telangana and in portions of Bengal and Assam.

In other countries, too, the agrarian masses have taken part, sometimes even decisive, in political movements. Tens of millions of peasants participated in such world shaking revolutions as the Russian and the Chinese. Large sections of Indonesian and Burmese peasantry also took part in a series of political struggles having national independence as their objective. Peasant masses constituted the preponderant social force of the resistance movements in France, Yugoslavia, Poland, Hungary and other European countries which developed during the period of occupation of those countries by Nazi Germany. Also in recent decades, the agricultural populations of Spain, Italy, Latin American countries and others have exhibited considerable political awakening, formed sometimes their own political parties and have launched numerous political struggles.

These events explode the misconception that agrarian population is politically a passive force.

In fact, the growth of political consciousness among peasant populations and their increasing political activity are striking features of the political life of mankind today.

The agrarian areas of a number of countries have been transformed into storm centres of militant political activity of the rural people.

Basic Problems and Issues

The following are the two main reasons why it becomes

imperative for the rural sociologist in India to study the political life of the rural people to-day.

(1) The Constitution of the now independent India has provided universal adult suffrage to the Indian people. Tens of millions of peasants who constitute the majority of the population thereby acquire a political status. Their will expressed through the ballot box would now considerably influence the political life of the nation. This is a unique event in the long history of the Indian humanity, for, it is for the first time that the people including the rural masses have secured the democratic right to determine who will rule them. The theory of the divine right of the king or a "providence ordained "imperialist power to rule the people has been ousted by that of the democratic right of the sovereign people to determine their political destiny. Universal adult suffrage serves as a powerful ferment in the life of the rural people making them politically conscious to a phenomenal degree. It is a momentous event in the history of the rural society.

The new situation has posed a number of fresh questions for the rural sociologist. How will the rural people, illiterate, ignorant and superstitious in the main, exercise their franchise? What social, economic, and ideological influences will determine their voting? What types of political organisations will the peasant masses throw up for implementing a programme embodying their conception of a good society by legislative means? What political parties will emerge in the rural area, corresponding to various layers of the existing stratified rural society? What repercussions will take place in the sphere of social and ideological life of the rural people due to the mass-scale growth of political consciousness and activity among them due to their acquisition of adult suffrage? How will this political equality affect caste and other social as well as cultural and economic inequalities?

The study of these new problems will form an integral part of the study of the Indian rural society.

(2) A proper understanding of the political life of the rural people is necessary also for another reason. Unlike in the pre-British period, the modern state plays a decisive role in deter-mining the life of the rural society. During the pre-British phase, the village, as we have seen previously, was an autarchic and almost autonomous unit. During the British period, it experienced a basic transformation. Its self-contained subsistence economy based on self-sufficient agriculture and artisan industry was undermined.

Further, the British Government established a centralized State with an administrative machinery which penetrated the hitherto autonomous village. This basically changed the political physiognomy of the village. It became a unit of the countrywide political and administrative system.

The consequences of this economic and political transformation were far-reaching. The village population no longer lived an almost hermetically seated existence but was drawn into the wider whirlpool of the national and international economic and political life. Thenceforward the economic, political, and other problems of the rural community had to be considered in the wider context of national and world politics and economy as well as of the policies of the Central Government.

A systematic study of the rural political life may be made on the following lines:

(a) The study of the governmental machinery in the rural area.

(b) The study of the non-governmental political organizations in the rural area.

(c) The study of the political behaviour of the rural people and its various sections.

A few observations on each of these are made below

(a) Governmental Machinery

The study of the governmental machinery can be divided into two parts:

(i) the study of the structure of the administration and its functioning within the village and

(ii) the study of the administrative machinery of larger units like Talukas Districts, Regions and States.

In the pre-British period, when the state did not interfere in the life of the village beyond claiming a portion of the village produce as land revenue and occasionally levying troops, the village administration was carried on by the village panchayat composed of elected or customary representatives of various castes, generally elders of the castes, or by village headman with the panchayat as the consultative body. The village panchayat was the link between the village population and the higher authority. The panchayat and the headman maintained peace in the village, settled disputes among the villagers, looked after the sanitation and other matters of common concern of the village population, determined and collected the share of the farmer family in the collective land-revenue to be paid to the State on behalf of the village, and also regulated the use of collectively owned pasture land and forest area in the periphery. Thus from the standpoint of administration the village was autonomous.

The administrative, judicial, policing, and economic func-tions of the village were, as seen above, performed by the village panchayat and the headman. So far as the personal, social and religious life of the village people was concerned, the customary law governing it was operated by various caste councils which regulated the behaviour-patterns of respective castes.

The disintegration of empires did not affect the administrative autonomy and general internal life of the village. This was because the State, even the Imperial State, restricted its intervention in the internal affairs of the village to the mere gathering of the tribute and the levying of the troops generally in war time. The State or the king looked after the inter-village administration and other vital matters affecting the people of the kingdom as a whole such as coinage, irrigation, and the maintenance and development of the network of roads.

With the advent of the British rule in India, as we have stated before, the Indian society began to experience a fundamental economic and political transformation. The new administrative machinery evolved and organized by Britain in India supplanted the old one which had functioned for centuries with little variation. The new state, the organ of British rule in India, stationed its own revenue, judicial, police and other officials in the village. The village lost its administrative autonomy and the caste councils, their penal powers. In the new political set up, the village became the basic administrative unit of a hierarchically graded countrywide administrative system.

The local village officials were independent of any control over them by the village population. Thus if the forest had to be cleared, wells to be dug or roads to be built in the village, it was not now the village panchayat which independently and of its own will evolved a scheme and mobilized the village population for implementing that scheme. It was the new village administration, itself a unit of the national administrative system and subject to the latter's control, that decided those questions.

Henceforward the social, political and economic life of the rural people, was largely determined by the State. Village problems became an integral part of the total problems of the nation and could not be solved in isolation by the initiative of the village community.

The character and policies of the government appreciably determined how those problems would be solved and hence what type of life the rural people would live.

After independence, the Indians retained the centralized State apparatus elaborated by the British in India. The rural sociologist needs to study the working of the administrative system inherited from the British in the new national situation. It should be noted that this administrative system had been devised by them as a lever to suppress or restrict the initiative of the people. A critical evaluation of this system from the standpoint of the solution of such problems of the rural population as their general economic advance, universal spread of education, cheap expeditious justice, awakening and play of the local initiative within the framework of the national plan, and others, has, therefore, to be made and a scheme of reconstruction of the existing administrative system evolved.

The study of the administrative system raises the following problems

(i) How far the administrative machinery is responsive to the opinions and wishes of the people.

(ii) How far the people are associated with it and participate in its functioning.

(iii) How far it is cheap, efficient, and sensitive to the problems of the people.

(b) Non-Governmental Political Organizations

It is further necessary to note that the governmental activity is only one aspect of the political life of the village population. Non-governmental political organizations also have emerged and are functioning in the rural area in modern times. Political parties thrown up by the rural people are principal among them.

It is very essential to study the various political parties operating in the rural area. These parties express the specific interests and aspirations of various classes and socio-economic groups composing of rural people such as landlords, tenants, land labourers, peasant proprietors and others. They voice their desire and determination to secure political power and use it to modify or overhaul the existing social system in consonance with their own interests and social objectives. The rural area becomes the arena of struggle between these parties. To have a concrete composite picture of the political life of the rural people it is, therefore, vitally necessary to study closely the ideologies, the programmes and the policies of these political parties and trace their roots. The general elections recently held in our country on the basis of the new Constitution have revealed the extensive growth of political consciousness among the rural people, the expansion of the old political parties and the emergence of new ones in the rural area and, above all, large scale participation of the rural people in the elections. Paradoxically enough, voting in some rural areas even exceeded that in urban zones. Further, large sections even of illiterate peasant women registered their vote, an event of great political significance.

The student of rural society should also study the changing political moods of the rural people and the resultant increase or decline in the influence of different political parties among them. He should further investigate, by means of a sociological analysis, the causes which bring about the rise and fall of political parties in the rural area. He can predict on the basis of such a study the tendency of the development of the political life of the rural people. Such a study is very vital since the victory of a political party in a country implies its capture of government machinery which it intends to use as an instrument to alter or replace the existing socio-economic structure of society in the interest of the class or the group which it represents. For instance, in India, the Socialist or the Communist Party desires to win political power so that it can use it to abolish capitalism and establish socialism. The Hindu Mahasabha aspires for political power to establish the Hindu Raj and reconstruct Indian society in conformity with the Hindu ideals. The Indian National Congress, the ruling party in India is working for a society based on a mixed social economy with two sectors, private and state owned, and Secular democracy.

(c) Political Behaviour of Rural People

Another aspect of the rural political life deserving study is the political behaviour of the rural people. The study must be made from two angles.

First, the rural sociologist should study the various programmes which various strata of the rural people or the rural people as a whole are striving to fulfil.

These programmes will disclose the basic social aspirations and the immediate needs of the rural people and its various sections. The nature of these aspirations and needs will also disclose the psychologies and ideologies of the rural people and its constituent groups at a given historical moment.

For instance, some decades back, the cultivating tenants in the zamindari tract considered the zamindari system as immutable and merely desired and asked for a humane treatment from the zamindars. Subsequently, increasing sections of them questioned the zamindari system itself and put forth the demand for the abolition of landlords and transfer of land to themselves. They also aspired for a workers' and peasants' Raj which they previously did not even conceive of.

The rural sociologist is required to concentrate special attention on the study of the programme and the political behaviour of peasantry since it constitutes the major section of the rural people and, therefore, would exert decisive influence on the future of the rural society. The peasant movements in a number of countries in recent times have been transforming the entire social, political, and economic landscape in the agrarian area.

Secondly, the rural sociologist should make a thorough study of the methods which the rural people have been adopting to realize their aims.

Targets for Welfare

Different sections of the rural people make use of different methods to implement their programmes at various times.

Indian rural society provides a classical laboratory for the study of a rich variety of these methods. The following are the principal among them.

1. Petitioning.
2. Voting.
3. Demonstrations and marches.
4. Hijrats or mass emigrations.
5. Satyagraha, passive resistance.
6. No-rent and no-tax campaigns.
7. Spontaneous elemental revolts.
8. Organized armed struggles.
9. Guerilla warfare.

Peasant populations in different countries in the present epoch have been employing diverse methods to implement their programmes. In India, too, as previously stated, these varied methods have been used in varying degrees by the agrarian population in different parts of the country in different periods. In the second half of the nineteenth century a section of the Maharashtrian peasantry took to spontaneous armed struggle known as the Deccan Peasant Riots against moneylenders and the government. Mahatma Gandhi organized a number of no-tax campaigns of the peasantry in various parts of India. Subsequently a series of peasant demonstration and marches have been organized by the Kisan Sabhas and the Socialist Party of India. In Telangana, a combination of the methods of open armed struggle and guerilla warfare was adopted by the peasantry led by the Communist Party only a few years back.

In the two General Elections held very recently, the rural population including millions of peasants, men and women have utilized the method of the ballot box and elected representatives to the State Assemblies and the House of the People.

Thus the rural people have used at various times parliamentary as well as extra-parliamentary methods of struggle to achieve their aims and demands.

A sociological analysis of the programmes of the rural people as a whole and its constituent strata as well as of the varied methods employed by them specially becomes necessary when the agrarian society is in a state of deep crisis and is simmering with great discontent of the rural masses in the major part of the world including India.

Since agriculture is the pivot of the rural economy and land is the most important means of production in agriculture, the struggle between the various groups of the rural society has mainly revolved round the question of the ownership of land. As has been almost universally recognized by sociologists and statesmen all over the world, the problem of land relations is the basic problem in all backward or semi-backward countries of Asia and even of some countries of Europe like Spain and Italy. The peasant movements in those countries have had as their basic objective the abolition of feudal or semi-feudal forms of land ownership and transfer of land to the actual tillers.

Struggle over the question of land has, in fact, provided the main dynamic to the political life of the rural society in the present period.

Different sections of the rural people hold different views on the land problems which are determined by their differing specific position in the socio-economic structure of the rural society. The view-points of the landlords, the tenants, the land labourers, the peasant proprietors, and the moneylenders and the merchants to whom the peasant debtors have mortgaged their land, vary widely. The divergence of views which expresses divergence of material interests of these groups, is the genetic cause of the economic and political struggles between them, struggles which now-a-days form an essential part of the political life of the rural people.

This inter-group struggle among the various sections of the rural people revolving round the land problem has not been adequately and scientifically studied hitherto by the student of the rural society. A historically progressive solution of the land problem is a crucial need since the future of the rural society, its retrogression of further advance, depends upon it.

Role of Caste System

In the Indian rural area where the occupational homogeneity of the caste is not still seriously undermined and where caste consciousness among the people remains stronger than in the urban centre, caste influences the political life to a much greater extent than it does in towns and cities. In recent times, however, due to the growth of class consciousness among various groups into which the rural population is divided on economic lines, the influence of caste on the political life is slowly diminishing. For instance, non-Brahmin landlords will politically ally with Brahmin landlords rather than with his non-Brahmin tenants since both the Brahmin and the non-Brahmin landlords stand for the defence of landlordism, their common economic interest. Similarly, the Brahmin and the non-Brahmin tenants will more and more come together and form a Kisan Sabha or a peasant party with the programme of abolition of landlordism and transfer of land to the tillers of land, both Brahmin and non-Brahmin.

In India, where the old caste system of the Hindus still exists and is strong, special attention should be paid to its role in determining political life. Often even when a caste is not occupationally homogeneous and does not, therefore, correspond to a socio-economic group, the caste allegiance among its members is so strong that they may politically support caste leaders who belong to another socio-economic group.

It should, however, be noted that, due to historical reasons, the caste and the socio-economic group often correspond to a great extent in various parts of the country. For instance, a good proportion of the farmers-tenants in Maharashtra happen to belong to the non-Brahmin caste while a good proportion of the landlords to the Brahmin caste. Due to this the party of the peasantry has an overwhelmingly non-Brahmin social composition. This often blurs the fact that, judged from the standpoint of the basic aim and demands of the organization, it is the party of a socio-economic group, a class. Caste in this case obscures the class content of the party. The specific weight of caste in the political life of the rural people is still great and the rural sociologist has to assess it carefully.

8

Agricultural Economy

This subject is usually discussed under the broad heading land reform or agrarian reform. There are many aspects of agrarian reform and I shall deal only with what I consider to be the core of agrarian reform in India, namely, organisation of agricultural production with particular reference to the size and structure of the unit of agricultural production.

The main constituents of the programme of agrarian or land reform currently undertaken by the State in India are classified as follows in the Progress Report for 1953-54 of the Five-Year Plan:-

(1) The abolition of intermediaries;

(2) Tenancy reforms designed:-

(a) To scale down rents to 1/4th or 1/5th of the produce;

(b) To give tenants permanent rights subject to the landlord's right to resume a minimum holding for his personal cultivation within a limited time;

(c) To enable tenants (subject to the landlord's right of resumption for personal cultivation) to acquire ownership of their lands, on payment of moderate compensation to the landlord spread over a period of years;

(3) Fixing of ceilings on holdings;

(4) Re-organisation of agriculture including the consoli-dation of holdings, the prevention of fragmen-tation and the development of co-operative village manage-ment and co-operative farming.

Many of the items included in the above have been subjects of attention and activity on the part of governments for many decades past. However, a number of important elements are of recent introduction and the programme has begun to look like an integrated attempt only within the last few years. An important feature which has received emphasis only since the attainment of Independence is the abolition of intermediaries, popularly regarded as equivalent to the abolition of zamindari.

While emphasising the primary importance of the abolition of zamindari it is necessary to remember that, in India, it affects, in the main, the distribution of the total agricultural product and not the size and organisation of the unit of agricultural production.

This is because, in the first instance, the abolition of intermediaries does not mean the break-up of large farms or farming estates or the redistribution of land and secondly because, even if this had been a part of the programme, there are, in fact, with the exception of a small number of regions, no large farming estates in India. The very description of the reform as abolition of intermediaries, emphasises this aspect of the redistribution of the product and reduction of the burden on the actual cultivator. It is conceived of essentially as establishing, as far as possible, a direct relation between the actual tiller of the soil and the State.

Tenancy reform or tenancy legislation has a much wider sphere of operation than legislation for the abolition of intermediaries.

Reform in Land System

Tenancy reform also, it will be obvious, does not affect the size and shape of the agricultural holding. It brings about, in the main, a redistribution of the total produce in favour of the tenant and also gives him a sense of security regarding the future which should react favourably on the economic and technical operation of the tenant cultivator. However, there is one important difference between tenancy reform and the abolition of intermediaries. The latter is, for the most part, a once-for-all operation; the former, on the other hand, has not only continuous effect but has further to adapt itself constantly to a changing situation. In consequence though tenancy legislation may not operate directly on the unit of agricultural production, the framing of tenancy legislation is always influenced by total land policy including policy relating to the size and structure of the unit of agricultural production. In India, tenancy legislation has to concern itself with problems such as those of sub-letting or of the alienation, transfer or inheritance of land; and all of these have relation with objectives of policy relating to the unit of agricultural production.

The fixing of ceilings on holdings is likely to affect the size of the unit of agricultural production much more directly than either the abolition of intermediaries or tenancy reform. Before proceeding further I may note that the omission to distinguish clearly between the ownership holdings and the cultivating holdings leads often to a confusion in thinking and exposition of the subject of land reform in India.

The immediate effect of the adoption of a ceiling for the future, on size of the production unit would, on the other hand, be negligible, except to the extent that it would encourage actual or notional division of existing large holdings among family members so as not to be affected early by the operation of the legislation. The long-term effects are problematical and would depend on the extent to which the existing or future situation otherwise favoured the formation of very large holdings.

Even the comparatively large estate of Kashmir and Telengana do not or did not contain elements of direct cultivation large enough for redistribution to effect sensibly the problem of the small peasant holding, in even restricted areas. Elsewhere the contrasts are much less glaring. The concept of the ceiling, if it is to be used in India must, therefore, be different in content and operation from that in countries with large landlord estates plantations or latifundia.

The concept of the economic holding or a minimum holding called by any name, like the concept of the ceiling, can form the basis of an immediate operation of reorganisation or can be confined to setting a limit to future transactions. In the latter alternative it may act as an effective means of preventing a worsening of the existing situation and may partly even help to improve it gradually in the future. These effects will, however, become apparent only slowly over a series of years and a limit for the future cannot help towards reorganisation, if the existing situation in itself is extremely unsatisfactory. A minimum holding or a floor has not been used in any State in India yet for bringing about immediate reorganisation of production units in lands included in units below the minimum size.

Consolidation as practised in India affects powerfully the internal organisation of a holding, though not usually its total size. The process of consolidation may lead to some saving in the land surface used for such purposes as boundaries or roads and may thus enable formation of a pool of land for specific common purposes. But the saving effected in this way is not likely to yield substantial acreage for distribution among existing holders. Co-operative farming or co-operative village management are yet chiefly in the stage of thought. What little action has been taken is experimental and nowhere has any legislation been formulated or contemplated which bases itself on the formation of co-operative farming units for at least a part of state policy relating to land management.

Legislation on land reform is essentially a matter for governments of States. Therefore, the programme is usually framed in the context of particular problems of each State. The activity of the National Planning Commission affords the chief occasion and instrument for integrating policies of different State Governments and for formulating a common Indian policy. Considerable importance, therefore, attaches to the views regarding land policy contained in the First Five-Year Plan. The problems of the policy are divided into two aspects; Land Management and Land Reform. It is evidently considered that there is some conflict between the two; for, it is said that "Land Policy should include both elements but should maintain a balance between the two."

The suggested land reform policy is again not uniform; it is evidently to change with size of land owning. The most important result is that the tenants of small and middle owners are recommended much less protection than the tenants of large owners. As middle owners are defined as owners of land upto three times the family holding the field of tenancy, protection is thus seriously narrowed. The main reason given for the maintenance of a large class of tenants-at-will in this way is that otherwise movement of people from agriculture and rural areas into other occupations and towns may be seriously checked. It is fortunate that most State Governments have paid little attention to this recommendation in their legislative programme.

In relation to the landless worker the main concrete reference is to the Bhoodan movement. "It offers the landless worker an opportunity not otherwise open to him." This can be only interpreted as meaning that the State itself considers it neither necessary nor possible to do anything for him. It is added that the problem of the landless worker must be considered in terms of institutional changes which would create conditions of equality for all sections of the population. The essence of these changes is described as a system of co-operative village management. Co-operative village management is referred to in the Plan in other context also. For example, after having formulated the important and unexceptionable proposition that "the basic condition for increase in agricultural production is increase in the unit of management of land" this also is said to be possible only through co-operative management at the village level. With regard to the small and the middle farmers again it is recommended that they should be encouraged and assisted to develop their production and organise their activities on co-operative basis. With this emphasis on co-operation it would be expected that co-operative organisation or cooperative village management would be described in specific detail and a programme sketched out for establishing it. The following extract summarises the ideas of the Planning Commission on co-operative village management.

"Broadly speaking, however, we envisage that the village panchayat should become the agency both for land reform and for land management in the village. In the first place it should be the body concerned with the management of land taken over from substantial owners, and also of village waste lands. The leasing of lands by small and middle owners should also be done through the panchayat and not directly. In this way the village panchayat may be able to provide cultivating holdings of economic size, at any rate for landless cultivators. The exercise of these functions would naturally lead on to the wider conception of the co-operative management of the entire land of the village and the undertaking of activities for creating non-agricultural employment in the village."

It is not necessary to comment on the above except to note that it does not deal with the problem in the comprehensive manner that might have been expected, that it is over-optimistic and also that the working model presented is obviously unsuitable and inadequate in most respects. Moreover, no concrete programme is provided for progress in the direction of co-operative village management even according to ideas contained in the Plan, beyond the Rs. 50 lakhs provided for study, training and experimentation. It would not be unfair in the circumstances, to suggest that the Plan proposes little of importance in relation to land management and that we have at present no effective programme in contemplation for dealing with what the Planning Commission itself recognises as the basic problem, viz., that of " the increase in the unit of management of land".

Not only is the subject treated unsatisfactorily in the Plan but also the subsequent activities of the Planning Commission and the Central Government do not indicate that it is currently held in importance or receives any special attention.

The Community Projects are supposed to be the special field of the Planning Commission and great reliance is placed on them in relation to agricultural development in the future. Not only do these projects pay no attention to land reform or land distribution but even experimentation in relation to land management appears to find no place in them. The complete absence of any attention to it in the programme of community projects is evidenced by its not having been necessary to devote any attention to the subject in the Evaluation Report on the first year's working of these projects. And the later report of the Evaluation Organization, "Community Projects-First Reactions" contains enough evidence to show how the project authorities completely ignore land management and land reform problems. In regard to co-operative organizations we have the following comment in the Evaluation Report. "While in the very initial stages of the formulation of community plans this aspect of mutual dependence between community development and co-operative organization was not so explicitly stated, during the course of the year increasing emphasis was placed by the Community Projects Administration on promotion of cooperative organizations." (p. 39.) The cooperatives to which increasing attention is reported are still the credit, purchase and sale and other organizations and not experiments in increasing scales of land management. The putting forward more recently of agricultural extension as the panacea for all rural ills is, perhaps, a reflection of the same attitude. It appears to be considered by the Planning Commission, as by many foreign experts, that all that is required to increase agricultural production in India adequately is to arouse enthusiasm and to transfer techniques. The problem as to whether conditions in the field are such as to favour generation of enthusiasm and the acquisition and continued practice of new techniques does not evidently need prior consideration. Finally, it is reported that in some States, the Central Government, presumably acting through the Planning Commission, was responsible for persuading Governments to modify their original ideas regarding immediate operation of a ceiling on holdings. All in all, one gathers the impression that while in its theoretic formulation the Planning Commission may recognize the existence of the problem of land management it is not ready to give this recognition any immediate or in concrete form.

As indicated above, the Planning Commission appears content to operate with the existing unit of agricultural production and does not propose to change in any radical manner the organization of land management and operation. The Congress Agrarian Reforms Committee also formulates its actual programme very largely in terms of the peasant farm and it does not appear to consider that a programme of reorganization involving large numbers of families and a considerable land surface is insistently called for. The experts appear to talk almost exclusively of the peasant unit and their ideas of land reform are confined mostly to abolition of intermediaries and dealing with large estates. In the circumstances, it becomes necessary to examine existing conditions carefully, especially with a view to throwing light on the strength and efficiency of the independent peasant farm as the unit of land management and agricultural production.

Farms and Produces

It is generally known that the size of the large bulk of farms in India is very small and that numbers of them cannot be called family farms in any valid sense of that term. However, no attempt is usually made to indicate with figures the dimensions of the problem. I shall, therefore, note certain salient features of the situation very briefly. My concern is with the unit of land management, the cultivated holding, and data relating to ownership of land are not relevant to my purpose. The data required are those relating to size, scale of operations and of investment, receipts and employment, etc., from farming, of the independent farming units.

According to the Survey a little over half of the cultivators reported a value of gross produce of farm business lower than Rs. 400 for the year. This then is a useful starting point of the description, that half or more of the farm units, i.e., independent units of land management in India may have a gross produce of farm less than Rs. 600 a year. The next step is to assess the relative importance of farming activity to the farm family. In the total number of cultivators reporting less than Rs. 400 of value of gross produce during the year two divisions were made representing those with a value of gross produce below Rs. 200 and those with a value of gross produce between Rs. 200 and Rs. 400. The former formed slightly more than 29 per cent of the total cultivators and the latter, group 21 per cent. Those reporting value of gross produce less than Rs. 200 reported total farm expenses which exceeded their value of gross produce and those in the latter class reported total farm expenses that were on an average only about Rs. 60 less than the average value of gross produce. The average reported cash receipts from sale of crops and fodder in the two classes were about Rs. 20 and Rs. 70 respectively and both classes reported cash farm expenses that were more than Rs. 50 on an average than the average cash receipts from sale of crops and fodder. Making all allowances for errors in reporting, etc., it is clear that the cultivators included in these groups earn little, if any, net cash income through their farming activity and the main advantage derived by them from farming is some contribution in kind to family living.

In the main, however, cultivators in the lower strata have much lower values of gross produce than those in the upper. Of the total borrowings of even the middle four deciles more than half represented borrowing for family expenditure items; for the last three deciles the corresponding proportion was almost 60 per cent. The capacity of the average cultivating family to undertake capital expenditure was obviously extremely limited. The average expenditure undertaken on all items such as bunding, reclamation, irrigation sources, implements, etc., including expenditure on repairs, maintenance and replacement was about Rs. 22 for families of the lowest three deciles and Rs. 51 for families of the middle four deciles; the corresponding amount was Rs. 311 for families of the first decile. But if this expenditure is taken together with expenditure on purchase of livestock by the respective groups of deciles and the total calculated on a per acre basis the expenditure incurred actually increases as one goes down the groups of deciles. This means that while the total outlays of the families of the middle and lower deciles are small and are known to be inadequate their burden in terms of per acre costs rules high.

It is not necessary to labour the point further. What I want to emphasise is that the size of farming business of at least half the cultivating families in India is such that it is futile to consider them as independent units of land exploitation in any plan for a developing economy. It is irrelevant in the light of the data cited above to talk in terms of family farms or economic holdings. Even the definition of basic holding of the Congress Agrarian Reforms Committee cannot cover these units. Therefore, a land policy for a developing economy must face up to the serious problem of the reorganization of these units. A vague recognition of these facts is seen in the general comments made in various contexts by numerous experts and committees on the "non-creditworthy" or the "marginal and submarginal" groups. This recognition must become more explicit and must lead on to a realisation of the inability of any supply or credit reorganization to deal with fundamental defects of the small size and turnover of the existing basic units and of the large numbers involved in any scheme of reorganization.

There appears at present general agreement on the nature of the problem and the main approach to its solution. The following statement by the Prime Minister, Pandit Jawaharlal Nehru, may be taken as representative of this.

"As agriculture is the principal occupation of the great majority of our people, it must be the first concern of the State. The abolition of the zamindari system has been the first reform and this must be expedited. But it must be remembered that this by itself is no solution of the problem Even before this abolition a very large proportion of land was self-cultivated. An addition to it, without any further reforms, will not help much. The small subsistence farm makes progress difficult. We have to think, therefore, and think soon, of other and further steps. There should be a diversion of a part of the agricultural population to other occupations. There should be a development of cottage and small-scale industries. But essentially the problem of agriculture needs co-operative cultivation and the application of modern techniques. This does not mean necessarily mechanising agriculture all over India, though some degree of mechanisation is taking place and is desirable. But there is no escape from some form of co-operative cultivation, if we are to make agriculture progressive."

Considerations of production economy do not seem to indicate any particular figures or proportions in this context. However, data from the Rural Credit Survey may be set out to illustrate the relative proportions involved. These data relate to all the cultivated holdings in the 600 villages selected for the survey in 75 districts. The cultivators were arranged, for the purpose, in order of the size of their cultivated holdings. When so arranged it was found that the first 10 per cent or decile of the cultivators held more than 25 per cent of the total land surface in almost all districts and held more than 30 per cent of it in 51 of the 75 districts. The first 30 per cent of three deciles taken together held more than 50 per cent of the land in almost all districts and in 48 districts they held more than 60 per cent; in no district was this proportion larger than 85 but in 6 it varied between 75 and 85 per cent. The middle four deciles held between 25 and 35 per cent of the total cultivated land in the large majority of districts. The holdings of the last three deciles included less than 10 per cent of the total cultivated land in the majority of districts; but in 27 out of the 75 districts they held between 10 and 15 per cent. Taking the broad division of cultivators into the upper half and lower half the relative size of their holdings of total land surface would be approximately 3:1.

The above taken together with the data relating to occupational distribution of families should give an idea of the overall dimensions of the problem. We may assume that about 60 per cent of families in rural India are cultivators in the sense of operating some cultivated land and that of the non-cultivators at least half depend for their support on agriculture and land. This gives about 80 per cent of rural families as interested in land management units and policy. We may, on the basis of data set out before, consider about half of the cultivators as having unsuitable units for independent land management, the proportion cannot at a minimum be put at less than a third of the cultivators. If we take the former figure the cultivating families together with the landless interested in reorganization, will form about half the total number of families in the countryside, and, if the latter, about 40 per cent of them. Working with the data for existing distribution of cultivating holdings and assuming a transfer, because of the operation of the ceiling, of the order of 5 per cent of the total cultivated land, we have the following figures of the extent of land surface and number of families affected by reorganization; if, half the units cease to be independent, about 50 per cent of rural families and 30 per cent of the cultivated land; and if, about one-third of cultivators are so affected, about 40 per cent of the rural families and about 15 per cent of the total land surface. These calculations are so broad as to be almost notional and they have been indulged in at this place only to give some idea of the dimension of the problem.

The two fundamental steps in reorganization of land management units in India are: (i) redistribution of the land surface and: (ii) formation of the larger consolidated units out of the pooled resources of the uneconomic units and surplus available for redistribution. The first step is an essential preliminary in almost all programmes of land improvement and agricultural development. Its importance is universally recognized in connection with the consolidation of fragmented holdings. It is, however, necessary from other points of view also. One can view the process of consolidation in a wider context as part of the process of a rational layout of the total land surface for agricultural and other utilisation.

This task is no doubt of vast dimensions. But tasks of somewhat similar dimensions have been undertaken in other countries and the total work indicated above is not more compli-cated or larger than the process of consolidation undertaken currently by many State Governments in India. As I visualise it the first stage in the process will be that of determining the general layout and the second of locating in this layout the independent farm units now fixed in location and made impartible, and the co-operative estates or farms.

The formation of larger units out of pooled land and other resources will have two aspects, one compulsory and the other voluntary. I have assumed that once the floor has been defined independent units of farm management smaller in area will not be allowed to exist. Obviously the enforcement of this must be by some sort of legislation. The measure of compulsion may vary. In the early stages the step may be initiated, as in some programmes of consolidation, only on the motion of a minimum number of families involved.

Both these tasks, that of redistributing the land surface and the formation of a small number of co-operative farms in each village are immense in extent and complexity. I would argue that not only are they a *sine qua non* of any programme of land reform but also that they are not beyond our capacity, if a sincere and concentrated effort is made. Consolidation is already generally accepted as a necessary part of the programme by everybody. The formation and proper functioning of co-operative farms is undoubtedly less generally accepted as part of universal policy and is somewhat more difficult. It is, however, equally necessary.

I shall, without elaborating them, briefly state a number of reasons in favour of this proposition. In the first instance, without cooperatives, collectives or state farms, an economic reorganization for operation of the existing numerous small units is impossible. Secondly, except as member of a co-operative the small farmer can never be in a position to avail himself of technical, financial, or other external aid of which he stands in need, more than anybody else. The findings of all studies; whether, e.g., of the Rural Credit Survey or the Evaluation Organization are that the bigger man gets the greater profit out of everything, government loans, co-operative finance or other financial or technical assistance of any type. One need not go into the reasons for this state of affairs; it is, however, clear from the studies that the scattered, weak units cannot really be helped effectively unless they come together. Also, as long as there is no consolidation of these weak units the balance in rural society will always remain against them. Any close study of the effects of recent land reforms legislation reveals large variations in its results, dependent chiefly on the strength of tenants and smaller holders in a locality or region. In a large number of instances legal protection and other devices prove cons-tantly fruitless because of the strength and ingenuity of the strong. It is sad to record that large deflection of original intentions, brought about by the strong, has been reported even in the working of the Bhoodan movement. The moral is that unless the weak acquire economic strength by joining together they could never stand up and get full advantage of state policy and state legislation. The formation of a small number of co-operative farming societies of the smaller holders and the landless in each locality is a necessary step in this direction. It will be noticed that I consider redistribution as only a part of the process in the formation of the large co-operative farms. I cannot see any virtue in merely tenancy co-operatives which perpetuate the smaller units of management. Leaving scope for allotments or kitchen gardens would be welcome but the main cropping operations must be in terms of the large units. The experience elsewhere, such as with the Ejido in Mexico, emphasises importance of this.

I do not think that widespread formation of such co-operatives is an impossible undertaking. In the initial stages the progress may be slow but once the movement gathers momentum the field could be covered fairly quickly. Wide extension of the activities of State governments in rural areas together with efforts made by the Central Government in directions of Community Development and National Extension already provide comparatively large staffs in the field; the work of this staff would come to have real meaning and purpose only if it is linked to a programme of the formation and operation of such co-operatives. Instead of chiefly conducting propaganda they would find in these co-operatives numerous local units which could prove centres of demonstration and experimentation. All governmental information and propaganda, aid and assistance could be directed towards and routed through these co-operatives. The special terms of assistance, etc., laid down for these co-operatives should combine the features of the programmes envisaged in the draft outline of the Five-Year Plan for the Registered Farms and for the Co-operative Farming Societies. Instead of receiving very little or nothing of government protection and assistance this step would ensure that the most disadvantaged received, as they should, the highest priority and the greatest assistance.

There are following basic propositions. That in relation to land management we are following, in this country today, a policy mainly of drift; that a programme of economic development requires more positive approach in respect of agricultural productive organization and units of land management; that a very large number of existing cultivating holdings are extremely unsuitable for functioning as independent units in a programme of agricultural development and that a rational layout of the land surface for its proper utilisation and a programme for the creation of large consolidated holdings are essential ingredients in any agricultural and land development policy. I may add finally that it would be impossible to deal with this problem except in term of bold steps and very large and strenuous effort. However, these would be no more radical and strenuous than those undertaken by many other countries in analogous situations, as evidenced, for example, by the Mexican Agrarian Revolution which redistributed land in favour of the Ejidos or the transformations brought about in countries of South and East Europe both during the inter-war years and in the period after the Second World War.

Village Industry

The weakest spot in our programmes of community development is the development of rural industries for providing employment to the unemployed and the underemployed. From the data available, it appears that only 2.5 per cent of the families have been benefited by our activities in the 80 blocks examined by us. These figures are too generous in that the benefit of employment to one man has been equated to benefit to one whole family; also the employment has been assumed to be full employment. Even so, this additional employment introduced in the village is insufficient to set off the two years' increase in population. The training-cum-production centres have been the main channel of opening new rural industries. Figures available, however, show that more than 50 per cent of the persons passing out of such centres do not take up the profession to which they have been trained. These disquieting facts have to be faced and our present approach to the problem has to be revised radically.

To this end steps have to be taken for:

(i) carrying out a rapid local economic and technical survey in each block in the possibility of specific industries;

(ii) training for improvement of existing technical skills and introduction of new ones in consonance with the findings of (i.) above;

(iii) establishment of pilot projects to demonstrate the technical feasibility and economic soundness of any particular industry or industries;

(iv) co-ordination of cottage, village and small-scale industries;

(v) rural electrification which could equally well serve irrigation purposes;

(vi) provision of credit for rural industry;

(vii) supply of raw material where necessary and of improved designs;

(viii) quality control and facilities for marketing; and

(ix) research, technical supervision and guidance.

Cottage, village and small-scale industries need a very considerable coordination in their working. They have their appropriate place in the rural economy but sometimes are apt to cut into one another. At the all-India level, a number of such indivi-dual industries are promoted by all-India boards which sometimes are inclined to work in separate compartments. It should not be difficult to make some effort to pool funds, personnel; agencies of supervision and inspection and marketing arrangements so that inefficiency and waste can be minimised. The all-India boards, themselves should function through State boards nominated by the State Governments in consultation with them. The State boards in their turn should function through the various State departments concerned with the industry and through local representative organisations.

In-house Industry

Taking up first those difficulties which are special to cottage industries, as distinguished from agriculture, three main items are obvious:

(1) Cottage industries have to face the competition of larger, better organized and technically much more competent units in the shape of the manufacturing industries situated in towns and cities.

(2) The market for cottage industries is much less assured than for the agricultural industry. Fortunately for the latter, food is firstly wanted by all, and secondly is still grown on land and not in factories. For cottage industries, on the other hand, the essence of the problem is to find a market and then not lose it to a more power-ful urban competitor.

(3) The other important special problem for many cottage industries is the finding of the raw material. Thus, one of the greatest difficulties of the handloom industry, except perhaps in periods of control, has been that of the purchase of yarn. A number of weavers' co-operative societies, it is interesting to note, are little more than societies for buying yarn and distributing it among their members.

Apart from these items, all of them grave and all of them important, the nature of the difficulties seems essentially the same for cottage industries as for agriculture when looked at from the point of view of the reorganization and rehabilitation of the industry on a co-operative basis. The main and still largely unsolved problem for co-operative cottage industry is, we suggest, the same that has been faced by co-operative agriculture, namely, how to make a combination of the very weak strong enough in relation to the much stronger. Just as there is the moneylender in the sphere of agricultural credit, so there is the Karkhanadar for each important cottage industry, with the difference that he combines in himself the handicraftsman and the financier. The karkhanadar is himself part of a wider system of private finance. Thus a whole set of private creditors, financing agencies, marketing agencies, etc., deal with the individual small weaver, as do the private traders and private financiers with the cultivator. We would, in this connection, quote from a note which appears in the First Annual Report (1954) of the All-India Handloom Board.

"Since, according to the Fact Finding Committee's Report, the unorganised condition of the industry is responsible for its abnormal high marketing costs and its consequent evils, it is but natural to accord pride of place to the organisation of the industry in all schemes aiming at the stabilization of the ancient industry and thereby ensuring the prosperity of the weavers." According to the Fact Finding Committee, the official agencies have fostered only co-operative organisations which have, speaking generally, suffered from financial weakness, inefficiency of management and inability to cope with fluctuation in yarn prices and with marketing of the finished product. The Committee has also emphasised the age-long social and business relations and, in most cases, ties of caste and creed between the master-weavers, sowcars and mahajans, on the one hand and the weavers on the other, which may have been primarily responsible for the half-hearted support accorded to the co-operative movement. It is also possible that the lack of credit facilities on social occasions such as marriages, pujahs, absence of any effective voice in the management of co-operative organisation and the smallness of the capital invested by him in the society did not evoke the enthusiasm of the weaver who preferred to eke out an existence as best as he could with the aid and support of the master-weaver or the sowcar mahajan. It is also not unlikely that co-operative organizations invited within their fold only the weavers and thus alienated the sympathy of the master-weavers and the mahajans.

"The next question of importance is the question of marketing. In so far as the independent weavers are concerned, they form the smaller proportion of the weaver population in the country; no tangible relief could be possible unless they join either the co-operative or any other organization which may be fostered. Their slender finances, chronic indebtedness and, therefore, complete dependence on the yarn dealer for the supply of yarn on credit leave them no option other than that of selling at the buyer's price. Unless, therefore, they are brought within the fold of such organisation as would supply them yarn on credit and take back the finished product at prices based on standard wages and replacement cost of yarn, they would in due course of time be relegated to the position of mere wage-earners.

"...The numerous types of middlemen and the functions of each has been dealt with fully by the Fact Finding Committee in paragraphs 60 to 63 of its Report, and the Committee has discussed the middlemen's profit in paragraph 124. The Committee has also come to the conclusion that `there are far too many middlemen participating in the trade and that their efficiency and individual turnover are much lower than they should be. At the same time, there are many middlemen who appear to be keeping their heads above water by taking a proportionately higher share of the gross profits of the industry than the weaver himself.' The Committee has emphasised that the cost of marketing of handloom fabrics is 'prohibitively high and that the middleman is largely to be blamed for this.' `The principal problem, therefore, so far as marketing is concerned, is how to reduce the marketing costs."

9

Agricultural Products

A little more than a decade has elapsed since this country launched upon a programme of planned economic development. According to the estimates of the Planning Commission, an investment of 10,110 crore rupees has been made in the economy between 1951 and 1961. The Third-Five Year Plan envisages an investment of another 10,000 crore rupees during 1961-65. It is legitimate to expect that all this investment and the organizational effort that goes with it, would not only accelerate the pace of economic development, but, in the process, also alter the structure of the economy. It would be interesting therefore to examine the nature and extent of change in the structure of the national economy during the last decade, by reference to some of the conventional economic indicators.

For the purpose of this Address, I should like to focus attention on the impact of the process of growth on the agricultural sector. The literature on the economics of growth visualizes a certain role for agriculture in the process of economic development, stage by stage, but a little more precisely in the early stage of development. Not that all writers are unanimous on the subject, but most of them agree on the importance or the crucial role of agriculture.

As a background to our main factual analysis of India's experience, it would be interesting to review briefly, first, some of the theories on the role of agriculture in economic development, and then, the thinking of the Indian planners on the subject, as revealed in the successive Five-Year Plans.

Fundamental Issues

The primacy of agricultural development is emphasized by some writers, because agriculture is not only the most populous but also the most depressed sector of the economy in most of the developing economies. This view is sometimes carried to the extreme of opposition to industrial development. It is argued that "the policy of industrialization will intensify the tendency for savings to be drained from the countryside by making investment in urban industries more attractive", and thus widen the range of inequality between the urban and rural standards of living. "Problems of over-population and unemployment, very low incomes, excessive urbanization, food shortages as well as certain social and political considerations would suggest that the policy of industrialization is premature and undesirable at the present stage of Asian development." The importance of increased supply of food and other wage goods is emphasized by a group of thinkers not merely on welfare grounds, but as a necessary investment in human capital. The `consumption multiplier', it is argued, is not less crucial than the conventional investment multiplier in the strategy of development.

Priority for agriculture is also favoured on the ground that the creation of investible surplus is technologically easier in agriculture and has much shorter gestation period. Increase in agricultural production in the initial period of development can be brought about through the application of resources which have a low opportunity cost and make no inroads on the critically scarce resources necessary for industrial development.

The point of departure comes on the question whether the economic surplus in agriculture should be retained within it for improving the standard of rural living or should be siphoned off for urban, industrial development. Those who advocate the latter are interested in agriculturists either forcibly or through lower prices. The non-violent strategy is expounded thus: "Increase in the output of foodgrains and other agricultural commodities sufficient to lower their price will make the terms of trade unfavourable to agriculture. The fall in agricultural prices will be steep, due to the fact that the demand for food is not infinitely elastic. If agricultural prices are depressed relative to non-agricultural prices, agricultural surpluses will go into the hands of non-agriculturists."

As against the agriculture-first school, those who emphasize the role of rapid industrialization in economic development argue that most of the underdeveloped countries are, in fact, so termed because of the predominance of agriculture in their national economy. The path of progress, therefore, must inevitably lie in the direction of a shift of resources, both capital and labour, from low-productivity enterprises to high-productivity enterprises. Agriculture is admittedly a relatively low-productivity sector even in most of the advanced countries; as such, the strategy of economic development would consist in gradually reducing the preponderance of the agricultural sector in the national economy through a process of industrialization. This, in any case, would be necessary inasmuch as with rising incomes, the community's demand-pattern will undergo a change in favour of industrial products.

International comparisons of shares of major sectors in national product "reveal a negative correlation between the level of income and agriculture's share in it, and a positive correlation between the level of income and the share of non-agricultural commodity production. As the level of per capita income increases, the share of agriculture in national product drops and that of industry rises." Analysis of long-term trends also confirms the results obtained by cross-country analysis. Thus, Prof. Kuznets found that with the secular rise of product per capita and per worker, the share of the agricultural sector in total product declines and the share of the manufacturing sector rises. The analysis in terms of distribution of labour force in the different sectors of the national economy suggests a significant positive association between the rate of growth in per capita and a shift away from agriculture in the structure of the labour force. One is therefore led to argue that "if real income per capita is to grow rapidly, the accompanying changes in the occupational structure of the labour force should be equally large. In the sample of eighteen countries, the total shift in the percentage distribution of labour force (including unpaid family labour) among the three major sectors (agriculture, manufacture, services) tends to be large in countries with high rates of growth of per capita income and vice versa."

These conclusions, however, should not be interpreted to imply that re-deployment of labour force would automatically, so to say, lead to higher per capita income. Kuznets' analysis has also revealed that a mere shift of the industrial structure of underdeveloped countries towards the pattern of developed countries-retaining the contrast between the high, relative, per-worker product in the manufacturing and service sectors and the low one in the agricultural sector-will not reduce the international differences in per-worker product. "To put in simply," he says, "the major source of international differences in countrywide output per worker (and per capita) between developed and underdeveloped countries is not that the full-time labour force of the former and of the latter are distributed differently among the several industrial sectors .... It is rather in the fact that within each sector proper within agriculture, within mining, within manufacturing, within transportation and trade, etc.-the product per worker in the underdeveloped countries is so much lower than in the developed." As a matter of fact, Kuznets himself has elsewhere argued: "Agricultural Revolution-a marked rise in productivity per worker in agriculture-is a pre-condition of the industrial revolution in any part of the world." Whatever be the motive or objective of economic development, welfare of the rural community or its surplus-generating-potential for overall economic development, there appears to be a fair degree of consensus regarding the crucial importance of agriculture in the initial period of economic growth.

Schemes and Plans

In the light of the foregoing discussion on the role of agriculture in economic development, it would be useful to review briefly the views of the Planning Commission on this question as stated in the successive Five-Year Plans. Writing about the pattern of priority in the First Five-Year Plan, the Planning Commission states: "The conception of priorities over a period has to be a dynamic one, the emphasis as between different sectors shifting as development in those taken up initially prepares the ground for development in others." Having laid down this broad principle, the Planning Commission proceeds to state: "For the next five-year period, agriculture including irrigation and power must, in our view, have the top-most priority. For one thing, this emphasis is indicated by the need to complete the projects in hand, and further we are convinced that without a substantial increase in the production of food and of raw materials needed for industry, it would be impossible to sustain a high tempo of industrial development. In an underdeveloped economy, with low yield in agriculture, there is of course no real conflict between agricultural and industrial development. One cannot go far without the other; the two are complementary. It is necessary, however, on economic as well as on other grounds, first of all to strengthen the economy at the base and to create conditions of sufficiency and even plenitude in respect of food and raw materials." Consistent with this approach, in the total Plan outlay of 2,356 crore rupees, as much as 15.1 per cent was allocated to agriculture and community development and 28 - 1 per cent to irrigation and power (16.3 per cent to irrigation, 11.1 per cent to power and 0.7 per cent to flood control, etc.) as against 7.6 per cent to industry and mining (6.3 per cent for large and medium industries and 1.3 per cent for small industries). It should, however, be mentioned that the Planning Commission, at that stage, held the following view: "The progress in industries, especially large-scale industries, would have to depend, to a great extent, on effort in the private sector, while the State would concentrate on the provision of basic services like power and transportation." Though it was stated that the State had also "special responsibility for developing key industries and heavy industries like iron and steel, heavy chemicals and manufacture of electrical equipments without which development in the modern world is impossible," no significant allocation was made for the development of these key industries in the public sector.

Agricultural production during the First Five-Year Plan increased substantially, though in retrospect it appears that the bulk of it was due to an increase in the acreage and to good weather conditions. At the end of the First Five-Year Plan, foodgrain production had increased from 55 million tons to 65 million tons, exceeding the target of 61.6 million tons laid down for the last year of the Plan. Prices of agricultural commodities also declined sharply. The comfortable situation on the agricultural front induced the Planning Commission to shift the emphasis towards industrialization, while formulating the Second Five-Year Plan one of the major objectives of the Plan was stated to be "rapid industrialization with particular emphasis on the development of basic and heavy industries". The other objectives mentioned in this context were a sizeable increase in national income, large expansion of employment opportunities and reduction of inequalities in incomes and wealth, but there was no specific mention of the development in agriculture. Arguing the case for rapid industrialization, the Commission state: "Low or static standards of living, under-employment and unemployment and, to a certain extent, a gap between the average and the highest incomes are all manifestations of basic under-development which characterizes an economy dependent mainly on agriculture. The core of development is thus rapid industrialization and diversification of the economy. But, for industrialization to be rapid enough, basic industries like iron and steel, non-ferrous metals, coal, cement and heavy chemicals as well as industries which make machines for making machines have to be developed rapidly." The approach of the balanced growth was not given up. It was stated that balanced pattern of industrialization requires well-recognized effort to utilize labour for increasing the supplies of much-needed consumer goods in a manner which economizes the use of capital.

Consistent with this view, the percentage of the developmental outlay (Rs. 4,800 crores) allocated to industry and mining was increased to 18.5 per cent (from 7.6 per cent in the First Five-Year Plan) and that for agriculture and community development was reduced to 11.8 per cent (from 15.1 in the First Plan). There was a similar reduction to 19 per cent from 28.1 per cent in outlay allocated for irrigation and power. The targets of agricultural production for the Second Five-Year Plan were also relatively modest. For example, the production of food-grains was to be increased from 65 million tons in 1955-56 to 75 million tons in 1960-61, an increase of 10 million tons in the five years of the

Second Plan as against an increase of 14 million tons achieved during the First Five-Year Plan. Soon after, however, it was realized that the target for foodgrain production in the Second Five-Year Plan was rather low and was raised to 80 million tons, without however, making any addition to the financial allocation for agricultural development.

Outlay in the Public Sector in the First, the Second and the Third Plan.

Head	First Plan		Second Plan		Third Plan	
	Outlay	Per centage	Outlay	Per centage	Outlay	Percentage
Agriculture & Community Development	357	15.1	568	11.8	1,068	14
Major & Medium Irrigation	401	17.0	486	10.1	650	9
Power	260	11.1	427	8.9	1,012	13
Village & Small Industries	30	1.3	200	4.1	264	4
Industries & Minerals	149	6.3	690	14.4	1,520	20
Transport & Communications	557	23.6	1,385	29.9	1,486	20
Social Services & Miscellaneous	533	22.6	945	19.7	1,300	17
Inventories/ Miscellaneous	69	3.0	99	2.1	200	3
Total	2,356	100	4,800	100	7,500	100

* Planned, not actual. Source: Five-Year Plans.

Though in the last year of the Second Plan, food-grain production nearly reached the revised target, in the preceding years, shortages were experienced resulting in a substantial increase in food-grain prices. The Third Plan, therefore, restored the primacy of agriculture in its development programme. Unlike in the Second Plan, the achievement of self-sufficiency in food-grains and increased agricultural production to meet the requirements of industry and export, found place in the principal objectives of the Third Plan. It was stated that in the scheme of development in the Third Plan, the first priority necessarily belonged to agriculture.

The experience during the period of the first two Plans, especially the Second, had shown that the rate of growth in agricultural production was one of the main limiting factors in the progress of the Indian economy. This, however, did not imply relaxation of emphasis on the development of basic and heavy industries. As a matter of fact, there appears to be a degree of ambivalence regarding the relative importance of agriculture and industry. On the one hand, it was stated: "The development of agriculture based on utilization of manpower resources of the countryside and the maximum use of local resources holds the key to the rapid development of the country." On the other, it was also stated: "There is no doubt that industry has a leading role in securing rapid economic advance." This was sought to be reconciled by the following statement: "The growth of agriculture and the development of human resources alike hinge upon the advance made by industry. Not only does industry provide the new tools, but it begins to change the mental outlook of the peasant."

Allocation of financial outlay to the different sectors in the Third Plan does indicate a slight shift in favour of agriculture. The share of agriculture and community development in the total financial outlay was increased from 11.8 per cent in the Second Plan to 14 per cent in the Third, while the percentage allocated to major and medium irrigation was slightly reduced. The percentage share of organized industry and minerals was stepped up from 14.4 to 20 per cent. It was, however, stated: "In formulating agricultural production programmes for the Third Plan, the guiding consideration has been that the agricultural efforts should not be impeded in any manner for want of financial, or other resources. Accordingly, finance is being provided on a scale which is considered adequate and further assurance is given that if for achieving the targets of production, additional resources are found necessary, this will be provided as the Plan proceeds." During the first two years of the Third Plan, progress of agricultural production was very unsatisfactory and when national emergency was declared, after the invasion of the northern frontier, the National Development Council sanctioned supplementary allocation for minor irrigation and soil conservation.

Viewing the three Five-Year Plans together, one can state that the only period during which the importance of agricultural development was not sufficiently appreciated was at the time of the formulation of the Second Plan. It may be perhaps more appropriate to say that during that period, the importance of the basic and heavy industries in national development came to be emphasized for the first time. It was interpreted as 'neglect' of agriculture. In this connection, it is important to mention that the allocation of only 6.3 per cent of the total financial outlay in the First Plan to the development of large and medium industries in the public sector was altogether too meagre and its step-up to 14.4 per cent in the Second Plan was, in a way, a correction of the 'neglect' of industrial development in the First Plan. It is interesting to note that, in retrospect, even the critics of the heavy-industry bias of the Second Plan agree that it would have been worthwhile to have endeavoured to establish a steel mill during the period of the First Plan.

In this connection, it is necessary to emphasize that it is inappropriate to judge the priorities accorded to different sectors, only by reference to the composition of planned public outlay or investment. Apart from the considerable non-monetized investment, particularly in the agricultural sector, so characteristic of underdeveloped economies, the quantum of private investment in different sectors constitutes an important component of the total investment in which the ultimate output would depend. According to the estimates given in the Third Five-Year Plan, during the period of the First Five-Year Plan (1951-56), the private-sector investment came to 1,800 crore rupees as against 1,560 crore rupees of public sector investment. The corresponding figures for the Second Plan period (1956-61) are 3.100 crore rupees and 3,650 crore rupees. It may also be noted that during the period of the Second Plan, private investment in agriculture and community development came to 625 crore rupees as against public investment of 210 crore rupees. In the case of major and medium irrigation, however, as expected, there was no private investment against an investment of 420 crore rupees by the public sector. Further, as Reddaway has rightly pointed out, "The only way of judging whether a development plan is well-balanced is by considering the flow of output of the various goods and services. Investment is simply one means of securing this balance and the character of the development cannot be judged by the way in which this one means is allocated between various industries. "The capital expenditures", he says, "are a very important means of helping to attain this output, but they are not objectives in themselves; if some other method of raising output could be discovered during the Plan period (e.g. by the use of better seeds instead of costly irrigation schemes), then, the essence of the Plan can be fulfilled even if the capital expenditure were far below the original figures."

Professor Reddaway has elaborated this point thus: "A five-year plan normally shows two main sets of figures: targets for the outputs of various commodities which should be attained in the last year of the plan, and plans for capital expenditure to be done in the whole period of the plan. Of these two, the capital expenditure is the thing which calls for direct and immediate action, and it tends, therefore, to be regarded as the essence of `the Plan'. This is, however, to mistake the means for the objective: the fundamental objective of the Plan is to attain the higher levels of output, and it is these levels of future output which have to be kept in balance as between one product and another, if the Plan is to be a coherent one."

After this rather prolix introductory background, we may concentrate on our main theme: the impact of the growth-process on Indian agriculture. Let us begin with the examination of the relative growth-rates in the agricultural and non-agricultural sectors of the economy. To keep quantitative analysis within a modest limit, ours will be only a two-sector analysis: agriculture-including animal husbandry, forest and fisheries -- and the rest of the economy which, for the sake of convenience, has been termed non-agricultural sector, unless otherwise stated.

Several factors influence the relative position of the two sectors in the process of development. Firstly, the growth-rates in the two sectors may vary. The impact of the differential growth-rates on per capita (or per worker) income will be modified by the sectoral transfer of labour-force. The change in the terms of trade will further alter the income-parity ratio of the two sectors. We shall

Investment (Private and Public) in the First, the Second and the Third Plan

Head	First Plan Investment				Second Plan Investment				Third Plan Investment			
	Public (a)	Private (b)	Total	Percentage	Public	Private	Total	Percentage	Public	Private	Total	Percentage
1	2	3	4	5	6	7	8	9	10	11	12	13
Agriculture & Community Development	234	363	597	18.0	210	625	835	12	660	800	1,460	13
Major & Medium Irrigation	250	(b)	250	7.2	420	(b)	420	6	650	(b)	650	6
Power	203	23	226	6.7	445	40	485	7	1,012	50	1,062	10
Village & Small Industries	31	101	132	4.0	90	175	265	4	150	275	425	4
Organized Industries & Minerals	62	392	454	13.5	870	675	1,545	23	1,520	1,050	2,570	25
Transport & Communications	421	78	499	15.0	1,275	135	1,410	21	1,486	250	1,736	18
Social Services & Miscellaneous	359	553	912	27.0	340	950	1,290	19	622	1,075	1,697	16
Inventories	–	290	290	8.6	–	500	500	8	200	600	800	8
Total	1,560	1,800	3,360	100	3,650	3,100	6,750	100	6,300	4,100	10400	100

Note:-Investment should be distinguished from outlay. The former represents expenditure on the creation of physical assets, the latter corresponds to revenue expenditure on Plan schemes.

(a) The break-up of investment in the private and the public sector for the period of the First Plan is not available. The break-up given in column 2 corresponds to the break-up of public outlay. The break-up in column 3 is worked out under the assumption that its pattern was the same as in the Second Plan.

(b) Included under agriculture and community development.

first briefly review the experience in regard to these three dominant factors during the last decade.

Progress at Fast Pace

A variety of statistical data, not always easily comparable, is available on growth-rates in agricultural production, and productivity.

We have the unadjusted and the adjusted figures of annual production in absolute terms. We have also the Index Numbers of Production, Area and Productivity which claim that they remove the non-comparability due to changes in statistical coverage and methods of estimation. As the measurement based on two specific points (years) would be influenced by seasonal conditions which are important in agriculture, linear growth-rates and compound rates have been calculated. One series is based on the three-year moving-averages of the index numbers for the period 1949-50 to 1961-62 and the other for the period 1952-53 to 1961-62.

All-India Compound Growth-rates in Percentages

Food-grains	3.45	2.46
Non-food-grains	3.57	3.88
All crops	3.49	2.94

The table reveals that agricultural production increased at the compound rate of about 3.5 per cent during 1951-61. If, however, a three-year average centred on 1951-54 is taken, the increase amounts to only three per cent per year.

The better results in the 1949-50 series are believed to be primarily due to the larger contribution of the increase in area. As there are grave doubts about the Index Number Series of Area (which incidentally is used as a deflator for calculating the Index of Productivity) it would be advisable to avoid going into the question of relative contribution of Area and Productivity to the growth in production.

For industrial growth, we have the Revised Series of Index of Industrial Production with the Base: 1956=100. After shifting the base to 1951, we get a linear rate of growth of 9.7 per cent per year.

That the growth-rate in the industrial sector should be higher than that in the agricultural sector, is to be expected in a developing economy. What is somewhat unexpected is the wide divergence between the two.

The national income data provide another source from which the sectoral growth-rates may be derived. The net national output in 1948-49 prices originating from the agricultural sector increased from 43.8 abja rupees (annual average of 1949-52) to 57.6 abja rupees (average of 1959-62) resulting in an increase of 31.5 per cent during these years (Table). For the corresponding period, the increase in the net national output in the rest of the economy (termed the non-agricultural sector) was from 45.6 abja to 68.3 abja, resulting in an increase of 49.8 per cent. If these figures are viewed from another angle, 37.8 per cent of the total increase in national output during the period was contributed by the agricultural sector and the remaining 62.2 per cent by the non-agricultural sector. It is apparent that the rate of growth was relatively small for the agricultural sector as compared with that for the non-agricultural sector. This would make the income-parity ratio between the two sectors less favourable to the agricultural sector over the decade; other factors such as labour-force movement and terms of trade remaining the same. This picture is slightly altered when the national output is measured in current prices. Under this method of calculation, the output in the agricultural sector shows an increase of 39 per cent as against an increase of 54.4 per cent in the non-agricultural sector. In other words; 42.1 per cent of the increase in the national output during this period was contributed by agriculture as against 57.9 per cent by the non-agricultural sector. The contribution of the agricultural sector to the total increase in national output was relatively larger (42.1 per cent) when measured in terms of current prices instead of constant prices (37.8 per cent). This difference can be attributed to the change in the terms of trade in favour of agriculture (Price-parity ratio 102.72).*

Growth in National Output

	1949-52	1959-62	Increase	Increase percentage	Share in total increase
	Constant prices (1948-49)				
Agriculture@	43.8	57.6	13.8	31.5	37.8
Non-agriculture@ @	45.6	68.3	22.7	49.8	62.2
Total	89.4	125.9	36.5	40.8	100.00
		In current prices			
Agriculture	48.0	66.7	18.7	39.0	42.1
Non-agriculture	47.2	72.9	25.7	54.4	57.9
Total	95.2	139.6	44.4	46.6	100.0

* Three-year average centred round 1950-51.

** Three-year average centred round 1960-61.

@ Includes animal husbandry, forest and fisheries.

@ @ The rest of the economy.

Labour force: The changes in the composition of labour-force between 1951 and 1961 as revealed by the population census, are presented in the following Table. There were, however, some drastic changes in the concepts and definition used in the two censuses, and extreme caution is needed in drawing conclusions based on these figures. Particular mention may be made of the marked increase in the labour-participation rates from 39 per cent in 1951 to 42.98 per cent in 1961. On the whole, it can be said that the increase in the labour-force between 1951 and 1961 revealed by the table exaggerates the situation due to an underestimation by the 1951 census and overestimation by the 1961 census. Anyway, the most significant factor which emerges from the table is that the proportion of the labour-force employed in agriculture remains almost the same (72.13 in 1951 and 71.79 in 1961) over the decade. This would imply that the change in the relative position of the two sectors due to differential growth-rates would not be affected by this factor inasmuch as there was no change in the disposition of the labour-force.

Terms of trade: The third factor which would affect the relative position of the two sectors would be the change in their terms of trade. Various methods have been used to determine the terms of trade: (a) of the agricultural sector vis-a-vis non-agricul-tural sector;

and (b) of the farmers in terms of the ratio of prices received to prices paid. The usual method used for the former is to study the relative movements in the prices of agricultural and non-agricultural commodities and the ratio between the two. This should not be strictly termed as terms of trade inasmuch as the weights used in the construction of the wholesale prices would be very different from the weights of the commodities entering into the trade between the two sectors. In any case, information regarding the movement in the prices of these two groups of commodities would be of some interest and is given in the following Table.

Price Indexes

	1949-52	1959-62			
Agricultural	100	107.45	107.45 / 104.60	=	102-72
Non-Agricultural	100	104.60	107.45 / 105.84	=	101.52
Total	100	105.84	104.60 / 105.84	=	98.82

Population and Labour-Force by Sectors

(Figures in million)

Year	Population	Working force	Agricultural workers*	Non-agricultural workers	% of agricultural workers to total workers
1951	356.88	139.52	100.63	38.89	72.13
1961	438.31	188.42	135.26	53.16	71.79
Change 1961-51	81.43	48.90	34.63	14.27	(-) 00 34

*(1) The term " agricultural workers " includes: (a) `cultivators', or the industrial category I of the 1961 census; (b) `agricultural labourers', or the industrial category II of the 1961 census; and (c) workers engaged in `livestock, forestry, hunting and plantations, orchards and allied activities' but not those engaged in mining and quarrying, or, in other words, only a part of the industrial category III of the 1961 census.

(2) The 1961 data are taken from: Census of India, Paper No. 1 of 1962, 1961 Census: Final Population Totals.

Employment, Output, Income Per Worker, and Income Ratio in Agriculture and the Rest of the Economy

Year force	Total Work- agriculture	Workers in non-agri- culture	Workers in agriculture	Output in non-agri- culture	Output in per worker	Agri. output output per worker	Non-agri. Agri. Non-agri.	Income ratio 1
1	2	3	4	5	6	7	8	9
		In millions	In Rs		prices	Rupees		
1951	139.52	100.63	38.89	43.4	45.3	431	1165	0.37:1
1960-61	188.4	135.3	53.1	59.1	68.9	437	1297	0.34:1
1970-71	237.7	170.7	67.0	77.14	99.70	452	1488	0.30:1
1970-71	237.7	165.6	72.1	77.14	99.70	466	1383	0.34:1
1975-76	266.9	191.7	75.2	88.13	119.93	460	1595	0.29:1

Assumptions: (i) Population increases at the compound rate of 2- 35 per cent per year; (ii) Work-force increases in both sectors at the same rate as that of population; (iii) Proportion of workers in the agricultural and the non-agricultural sector remains the same as in 1961 (71.8 and 28.2); (iv) Output in the two sectors increases at the same rate as experienced during 1948-49 to 1960-61 (agri. 3.7 per cent per year compound, non-agri. 3.76 per cent, National Income Data); *(v) In row IV in the Table, figures are worked out on the assumption that the ratio of the agricultural and the non-agricultural income in 1971 remains the same as in 1961.

By and large, the movements in the prices of the two groups of commodities have been on parallel lines. In the year 1955, however, the index for the agricultural commodities declined by as many as 12 points from the base year but that for the non-agricultural commodities fell by only one point. From this year onwards, the rise in the price index of the agricultural commodities has been somewhat steeper than that of the non-agricultural commodity price-index. In the year 1961, the two indexes stood almost at the same level.

Index Numbers of Wholesale Prices of Agricultural to Non-Agricultural Commodities.

(Base: 1951-53 = 100)

Weights	Agricultural commodities (680)	Non-agricultural commodities (320)	All commodities (1000)
1950	113	99	109
1951	122	117	120
1952	102	104	102
1953	107	99	104
1954	99	100	100
1955	88	99	92
1956	102	105	103
1957	109	108	109
1958	112	109	111
1959	118	111	116
1960	124	121	123
1961	126	127	126

Source: Economic Survey, 1960-61, Directorate of Economics and Statistics, Ministry of Food and Agriculture, p. 56.

Information regarding the ratio of prices received to prices paid by the farmers is available only for a few regions. (see Table.) The Punjab Board of Economic Enquiry has been compiling this information for the last 25 years. Similar information is available for the last decade in some other states like Assam, Kerala, Orissa and West Bengal. Extreme caution should be exercised in making use of this information without a detailed scrutiny of the methods and techniques used in the construction of the index. The differences in the crop patterns of these regions are significant. Orissa, Assam and West Bengal are predominantly rice-growing

areas, while the major crops in the Punjab are wheat and gram. Kerala's 'agriculture' is dominated by coconut, tapioca and pepper. Weights given to different commodities in the construction of the indexes of prices received naturally vary, as they should. But the marked variations in the weights given to commodities entering into the indexes of prices paid, particularly in regard to family consumption.

Index numbers of parity between prices received and prices paid.

Year	Assam (1944- = 100)	Kerala (1952-53 = 100)	Punjab (1938-39 = 100)	Orissa (1939- = 100)	West Bengal (Previous year= 100)
1951-52	131.6*	91.7	-	-	
1952-53	103.9	98.5	110.02*	-	
1953-54	102.1	95.2	101.2	103.02	-
1954-55	99.6	85.2	89.9	113.81	101.1*
1955-56	96.4	82.4	99.1	126.24	98.9
1956-57	106.7	83.4	102.7	135.54	-
1957-58	118.6	81.9	96.9	123.92	-
1958-59	109.3	83.0	103.2	121.84	107.3
1959-60	99.1	92.8	94.8	-	98.2
1960-61	107.3	92.1	95.3	-	102.6
1961-62	115.5	88.8	87.8	-	98.7
1962-63	105.6	84.1	84.9	-	97.9

* Calendar years, e.g.. 1951 is identified as 1951-52 and so on, in column one.
Source: Directorate of Economics & Statistics, Ministry of Food & Agriculture, Government of India.

48 per cent for clothing in the Punjab and eight per cent in Bengal—are difficult to explain. Similarly, the basis for weights given to commodities purchased for farm production is quite arbitrary in some cases. Apart from the technicalities of the construction of the index numbers, the method of collection of the data and their dependability leave much to be desired. However, for the sake of completing the record of available information, the parity indexes for these states are given in Table.

The statistical evidence regarding the terms of trade, apart from its inadequacy and qualitative deficiencies, does not lead to any firm conclusions. The sectoral national-income estimates in constant and current prices, indicate a positive shift of the terms of trade in favour of agriculture. Perhaps there is something in the (national-income-estimation procedures, which has such a built-in bias. The question needs a more careful and critical examination. Conclusions based on the wholesale-price index, would depend upon the year from which the trend is measured. Of the 12 years for which the data are given in above Tables years, the price index was favourable for agriculture, and the positive difference in its favour was, on the whole, larger than the negative difference against it. The data on the parity of the prices received to prices paid for Kerala and the Punjab definitely indicate that the terms of trade have gone against the former; Orissa shows exactly the opposite trend, and West Bengal a mixed trend.

The experience of the progress in the agricultural and non-agricultural sectors during the period 1951-61 may be summed up as follows:

(1) The gross product derived from the agricultural sector increased at the compound rate of 2.7 per cent; the growth-rate in the non-agricultural sector was 3.76 (1948-49 to 1960-61 National Income Statistics).

(2) The proportion of workers engaged in the agricultural sector declined fractionally from 72.13 in 1951 to 71.82 in 1961. Consequently, there was an insignificant increase in the proportion of the work-force engaged in the non-agricultural sector, from 27.87 in 1951 to 28.18 in 1961.

(3) The incomes per worker in the two sectors in 1951 were 431 rupees and 1,165 rupees respectively. In 1961, they had crept up to 437 rupees and 1,297 rupees respectively. As a result, the income parity of the workers in the two sectors declined from 0.37:1 to 0.34:1. It should be mentioned that the paltry rise of only six rupees in the per-agricultural-worker income is, in some measure, due to the sharp increase in the agricultural work-force, a part of which may be purely definitional. If the 1961 participation-rate is applied to the 1951 population-data, the work-force in 1951 would be larger and the per-worker

income would be smaller (approximately Rs. 392). In that case the increase in the per-worker income in agriculture, during the decade, would amount to 45 rupees.

Hard Facts

We may now examine some facets of the situation as it will emerge after a ten-year period ending 1971 and a 15-year period ending 1976; under certain specific assumptions. The projection examines the impact on the per-worker-income ratio of the two sectors under following assumptions

(1) Population will grow at the compound rate of 2-35 per cent during this period;

(2) The growth-rates in the two sectors will be the same as observed during the decade 1951-61; and

(3) The proportion of workers engaged in the two sectors will remain the same as in 1961.

The result of the projection shows that after a ten-year period, i.e. in 1971, the per-worker-income ratio in the agricultural and the non-agricultural sector will decline from 0.33: 1 in 1961 to 0.30: 1 in 1971, and to 0.29: 1 in 1975.

Apart from the deterioration in the relative position of the worker in the agricultural sector, as revealed by the above projection, the implications of our assumptions, that the ratio of the work-force in the two sectors will remain constant, need to be examined. On this assumption, the work-force in agriculture would expand from 135.3 millions in 1961 to 170.7 millions in 1971-resulting in an increase of 35.4 millions; in 1975 it will reach 191.7 millions-resulting in an increase of 56.4 millions in 15 years. The current pressure of population on land is already excessive, and one of the objectives of planned economic development is to reduce it. As we saw in Section III, we have not succeeded in doing so during the last decade. The above mentioned calculations indicate the magnitude of the task the agricultural sector will have to face in the next decade in regard to the employment situation.

Faced with this situation, it will be convenient to argue that the transfer of workers from agriculture to industry should be accelerated. But the industrial sector faces an equally difficult task. Under the assumption of no change (from 1961) in the proportion of workers in the two sectors, by 1971, the non-agricultural sector will have to find employment for 13.8 million people. If the income-parity ratio is not to deteriorate for the agricultural sector, it will have to take in additional five million persons. If the workers' proportion in agriculture is to come down to 65 (instead of 71.8 in 1961), the total absorption by the non-agricultural sector will have to be of the magnitude of 28 million workers in 1971. We have not worked out the capital requirements of employing such a large number in industries. It will depend on the pattern of industrialization, a discussion on which will lead us into the controversy of employment-oriented v. surplus-generating industrialization.

The situation as is developing presents an awkward dilemma for the planner. If industrialization is not speeded up, the employment and the income situation in the agricultural sector will become explosive. With the acceleration in the rate of population-growth in the current decade, if the growth-rate and the rate of labour-transfer remain the same as in 1951-61, there will be an increase in the per-worker income in the agricultural sector of only six rupees in 10 years (1971). The situation will improve only if the growth-rate is significantly stepped up or there is a massive transfer of workers from the agricultural to the non-agricultural sector or both. The experience of the first three years of this decade has demonstrated how difficult it is to step up the growth-rate in agriculture. I am not suggesting that this experience of the first three years would be typical for the entire 1961-71 decade. Far from it; but neither would any facile optimism be in order. It is also necessary to point out that there are limits to the expansion of agricultural commodities from the demand side as well. Though in the context of the present shortage this aspect of the problem may not be immediately relevant, its relevance for long-term planning should not escape attention. Agricultural surpluses can be quite embarrassing, not only in the developed countries, but also in the developing ones. Not only are the export prospects of primary commodities somewhat dim, but the income-elasticity of domestic demand also will, sooner or later, begin to exercise a curb on expansion. As and when this happens, the gains of improved production may be lost through adverse terms of trade. Transfer of workers from agriculture to other sectors of the economy-which themselves are not free from the growing problem of unemployment and under-employment-is also not easy. Apart from the social and the psychological problems involved in it, the magnitude of capital requirements for employment in large industries, and organizational effort that would be needed if employment is to be found in decentralized and small-scale enterprises, would be stupendous. The situation demands a highly competent and wise economic statesmanship.

10
Farm Sector

Until recent decades, agriculture in India had seldom been regar-ded as a business enterprise. It has been looked upon merely as a source of meager livelihood for the mass of petty peasants, who carry on production chiefly for subsistence and largely with family labour. They are of course known to be working under severe handicaps since the classes of landlords, moneylenders, and traders oppress and exploit them brutally and claim all their produce beyond a bare subsistence for the family and the cattle, often not even that. But they are generally regarded as insulated against the operation of the laws of the free market, and beyond the orbit of economic processes of commercialization and monetization, since they are believed to have little to sell in the market for money or invest in agriculture except on the fringes.

Background

This view of Indian agriculture has conjured up a rather simplified image of Indian agrarian society. On the top are seen only the layers of intermediaries, moneylenders, and traders, and at the bottom a mass of small peasants, more or less equal and homogeneous in their land and produce and suffering from the burdens of rack rent, usurious interest rates, and middlemen's profits in trade. The solutions derived from this image also have an appearance of naivete. It is perhaps believed that if only the intermediaries are eliminated rent-burdens reduced, interest charges regulated through co-operatives and middlemen's profits brought down through co-operative marketing, there will prevail a regime of social and economic harmony in Indian villages. And this harmonious mass of small peasants, aided with improved seeds, fertilizers, irrigation, credit, and extension services, and somehow persuaded to join the farming co-operatives, would be able to march forward smoothly towards economic prosperity and socialism.

This image of Indian agriculture might have been close to realities at some remote time in the past. But it holds sway over most minds today as if these realities have remained unchanged. However, in recent years, for the first time, ample data have become available which provide an altogether different picture of contemporary realities in Indian agriculture. These data show that this view of Indian agriculture is at best facile, and partial. The realities are far more complex. An attempt has been made in this paper to present these data and discuss some of their implications.

All recent studies about Indian agriculture strike at the root of the mythical harmony and homogeneity of Indian agrarian society. They reveal that it is composed not merely of intermediaries, money-lenders, and traders or of a mass of petty peasants, more or less homogeneous in their social and economic conditions, but of a peasant mass, characterised by a wide hetero-geneity, and bitter mutual strife. They show that the conditions of life of peasants, vary widely not merely from region to region or village to village due to natural factors but even from farm to farm and peasant to peasant within the village, due to socio-economic compulsions.

The farming community of an average Indian village in these studies is found to be composed of several strata of cultivators, highly differentiated from each other in respect of the size of land owned or cultivated, number of draught and milch cattle possessed, nature and amount of capital invested in farming, types of tools and implements used, amount of family or hired labour employed, techniques of cultivation practised, extent of surplus produce sold in the market, amount of gain or loss from farming business and the volume of savings or deficits made. Moreover, the studies also reveal that these strata are no longer the 'parallel social strata' of H. S. Maine's times which were scarcely distinguishable from each other except in the length of time over which they had been absorbed in the village community. On the contrary, they are today very much unlike each other in almost all aspects of their economic and social life. They present the curious spectacle of being engaged in a bitter economic and social strife which affects not only their mutual social relations but also their economic fortunes, standards of living and social welfare. And if one has to grasp the essence of contemporary developments in Indian agriculture, which often appear to pull into contrary directions, one has to look upon Indian agriculture not as a sector aggregate of small, uneconomic and subsistence peasant units of production but as one in which production units of different types and sizes with wide differences in their character of farming, techniques of cultivation, forms of employment of labour power, profitability, saving, investment and consumption, compete with each other and in which laws of the free market operate sluggishly but as ruthlessly as in the other sectors of the Indian economy. The following paragraphs illustrate these aspects with data.

The first and the foremost basis of differentiation amongst the peasants which causes differentiation amongst them even in other aspects, is the ownership and cultivation of land. The distribution of owned land in present day India is 'extremely concentrated with a small minority owning most of the land'. During last few years, three nation-wide surveys, viz. the National Sample Survey, the First Agricultural Labour Enquiry and the Census of Landholdings, have thrown up a mass of data on the pattern of land ownership in India. All these surveys reveal a high degree of differentiation amongst present households in respect of their ownership holdings, as shown in the following Table.

Distribution of Ownership Holdings amongst Rural Households According to size-groups Crop Season (Percentages)

Household Ownership Holdings				
Size-group (acres)	P.C. of holdings to the total	Cumulative P.C. of holdings	p. c. of area to total area owned	Cumulative percentage of area
0.00*	23.09	-	-	-
0.01 – 0.99	24.17	47.26	1.37	-
1.00 – 2.49	13.98	61.24	4.86	6.23
2.50 – 4.99	13.49	74.73	10.09	16.32
5.00 – 9.99	12.50	87.23	18.40	34072

10.00–24.99	9.17	96.40	29.11	63.83
25.00–49.99	2.66	99.06	18.63	82.46
50.00 or above	0.94	100.00	17.54	100.00
Total	100.00	-	100.00	-

* Includes households owning an area of .005 acres or less

Thus, while at the bottom about three-fourths of all rural households own less than 5 acres of land, and hold less than one-sixth of the total area owned, on the top, one-fourth of all rural households hold 83.68 per cent of the total area in size-groups above 5 acres. Even amongst them, 12.77 per cent of all the rural households hold as much as 65.28 percent of the total owned area in size-groups of more than 10.00 acres. And in the collection of data, ownership of land was defined as 'the right of permanent heritable possession with or without right to transfer the title' which means that even secure tenants of the State or of private individuals, who enjoyed rights, of permanent heritable possession, have been included as owners.

The data of household ownership holdings pertain to the year 1953-54, when the abolition of intermediaries in most parts of India was either in progress or almost completed. Thus ownership of land has remained so concentrated despite the abolition of intermediaries. This may be due to an aspect of ownership which may be noted. Before the abolition of interme-diaries, ownership of land was generally vested in a heterogenous class of intermediaries and was very uneven and highly concen-trated. It is usually thought that these ownership holdings were almost entirely cultivated by tenants, and the intermediaries were merely a class of functionless parasites. While it was true for the large bulk of land of the intermediaries, they also held some land as their Sir and Khudkashtland unevenly distributed on which they could carry on cultivation with their family labour or hired labour, and in which no tenancy rights could arise, even though a small part of these lands were let out to tenants. The bulk of these lands was cultivated by the zamindars personally with family labour or hired labour.

The average size of Sir and Khudkasht land varied widely between different zamindars. For instance in U. P. it ranged over 1.09 acre to 280.05 acres per zamindar. With such wide differences in the extent of Sir, it was natural that the Sir lands also should have been let out especially when there were no restrictions on leasing. Nevertheless, it may be emphasised that most zamindars engaged in direct cultivation on their Sir and Khudkasht lands with their own family labour or hired labour, in addition to realising rents from their tenants. Confronted with the prospect of abolition of their privileges as landlords a couple of years before the advent of Independence, the zamindars took measures to expand the area under Sir and Khudkasht cultivation to retain the maximum possible area for personal cultivation, and not let it become the property of the State. The age-old struggle of the land-lords and tenants for land was thus left by the government to be fought between themselves for some years before they enacted and implemented legislation taking over the intermediaries' lands.

As a result, while the State acquired a substantial area in ownership, the zamindars also retained large areas, as unevenly distributed as before. And not many tenants acquired ownership rights by paying compensation. Consequently, no significant change in the distribution of owned land took place after the zamindari abolition.

However, an important result, generally unnoticed and scarcely written about, has been that the ex-zamindars have been forced into a new way of life, and are on their way towards changing their character as a class. Deprived of the sources of land rent and prohibited from leasing out Sir lands, they are obliged to take even more interest in direct cultivation of land, and gradually convert themselves into peasant proprietors or capitalist farmers depending on the size of their holdings, and their social and economic position.

New Trends

A close examination of the laws relating to abolition of zamindari in most States suggests that the governments have gone out of their way to provide for their gradual conversion into cultivators of their own lands by making special provisions for resumptions, evictions, by leaving numerous loopholes and gaps in the land laws, and by delaying implementation. Provision of compensation is also a means to provide them with capital for investment in agriculture. Measures for imposition of ceilings and the manner of their implementation are also devised to compel them to take up farming by leaving only as much land with them as may be cultivated with hired labour on the basis of the technology in vogue, and insufficient for being leased out.

Of course, all intermediaries have not responded alike to these measures. Nor have they all been affected alike since the majority are only petty intermediaries with small holdings. But the bulk of the land retained for self-cultivation is in the hands of a small minority and their conversion into entrepreneur farmers depends on a host of factors, such as the availability and extent of non-farm sources of income, caste prejudices and attitudes towards cultivation, and personal competence to take up various tasks of agricultural enterprise. And for these reasons, variations arise in different regions of the country in the extent and manner in which this small minority takes to self-cultivation.

However, several careful observers of the Indian rural economy have drawn attention to the change in the position of the ex-intermediaries since their abolition. For instance, Daniel and Alice Thorner write:

> ...there are cases where these ex-landlords have used the money paid them as compensation for the taking over of their lands to buy tractors and go in for modern-style agriculture.

Dr. A. M. Khusro, summarising the group discussion held at the Annual Conference of the Indian Society of Agricultural Economics at Pilani, observed that:

> In Punjab and U. P. a substantial fraction of ex-zamindars who became bhumidars or resumed their lands is known to have taken to managerial type of cultivation and a new brand of farming, often termed 'capitalist farming', seems to have been emerging.

Similarly Dr. Otto Schiller has remarked that:

> ...the number of tractors in India has increased many of

> them are being introduced by big landowners who have become aware of the great possibilities offered by modern techniques. With the help of tractors, they have started to farm land which previously was cultivated by tenants. As a result some of the tenants have had either to work for the landowner on a hire basis or to look for other employment unless they could find other land which they could lease.

This process of conversion of erstwhile intermediaries into 'capitalist farmers' has developed unevenly and at varying speed in different regions of the country. But it has created pre-conditions for vital changes in the agrarian economy and its functioning. By narrowing the gap between ownership and cultivation of land, it has considerably diminished the scope for rack renting of the tenants in future, except covertly under the law, and provided them a sense of security. But, at the same time, it has helped the distribution of total cultivated area remain highly unequal and aggravated the differentiation of peasants in respect of the size of their cultivation. The following Table shows the distribution of cultivated area in India.

Distribution of operational (cultivated) holdings amongst Rural Households according to size-groups Crop season (Percentages)

	Household Operational Holdings			
Size-groups (acres)	Percentage of holdings to the total	Cumulative percentage of holdings	Percentage of area the total	Cumulative to percentage of holdings
0.00*	10.96	-	-	-
0.01–0.99	31.12	42.08	1.20	1.20
1.00–2.49	14.07	56.15	4.38	5.58
2.50–4.99	15.08	71.23	10.02	15.60
5.00–9.99	14.19	85.42	18.56	34.16
10.00–24.99	10.36	95.78	29.22	63.38
25.00–49.99	3.12	98.90	19.54	82.92
50.00 and above	1.00	100.00	17.08	100.00
Total:	100.00	-	100.00	-

It is evident that the distribution of cultivated area also is concentrated in the hands of a small minority. At the bottom, as many as 71.23 per cent households cultivate only 15.60 per cent of the total cultivated land in size-groups of less than 5 acres, while at the top, a small minority of 14.48 per cent households operate upon 65.85 per cent of the total cultivated area in size groups of 10 acres and above.

The pattern of distribution of operational holdings is quite close to that of the ownership holdings. And the bold fact emerges that concentration of ownership in land signifies simultaneously a concentration of the operated area. How little has been the change in this pattern as a result of zamindari abolition is shown by the data regarding distribution of cultivated area prior to and after abolition of zamindari in some sampled villages of Western, Central and Eastern U. P. as follows:

Percentage distribution of cultivating households and cultivated area according to size of holdings before and after zamindari abolition in sample villages of U.P

Before Zamindari Abolition				
Size-group	Percentage of house-holds	Percentage of area	Cumulative percentage of house-holds	Cumulative percentage of area
Less than 5 acres	51.53	16.95	51.53	16.95
5 – 15 acres	37.27	40.17	88.80	57.12
15 acres and above	11.20	42.88	100.00	100.00
After Zamindari Abolition				
Size-group	Percentage of house-holds	Percentage of area	Cumulative percentage of house-holds	Cumulative percentage of area
Less than 5 acres	51.89	18.25	51.89	18.25
5 – 15 acres	37.39	43.55	89.28	61.80
15 acres and above	10.72	38.20	100.00	100.00

Means of Cultivation

Let us examine whether cultivation on such a highly differentiated pattern of operational holdings would really be with family labour and for subsistence, and how far, so long as this pattern remains substantially intact, the objectives of agrarian policy laid down by the Congress Agrarian Reforms Committee can be really achieved. The extent of use of family labour on different size-groups of holdings largely depends upon the number of household members. The following Table shows the relationship between the size of operational holdings and the average household size in the respective size-groups.

In the following Table, the average household size shows an increasing trend with the increase in the size of household operational holding. But the increase in household size is much less (only a little more than twofold) relatively to the increase in the size of household operational holding (about 50 fold).

Average household size by size of household operational holdings

Size of Operational Holdings (acres)	Average Household Size
0.00	3.91
0.01- 0.99	4.14
1.00- 2.49	4.81
2.50- 4.99	5.24
5.00- 7.49	5.76
7.50- 9.99	6.16
10.00-14.99	6.34
15.00-19.99	6.76
20.00-24.99	6.86
25.00-29.99	7.15
30.00-49.99	7.23
50.00 and above	8.30
Average	5.01

If we assume that the proportion of family workers in an average household size of 5.01 is 2-0 and apply this proportion uniformly to all size-groups and compute the operated area per family worker in different size-groups dividing the average size of household operational holding by the number of family workers, we get the following result :-

Average size of holdings, Average number of workers and operated area per worker according to size-groups of household operational holdings

Size-group (Acres)	Average size of holding*	Average number of family workers per household	Operated area per family worker
0.00	-	1.56	-
0.01- 0.99	0.21	1.65	0.13
1.00- 2.49	1.69	1.92	0.83
2.50- 4.99	3.62	2.09	1.73
5.00- 7.49	6.12	2.30	2.66
7.50- 9.99	8.68	2.46	3.53
10.00-14.99	12.18	2.53	4.81
15.00-19.99	17.29	2.70	6.40
20.00-24.99	22.21	2.74	8.11
25.00-29.99	27.40	2.85	9.61
30.00-49.99	37.98	2.89	13.14
50.00 and above	83.54	3.31	25.24
Average	5.43	2.00	2.71

It is evident that the availability of cultivated land in different size-groups of holdings varies widely between 0.13 to 25.24 acres per family worker. In the higher size-groups of holdings, it is so large that family workers would find it impossible to cultivate it only by themselves and would necessarily depend on the regular use of hired labour. Moreover, if the family workers of households with large operational holdings prefer to abstain from physical participation in agricultural operations for reasons of their traditional status as zamindars, caste, etc, and remain content only with supervision and management, the need for hired labour is further aggravated.

From the data collected in the Farm Management Studies, one finds that the use of hired labour increases with an increase in the size of operational holdings, as, for instance, is shown in the following Table:-

Percentage classification of farm labour into family and hired labour on some sampled holdings in U. P. (Survey Sample)

Size-groups of holdings (acres)	Percentage contribution by		Total
	Family Labour	Hired Labour	
Below 5.0	87.8	12.2	100.0
5.0-10.0	79.2	20.8	100.0
10.0-15.0	68.2	31.8	100.0
15.0-20.0	58.0	42.0	100.0
20.0 and above	47.0	53.0	100.0

Now, if we regard the optimum work unit for an average household-sufficient to provide full employment for all the family workers to be, on the average, between 7.5 acres and 10.0 acres, then, under the present distribution of operational holdings, cultivation on 65.84 per cent of the total cultivated area in India must necessarily be done with the regular use of hired labour, permanent or temporary, on cash or kind wages. And it is no wonder that India had 17.9 million agricultural labour households in 1950-51 which constituted 30.39 per cent of all rural households and whose major source of livelihood was wage-labour in agriculture. Amongst them, bulk of the permanent farm servants were found to be employed on holdings of 10 acres or above in size, as is shown in the following Table.

From the Table, it is evident that 64.3 per cent of total permanent farm servants are employed on farms of 10.0 acres or more, and most of the remaining, employed on farms of less than 10 acres must be usually on holdings of small intermediaries or others who either do not touch the plough for reasons of caste, traditional status as zamindars or personal incapacity, or are engaged in non-farm occupations and get their holdings cultivated by permanent farm workers.

Percentage distribution of households, operated area and permanent farm servants by size-groups of operational holding in India (July 1953-June 1954)

Operational Holding Size (Acres)	Percentage of total number of households	Percentage of total operated area	Percentage of total farm servants
0-00 (a)	10.9	0.0	0.0
0.01-2.49	45.2	5.9	6.5
2.50-4.99	15.5	10.6	9.6
5.00-7.49	8.8	10.1	10.4
7.50-9.99	5.5	9.0	9.2
10.00-14.99	5.5	12.8	13.5
15.00-19.99	3.0	9.7	10.1
20.0 and above	5.6	41.9	40.7
Total	100.0	100.0	100.0

(a) Includes households who operate 0.005 acres or less

1. Total number of households = 63,532,000
2. Total operated area = 335,711,000 acres
3. Total No. of farm servants = 7,523,852

It thus appears that use of hired labour in Indian agriculture is not merely on the fringes or marginal but wide-spread. And the prevailing pattern of distribution of operational holdings makes it impossible for the small minority of farm operators (14.8 per cent) who hold about two-thirds of the total operated area (65.84 per cent) to cultivate their holdings merely with their own resources of family labour and necessitates regular use of permanent hired labour in farm operations.

Now let us examine whether agricultural production on the bulk of arable land is carried on for subsistence or for sale. If we estimate the amount of land (of average productivity) required to produce average foodgrain requirements for the average household in different size-groups holdings, we get the following result:-

Estimates of land sufficient to produce household foodgrains requirements in different size-groups of holding and land producing crops for sale

Size-Groups (acres)	Average size of household operational holding	Average household size	Requirement of food grains for an average household per year	Average amount of land sufficient to produce foodgrains requirements household.	Amount of land production on which is likely to be for the market.
0.00	-	3.91	1632	2.36	-2.86
0.01- 0.99	0.21	4.14	1728	3.03	-2.82
1.00- 2.49	1.69	4.81	2008	3-52	-1.83
2.50- 4.99	3.62	5.24	2188	3.83	-0.21
5.00- 7.49	6.12	5.76	2405	4.21	1.91
7.50- 9.99	8.68	6.16	2572	4.50	4.18
10.00-14.99	12.18	6.34	2647	4.64	7.54
15.00-19.99	1729	6.76	2822	4.94	12.35
20.00-24.99	22.21	6.86	2864	5.02	17.19
25.00-29.99	27.40	7.15	2985	5.23	22.17
30.00-49.99	37.98	7.23	3018	5.29	32.69
50.00 and above	83.54	8.30	3465	6.07	77.47
Average	5.43	5.01	2092	3.66	1.77

From this Table certain interesting conclusions emerge. First of all, we find that according to our estimates, 67.0 per cent of an average household operational holding would have to be devoted for the production of the foodgrains requirements of an average size household. And thus an average peasant household would have too little land to produce any substantial amount of crops for the market. But if we look at the estimates for the different size-groups, it is evident that households with operational holdings of less than 5 acres (71.23 per cent of all rural households, and operating only 15.60 per cent of the total operated area) would not have land sufficient even to produce their foodgrains requirements. But house-holds with holdings of 10 acres or more (14.58 of all rural households and operating 65.84 per cent of total operated area) would be devoting more than 50.0 per cent of their total holding to the production of crops for the market. It would thus appear that crop production on about two-thirds of the total land is mainly for the market.

In fact, even on holdings below 5 acres, cultivators of which do not have sufficient land for producing their foodgrains requirements, crop production is likely to be for sale. In the first instance, these households are compelled to make 'distress sale' of their produce to meet their money obligations like land revenue, rent and debt service, and to purchase such necessities of life as salt, kerosene and cloth, and for that reason, it has been estimated that the holders of land below 5.0 acres sell a relatively larger proportion of their produce than the cultivators of large holdings. Moreover, these cultivators, in the absence of adequate availability of foodgrains requirements for the household, try to raise cash crops with the help of which they purchase foodgrains for consumption. Such is the situation in areas like Eastern U. P. where cultivators of lands even below an acre or a half raise sugarcane and purchase paddy from fair price shops. In case they resort to neither of these expedients, they depend on money incomes from non-farm sources, like wage-labour in agriculture or non-farm small jobs outside the village or petty trade. In fact, it has been found in most recent studies that small cultivators generally take recourse to subsidiary occupations. For instance, we read in the Report of the All India Rural Credit Survey:

> The smaller the holding he (the cultivator) cultivates, the more is his dependence on other forms of earnings; the small cultivator, for instance, has often to resort to carting or agricultural labour. It appears that it is only a small section of the farming community cultivating 14.19 per cent of all rural households and operating in all 18.56 per cent of the total operated area, and holding lands in size-groups of 5.0 to 10.0 acres that devotes more than half of its operational holding size to the production of its own foodgrains requirements. But on the remaining 81.44 per cent of the operated area, particularly on the 65.84 per cent held in size-groups of 10 acres or more, crop-production is generally for the market.

Thus, it is evident that the character of farming, whether farming is based on family labour or wage labour, and whether crop-production is for subsistence or for the market-depends essentially on the size of operational holding, and that over bulk of the land, operated by a small minority of all rural households in size groups of 10 acres or more, is characterised by regular use of wage-labour and production for the market.

Let us now analyse the economics of the farming business in the light of the differentiation in operational holdings, and the characteristics of farming, analysed in the foregoing paragraphs. So far, only a few studies were available in which farming as a business enterprise was examined. But since these studies pertained only to a few selected holdings in small local areas, and there were wide differences in the concepts used and methods followed for collection, tabulation and analysis of data, they could hardly be used to derive general inferences about the economic efficiency of cultivation in different parts of the country. However, in recent years, a series of investigations with uniform concepts, methods and proformas were conducted into the economics of farm management in 'six' typical regions of peasant agriculture' in the States of U.P., Punjab, West Bengal, Madhya Pradesh, Bombay, and Madras. These have provided valuable and useful data for our purpose. From these studies one can derive a fairly general picture of the economic aspects of farming business in different States of India.

The Prosperity

These studies strikingly reveal that the economic efficiency of the farming business depends to a considerable extent on the size of the operational holding. In all States, the size of the farm has been found to have a decisive influence on the nature and extent of capital employed, forms of employment of labour, techniques of cultivation, input output coefficients, profitability or remunerativeness of the farming business, savings and consumption expenditure of the farming household and the nature and extent of capital formation on the farm. And the relative economic efficiency on different size-groups of operational holdings has been found to be essentially in a similar direction in all States though there are quantitative variations from State to State. Since our purpose is not to examine the quantitative aspects of these data but only to analyse the data bearing upon the relative economic efficiency of farming business on different size-groups of holdings, and since the findings in all States are more or less in a similar direction, we shall utilize data only for U. P. for the year 1955-56 for illustrating the basic economic relationships that obtain on different size groups of operational holdings.

In this Table, some of the important economic relationships essential for the determination of economic efficiency of farming have been shown. Per farm resources of land, labour and capital are obviously necessary for this purpose. And we find that the range of variation of these resources per farm is very wide, as, is also the case for the average size per farm in different size-groups of holdings.

While the average size of farm in the sampled holdings was 9.1 acres, the lowest size farms were as small as 1.5 acres and largest size farms as big as 34.8 acres. On these farms, while the average number of draught cattle per farm was 2.5, and of milch cattle 1.5, the small farms below 5.0 acres had much less than the average number, while farms above 10.0 acres had much more than the average. The farms below 5.0 acres possessed less than even 2.0 draught cattle per farm, which is the minimum necessary for independent and efficient cultivation from an individual peasant's point of view. This means that these farmers must either be sharing bullocks of others on an exchange basis, or hiring them from other farms. This would usually involve difficulties in the timely performance of farm operations like ploughing, sowing and irrigation and consequently even loss of potential produce. It would also mean delays in operations like threshing, crushing of sugar cane, and transport of produce, since they must adjust their operations to the convenience of those who provide bullocks to share or on hire. The farmers in the range of 5.0 to lb 0 acres size-groups would not suffer from such disabilities. And the farmers of 10.0 acres or more would not be handicapped in this respect in any sense.

More or less similar pattern of distribution is seen in case of the milch cattle. While the cultivators of lands between 5.0 to 10.0 acres possess only the average number of milch cattle, those cultivating below 5.0 acres possess only 1.0 or even less than 1.0

milch animal and those cultivating above 15.0 acres possess 2- 0 or more.

Data on the value of investment in livestock per farm indicate that while farms below 5.0 acres in size possess livestock of poor quality, much less than the average, and farms between 5.0 to 10.0 acres have livestock close to the average, the farmers of 10 acres have much better quality animals.

The data of investment on implements, farm buildings and fixed assets again shows that while farms of 5.0 to 10.0 acres have made investments on these items more or less close to the average, farms below 5.0 acres show much less investment per farm, and farms above 10 acres show investment much more than the average. In fact, farms of 15.0 acres and above have invested in implements Rs. 1,111 per farm, against the average of Rs. 407, in farm buildings Rs. 2,643 against the average of Rs. 690, and in all fixed assets (including livestock, implements, farm buildings and miscellaneous equipment but excluding land) Rs. 7,251 against the average of Rs. 1,963.

The fact that value of capital investment per farm increased considerably with an increase in the size of the operational holdings suggests that the capital-intensity of large-sized fauns is much more than of the small farms. Ipso facto they also command bulk of the total capital resources employed in farming. And thus, concentration of land simultaneously brings about a concentration of capital resources.

The data in value terms do not bring out the variations in the numbers and quality of capital employed in farms of different sizes. But it has been found that the small farms have generally a much less number of implements and of very poor quality and large farms possess more and better implements. For instance, in the region of U. P. under study, we find the following pattern in the distribution of some' improved implements'.

Percentage of farms possessing various types of improved implements according to size of holdings

Size-Groups (acres)	No. of farms in the size-group	Percentage of farms in various size-groups having Iron-ploughs	cultivators	Bullock operated chaff-cutter	Pneumatic tyred bullock cart
Below 2.5	47	-	-	-	-
2.5- 5.0	130	2.3	3.8	-	-
5.0-7.5	111	4.5	1.8	-	1.8
7.5-10.0	104	4.8	3.8	-	1.9
10.0-15.0	103	6.8	4.9	-	2.9
15.0-20.0	52	13.5	9.6	-	13.5
20.0-25.0	25	16.0	16.0	4.0	16.0
25.0 & above	25	8.0	24.0	12.0	32.0
Total	497	5.5	5.2	0.7	4.4

It is evident that the use of improved implements has been much more on the large-sized farms. And, in fact, large farmers have more of these improved implements per farm. For instance, out of 33 farms having iron ploughs, four had more than one. A farmer in the size-group of 25 acres and above has two iron cultivators.

Labour Problem

The resources of family labour per farm also increase with an increase in the size of holding like the resources of land and labour. But the extent of increase even for the highest size-groups of farms is not more than about two-fold, which is much less than the increase in per farm resources of land or capital. Consequently, need arises to employ hired labour in bigger size-groups on a regular and permanent basis. And, we have already seen that the proportion of hired labour to the total farm labour increases considerably on farms of 10-0 acres or more, and about two-thirds of all the permanent farm servants are engaged on those very farms.

However, despite an increase in the quantum of hired labour employed with an increase in the size of farm, since the resources of capital per farm increase more than proportionately to the increase in labour, the value of capital investment per worker increases with an increase in the size of farms. The following Table illustrates this point fully.

It is evident that on farms below 5.0 acres and even on farms of 5.0 to 10.0 acres, investment per worker is less than the average. But on farms between 10.0 acres to 20.0 acres, it is higher than the average, and highest on the farms of 20.0 acres and above. The investment per worker (excluding land) in the highest size-group is more than double of that in the smallest size-group.

From these data, and from the variations in the nature and quality of capital employed on different sizes of farms, it follows that techniques of farming on small farms are labour-intensive and tend to become relatively capital intensive as the size of farms increases. We have already seen that the proportion of hired labour in total farm labour increases considerably with an increase in the size of farms. Thus it appears that increasing employment of hired labour and increasing investment of capital per worker co-exist together. This co-existence suggests that an increase in capital investment per worker with an increase in the size of farm may be due to the efforts of the large farmers to increase productivity of hired labour by providing them relatively more and better capital. Since the large farmers have to pay a wage to hired labour, they like to extract the maximum output from them, and for this reason provide relatively better tools and implements, better means of irrigation and better types of inputs. A small farmer dependent only on family labour has neither incentive nor compulsion nor even resources to economise on family labour since it is surplus and there is no payment of wages. But as the size of farm increases and the share of hired labour in total farm labour increases, the farmer is obliged to consider whether it would provide him sufficient additional output to compensate for the payment of the wage.

Capital investment (fixed and operating excluding land) per worker according to size-groups of holdings

Size-Groups (acres)	No. of workers per farm	Investment of capital (fixed & operating including land) per farm Rs.	Investment of capital (including land) per worker per farm Rs.	Investment of capital per farm (excluding land) Rs.	Investment of capital (excluding land) per worker Rs.
1	2	3	4	5	6
Below 5.0	2.0	4236	2118	1718	859
5.0-10.0	2.8	7077	2528	2059	735
10.0-15.0	2.6	13377	5145	4432	1705
15.0-20.0	3.9	20608	5284	5680	1456
20.0 & above	4.6	37445	8140	9000	1957
Average	2.9	11892	4076	3477	1199

Moreover, since bulk of production on large farms is destined for the market, large farmers are compelled to maximise their net money income by extracting maximum possible work, from their hired workers. In times before abolition of zamindari when the zamindars had almost an unbridled and despotic command on farm labour, the exploitation of the farm worker used to be in the form of being made to work for the longest possible hours under conditions of bondage and servitude and providing forced labour himself and by his dependents. But since after the abolition of zamindari, such bondages of servitude and forced labour have practically disappeared. The zamindars, being obliged to convert themselves gradually into entrepreneurial farmers, have lost their earlier over- lordship of farm labour. They are now also obliged to change or modify their forms of exploitation. Despite persistence of old practices of oppressions on farm labour in some regions, they now generally seek to increase the productivity of the farm worker by employing more and better capital equipment unlike before by keeping him attached to their farm in servitude.

Of course, with such extreme concentration of total cultivated land in the hands of a small minority consisting mainly of ex-intermediaries and big peasants, plentiful supply of cheap labour and stubborn persistence of the earlier forms of exploitation of farm labour are bound to remain with us for a long time. Under these circumstances, a rapid or widespread movement for increasing productivity by investment of more capital per worker, amongst the large farmers, is hardly likely to gather momentum since the cost of labour would generally remain lower than the cost of capital until the pace of industrialisation and absorption of surplus labour from agriculture into non-farm sectors of employment becomes very fast. But the prevailing pattern of distribution of operational holdings has made such a development almost inevitable. One witnesses an increasing use of tractors and other farm machines in Indian agriculture. For instance, the number of tractors in India increased from 4,524 in 1945 to 35,000 in 1961 about an eight-fold increase; the number of electric pumps for irrigation from 8,561 in 1945 to 46,930 in 1965, a more than five-fold increase; and the number of oil engines with pumps for irrigation from 12,062 in 1945 to 1,22,230 in 1956, a more than ten-fold increase. These machines are employed mainly by the large farmers, and make their techniques of farming highly capital intensive. They replace farm labour from substantial areas and make surplus labour and unemployment accumulate amongst the lowest strata of the Indian agrarian society.

Turning away from per farm resources of land, labour and capital, let us now examine the relative availability of labour and capital resources per unit of land. Despite an increase in per farm resources of labour and capital with an increase in the size of farms, per unit of land, these resources decline with an increase in the size of the farms, as shown in the Table below.

These data reveal that while small farms possess much less capital and labour relative to the large farmers, they have too much capital and labour per acre, relative to the large farms. One finds that farms below 5.0 acres possess resources of labour and capital per acre much above the average, farms of 5.0 to 10.0 acres a little more than the average, and farms of 25 - 0 acres and above employ the least resources of labour and capital per acre.

This aspect of farm structure has an important bearing upon the costs of production, input-output coefficients, and profitability or remunerativeness of the farming business in different size-

Input-Output relationships, costs of production and profits or losses of farming on 400 holdings (Survey Sample) in U. P. according to size-groups of farms.

	Value of inputs per acre (Rs.)													
Size-Groups (acres)	Average size of farm	Bullock labour	Human labour	Seed	Fertilizers & manures	Upkeep of implements	Rent & Cess	Irrigation on charges	Interest on fixed capital	Total of inputs per acre	Total of output per acre	Output/Input ratio	Total amount of profit per farm	Net profit or loss as percentage of output
1	2	3	4	5	6	7	8	9	10	11	12	13	14	15
Below 5.0	3.2	137.9	56.8	18.6	8.5	17.4	9.7	9.8	10.9	269.6	291	1.08	75	8
5.0-10.0	7.2	94.3	50.2	17.0	7.4	12.3	9.5	9.0	8.2	208.9	253	1.21	314	17
10.0-15.0	12.1	76.8	45.9	16.0	7.0	11.0	10.0	9.5	6.8	183.4	241	1.31	691	24
15.0-20.0	16.8	74.4	43.8	15.5	6.8	10.1	9.3	8.3	6.7	174.9	216	1.23	678	19
20.0 & above	28.6	60.1	36.8	13.5	5.9	7.6	8.4	5.8	6.2	144.3	190	1.32	1299	24
Average	9.1	84.3	45.9	16.0	7.0	11.1	9.3	8.4	7.5	189.5	234	1.23	407	19

groups of farms. As a result of this farm assets structure, the inputs of labour and capital per unit of land decline and the costs of production per acre go down with an increase in the size of farm. In fact, the inputs per acre even of other resources such as seeds, fertilizers, manures and irrigation decline with an increase in the size of farm, leading to a considerable decline in total inputs per acre. Evidently, the output-input coefficient is more favourable on larger farms and the profitability of remunerativeness of farming increases with an increase in farm size, despite a somewhat larger gross output per acre on small farms. The following Table illustrates these points.

The costs of production per unit of land, as well as per unit of output are lower on large farms, and higher on small farms. The profits per farm and net profit or loss as percentage of total output also increases with an increase in the size of farm. Thus the farming business is more economic and efficient on large farms than on the small farms.

It was further found that 'farms incurring loss are most numerous among those below 10 acres and form about 80 per cent of total number (of farms) showing loss in both samples'. It thus appears that farms smaller than 10.0 acres have not merely made less profits but have also incurred losses, whole larger farms have made much greater profits and relatively suffered much less losses.

The calculation of profitability or remunerativeness of farming business by 'imputing' values to the contribution of family labour at the current wage rate for permanent labour and including it as an input factor for calculating the output-input co-efficient has been criticised recently. This is because, by following this method, much of Indian agriculture appears un-remunerative. In fact, even the authors of the farm-management studies, who have done much to apply and popularise this method of calculating farm profitability, themselves felt the need to develop some other concept of cost which may provide the explanation for continued production in spite of sustained losses' (on the basis of the method of calculation followed). However, no satisfactory concepts of cost, or criteria of economic efficiency have yet been developed.

Only Dr. A. K. Sen, in very brief-in fact too brief outline has suggested that since 'there may be no alternative employment opportunities, at the margin' for family labour, the factor that makes the crucial difference is the system of farming viz., whether it is wage-based or family-based, and non-wage family farming has some efficiency advantages, since it would enable family labour to be applied to a piece of land upto the point where net marginal product of labour becomes almost equal to zero.

Even if one agrees that imputation of value to family labour at the prevailing market rate for permanent labour exaggerates the costs of the small farmer, it nevertheless remains necessary to develop a method which may provide a uniform basis for comparison of economic efficiency on different farms, so heterogenous in their assets structure, forms of employment of labour and techniques of cultivation in which it is often difficult to distinguish a purely family-based and purely wage-based farm since all farms make use of both family and hired labour though in different proportions. It appears that if instead of taking into account the profit or loss per farm in this fictional sense, we take into consideration the farm business income, also computed in the farm management studies, which is the measure of earnings of the farmer and his family for management, risk, their labour, and capital investment and is obtained by adding the family labour income, the unpaid interest on owned capital and unpaid rent on owned land, we might bet a better measure of economic efficiency of different farms.

Some other measures of farm efficiency are also available in the U. P. Farm Management study. These measures are not given as alternative criteria of economic efficiency of farm business but have nevertheless been calculated. And we can use them also for a comparative picture of farm efficiency according to the size-groups. These are return per labour-day of family members, output per earner, or return per worker per year (including among workers both family and hired workers).

Economic efficiency of different size-groups of farms according to diferent criteria.

Size-Group	Farm Business income per farm Rs.	Farm Business income per acre Rs.	Farm Business income as p.c. to total output	Output per earner Rs.	Return per worker per year Rs.	Return per labour day of family members Rs.
1	2	3	4	5	6	7
Below 5.0	497	155.3	54	459	136	1.3
5.0-10.0	779	108.2	43	758	245	1.5
10.0-15.0	1396	115.4	47	1074	334	1.6
15.0-20.0	1520	90.5	42	1252	327	1.7
20.0 & above	2302	80.5	42	1359	595	3.1
Average	940	103.3	44	868	304	1.7

In the above Table the relative efficiency of different size-groups of farms is shown according to these criteria.

Thus it appears that even if we ignore the criterion of economic efficiency in terms of profit and loss altogether, we find that large farms yield much larger total farm business, income per farm, although the small farms yield more farms business income per acre than the large farms. Similarly, in terms of output per earner, return per labour day of family members or return per worker both family and hired, large farms have a distinct advantage in terms of economic efficiency and productivity of family or hired labour, and yield a much higher income per family member than the small farms, despite the fact that the proportion of hired labour on large farms increases. This means that family members obtain larger incomes for themselves even while employing hired labour and productivity per worker on large farms increases even when a larger proportion of them are hired. This fact dispels the myth that application of family labour in agriculture is inherently superior and more productive than hired labour, because the latter lacks personal interest and requires supervision.

The only advantage of small farms appears to be their ability to extract more output per unit of land, though not per unit of labour. But since these farms operate within a competitive market mechanism, and compete with the produce of large farms, this advantage would only be temporary. It would last only during the period until the large farms, which are slowly ascending the scale of entrepreneurial agriculture in the wake of zamindari abolition, by investing more capital, employing better tools and implements, using improved methods of farming, and raising the productivity of both hired and family workers outstep the small farms even in output per unit of land. We have seen that in a strictly economic sense, the costs on the small farms are not compensated even by higher gross output per acre. But the small farms continue in production because they do not calculate their profits or losses in the economic sense but only look to their total farm business income. And since the size of their land is extremely small, they try to extract the maximum output. But despite that they have to depress their standards of living to the lowest level and they have little to invest in land or its cultivation. Consequently, in the long-run, they are bound to lose in the race so long as their economic fortunes are determined by a competitive market system. The following data in following Table brings out these aspects.

Living expenses per family and per member and savings per family on (197) holdings (Cost Accounting Sample) in U. P.

Size-Groups (acres)	Average	Living ex- number of family	Living ex- penses per family	Savings ex- penses per member	per family
Below 2.5	6.1	772	126	-	302
2.5- 5.0	6.5	941	145	-	132
5.0- 7.5	5.5	1399	154	-	433
7.5-10.0	7.1	1216	171	-	19
10.0-15.0	6.8	1564	230	-	360
15.0-20.0	9.5	1998	210	-	356
20.0-25.0	14.1	2404	170	+	430
25 and above	12.5	2541	203	+	713
Average	7.6	1446	190	-	186

It is evident that living expenses per family as well as per member are much lower in the small farms than on the large and increase with an increase in farm size. And despite such a depressed standard of living, the small farmer is unable to make both ends meet even with his total farm business income, because of his high input costs and high living expenses. Even farmers between 10.0 to 20.0 acres suffer from the same difficulty. And only farmers of lands above 20.0 acres have savings for capital accumulation or investment on land or in cultivation. Thus, despite the initial advantage of higher gross output or farm business income per unit of land, the small farmer tends to lose this advantage in course of time, because the large farms, in the meanwhile accumulate capital and improve farm productivity.

The inability of the small and the medium farmer to make any savings or capital investment is also revealed by the Rural Credit Follow-up Surveys. For instance, we read that:

The capital formation reported by cultivators resulted in a substantial measure, through the efforts of big and large cultivators. The performance of medium and small cultivators, especially the latter group, was poor, barring one or two districts. It is significant to note that even in the districts in which big and large cultivators found it possible to undertake substantial capital formation expenditure, the performance of medium and small cultivators was generally poor. Medium and small cultivators had generally to finance a fairly large proportion of even their small capital formation through borrowings.

And yet another place, we find that:

The data for the four classes of cultivators clearly show that generally it was only among big and large cultivators that any net investment took place during the year. Medium and small cultivators generally recorded, disinvestments in the districts barring Mandsaur, East Khandesh, and Coimbatore.

And with disinvestments, the small and the medium farmer will not be able to retain their advantage of a higher gross output or farm business income per acre for very long.

Sale of Produces

Let us now examine as to how these farming units, with such wide differences in their assets structure, costs of production, input-output coefficients, farm business income, productivity per worker, and savings and investment potential, would fare under

Estimates of the likely amount of output per farm sold in the market according to size groups of holdings (Survey Sample).

Size of the farm	Output per farm	% of actually incurred cash & kind exp. to total output	Living expenses purchases and other payments	% of actual exp. in purchased for the purpose of Col. 3	Account of output exchanged for the purpose of Col. 5	Amount of output exchanged for the purpose of Col. 5	Amount of output exchanged	Total amount of output to total	% of exchanged
1	2	3	4	5	6	7	(6+7) =8	9
Below 5.0	918	36.7	895	38.9	337	348	685	74.6
5.0-10.0	1818	38.3	1293	40.0	696	517	1213	66.7
10.0-15.0	2904	43.9	1564	40.3	1275	630	1905	65.6
15.0-20.0	3630	39.0	1998	39.1	1416	781	2197	60.5
10.0 & above	5437	42.9	2476	44.2	2333	1094	3427	63.0
Average	2135	40.2	1446	39.6	854	573	1427	66.8

a competitive market mechanism. The output of all these production units competes in the market where a given price prevails. And those whose costs of production per unit of output are the lowest, productivity per worker the highest, and output-input co-efficient most efficient, derive the maximum profits. The large farmers are thus very favourably placed in a competitive market for agricultural produce while the small farmers face heavy odds in competition against them. And the middle group of farmers, since they are generally average in all aspects of farming, are in a state of continuous instability and flux due to the uncertainties of the market prices which affect them for the better or for the worse from time to time. The natural tendency of a competitive market is to impoverish the small farmer, enrich the large farmer, and to push the group of average or middle farmers into contrary directions, depending upon the numerous economic group of middle farmers gets drawn gradually into the whirlpool of economic competition, and is unable to remain close to the average and is slowly and gradually split up, some of them rising in the scale to become large farmers, and others, the bulk of them, dwindling into the position of small farmers.

This view of the impact of a competitive market on different types of farming units refers only to a long-term tendency. It is only the abstraction of an extremely complicated and protracted process which passes through complex stages and manifests itself in various forms. For instance, the impoverishment and economic ruin of the small farmer may express itself-and that too after a fairly long time-not in his complete elimination from the farming business but in his increasing dependence on non-farming subsidiary occupations, increasing burden of indebtedness or increasing liquidation of his farming assets. Gradually, he might turn to leasing out his land for a crop-season or a year, and may return to farming again depending upon the regularity and adequacy of his alternative employment. He may also continue to remain in the farming business by depressing his standard of living to the lowest possible level. These processes may also take long to become manifest on a considerable scale in a large country like ours. Similarly, the process of gradual splitting up of the middle group of farmers into small and large farmers may never come to light in the absence of two-point studies of a selected group of middle farmers over a reasonable period of time. The enrichment of the large farmers may also proceed slowly over a long period and remain disguised for a long time in the absence of any data regarding the changes in the distribution of land, capital investment, total output, savings, and few capital formation in the countryside. But a competitive market, un-checked by any counter measures, is likely to lead into these directions, is certain and well-known. So long as the market remains an effective regulator of the economic fortunes of the farming units, the direction of the movements of the small, middle, and large farmers would be along these lines.

If this view of the competitive process be correct, we should expect a bitter economic strife to prevail amongst peasants. There must exist a movement in opposite directions in India's agrarian society-a process of economic prosperity and ruin, improvement and decay, progress and regress. Some in the rural society, possessed of ample resources of land and capital, and using hired labour for farm operations, would make large profits, accumulate capital and expand output. Propelled by the motive to maximise their net money returns, they would take all steps conducive to economise on costs, enhance productivity of labour and output including the efforts to enlarge the scale of their farming business by taking more land on lease or buying it up from others, subject to the legal maxima. Another group-designated as the middle group-though not having such large resources of land and capital, but only a little more or less than the average, would also be drawn into the process of improving output, reducing costs, and investing capital in farming in order to be able to take the maximum advantage of the competitive market mechanism. And a few who are more skilful, hard-working and enterprising amongst them, by using inexpensive techniques of farming, and improved implements would succeed in expanding their scale of farming, make some profits and accumulate some capital. But because of their limited resources of land and capital and because of the severe competition from the top-group who command the bulk of the land and capital resources and reap much larger profits per farm, most of them would be gradually sliding down the scale of economic efficiency and welfare. And lastly, the vast majority of farmers, having only a small fraction of the total resources of land and capital, and with vast resources of surplus manpower, and suffering from acute pressure of population on their small holdings, would be fighting a losing economic battle against their formidable adversaries and would gradually face economic ruin and impoverishment. Sustained losses in the farm business, and inability to depress their standards of living beyond a given minimum will drive them to seek non-farm sources of income, thus diminishing the importance of cultivation as a source of livelihood for them, even leading them to lease out their small fragments to those who are expanding their scale of farming business.

This contradictory movement is likely to proceed only if there are no counter-checks or hindrances against it. However, in actual situations, numerous hindrances arise, and many counter-checks are applied against this natural tendency. For example, in economies with a large agricultural population, a highly unfavourable man-land ratio and without any alternative avenues of employment, this process does not lead to elimination, of the small farmer from cultivation despite such heavy odds against him but only intensifies his exploitation as share-cropper, tenant-farmer or agricultural worker. Nor is the movement for increasing the productivity of human labour by investment of capital or by improvement of technology very rapid.

In some agrarian economies, conscious counter-measures may be planned against this movement. For instance, the State may guarantee minimum prices for agricultural produce at a level at which most of the small farmers may continue in production despite all the diseconomies of their farming business. Even though it might lead to increasing disparities of income and wealth, since the large farmers would benefit more from the guaranteed prices, it may at least stabilise the small farm economy and arrest the process of its decline and economic ruin. Or limits may be imposed on the expansion of scale or farming by imposition of ceilings on the size of the operational holding, thus preventing complete alienation of the uneconomic farmer from his land, despite all disadvantages. Ad hoc measures like provision of subsidised inputs-irrigation, seeds fertilisers, manures, credit and extension-may be provided which also, to some extent, may check these contradictory processes. However, so long as production is destined for a free market, and the market plays a dominant role in determining the economic destiny of the farming units, the process must tend to assert and manifest itself.

In India, in the context of the present-day distribution of operational holdings, the process is likely to work out with particular severity. The group of large farmers with adequate resources of land and capital consisting only of those having farms of 10.0 acres or more, is extremely small only 14.58 per cent of all rural households, which commands 56.84 per cent of total operated area. Even amongst them, only 4.22 per cent of households hold as much as 38.62 per cent of the total operated area. And this small group is likely to ascend the economic ladder. The next group of middle farmers, holding farms between 5.0 to 10.0 acres which forms about 14.19 per cent of all rural households and holdings about 18.56 per cent of the total operated area, though drawn into the economic strife, is scarcely likely to make much headway, except for a few. And the vast mass of the small peasant households, with lands below 5.0 acres, forming 71.23 per cent of all rural households and possessing only 15.60 per cent of the total operated area, must face economic ruin and utter impoverishment if they are left entirely to the free winds of a competitive market.

Had the pattern of land reforms been different, and the monopoly of cultivated land by a small group of persons was liquidated at the time of abolition of intermediaries, or even later, the impact of the competitive process would have been far more widespread, rapid, and much less iniquitous. The movement for improving production and productivity, improvement of technology and investment of capital in agriculture would have embraced a far larger number of peasants than at present, and some of the anomalous developments currently apace in the countryside could have been avoided. But the path appears to have been laid, and unless it is reversed, must work itself out even though slowly, sluggishly, yet tortuously.

In recent years, there has been some evidence of these opposite processes developing simultaneously in the countryside. But this evidence is relevant only for small areas since no countrywide impirical investigations have been conducted for this purpose. The data about area and agricultural production, yields per acre, livestock, agricultural machinery and equipment and national income are collected only on an aggregative basis. No serious attempt has yet been made to collect these data according to broad socio-economic groups, or by size of operational holdings, which alone can reveal changes of opposite character in case of different groups. Nor have data been gathered in the decenial census to gauge these changes, even broadly. However, there are some studies, which do reveal some aspects of these contrary processes of growth and decay. We shall analyse them for whatever they are worth.

It is well known that Indian agriculture has shown considerable dynamism during the last decade since 1950-51. The index of agricultural production has risen by 45.5 per cent and agricultural output has risen at the simple rate of about 4.5 per cent per annum, or at about twice the rate of population growth. This rate of increase is in sharp contrast to the rate of growth of agricultural output during the half century before 1950-51 when it was scarcely more than the rate of growth of population. However, it has been estimated that out of the total increase of Rs. 1700 crores in agricultural income during 1949-50 to 1958-59, the share of the upper-income in the agricultural sector (accounting for only about 3.0 per cent of the rural population) in the increase of income at current prices may have been Rs. 600 crores or more (35.3 per cent of the total, increase).

It is already well-known that the benefits of the community projects have chiefly gone to the large landholders. For instance, we read in the Report of the Team for the Study of Community Projects and National Extension Service.

In nearly all the facilities that have nothing to do with agriculture and animal husbandry one notices that there is a direct relationship between the size of landholdings for a group and the proportion of respondents from that group that derive benefit from the particular facility. Thus we see that 66 per cent of the large owner-cultivators, 46 per cent of the medium owner-cultivators and 22 per cent of the small owner cultivators have derived benefit from the programme of improved seed supply. The same is found to be true about manures and fertilisers, improved methods of cultivation and pesticides. This implies that the better of group of farmers tends to be represented in higher proportion among the beneficiaries of agricultural facilities.

Now, if we relate these observations with the gradual conversion of ex-intermediaries and a few big peasants into entrepreneurial farmers, who seek to raise output and productivity, by employing agricultural machinery, hired labour, etc. It is natural that the large farmers should have more or less monopolised over the benefits of the Community Projects and contributed a major share in the total additional agricultural output. It has been suggested that the percentage increase (of agricultural output per acre) has most probably been greater in the bigger than in the smaller farms. And it should cause no surprise since bulk of the capital investments must also have been made by the large farmers, and bulk of the increased inputs like seeds, fertilisers, irrigation etc., must have also been applied by them. The large increase in the number of tractors, electric pumps and oil engines for irrigation, iron ploughs, bullock carts and other implements during the last 15 years suggests that large farmers, amongst whom there are ex-intermediaries and large peasants, have made considerable capital investment in the farming business. The investments are not only large in amount but also larger in per acre terms as compared to the small farmers. For instance, we find that

Big cultivators, who numbered 10.0 per cent of the cultivating families accounted for more than 40 per cent of the total capital formation reported by cultivators in Ferozepur, Broach and West Godavari. In all these districts the share of big cultivators in the total capital formation was marked higher than their share in the total area of cultivated holdings.

Apart from making capital investment in agriculture, large cultivators have also been taking lands on lease. For instance, the N. S. S. data show that of the total area taken on lease (which forms 21.0 per cent of the total operated area), three-fifth is with households operating farms of 10.0 acres or more, one-fifth with farmers of 5.0 to 10.0 acres size holdings, and only one-fifth with cultivators of holdings below 5.0 acres. Evidently, cultivators of farms of 10.0 acres or more do not take land on lease for eking out their subsistence, for which their own holdings are more than sufficient, but for commercial cultivation.

Similarly, the increasing use of hired labour in Indian agriculture, since 1950-51, is revealed in the data of the Second Agricultural Labour Enquiry. According to the Report, the total agricultural wage paid employment of agriculture since 1950-51 is revealed in the data of the 189 days per annum in 1950-51, to 194.26 days in 1956-57, despite more rigorous norms of working hours and intensity of employment having been used for determining a day of wage labour than in the First Enquiry. Again, wage paid employment for women workers in agriculture also increased during the period from 120 to 131 days per worker per annum. These data show that during the six years period, there has been relatively greater availability of wage employment, even though the level of total employment per worker per annum has gone down. Of course, the extent of increase is not much, but the significant aspect of this fact is that it has taken place only over six years, and within 3-4 years after the abolition of zamindari. As years roll by, its magnitude is likely to increase although in view of the plentiful supply of cheap labour, the increase in the figures of employment per worker per annum may yet be small and may not reflect its full significance.

Taking all these data together, one can form a broad view of the direction in which Indian agriculture has been moving in recent years. It is manifestly a path towards the development of the system of farming, often called, 'capitalist farming', in which a very small group of farm holders are becoming economically more prosperous and socially and politically more powerful in villages.

Unfortunately, not much data are available specifically about the relative performance of the small farmers during the last decade, since attention has been confined only to the new emergent group of prosperous farmers. Yet some symptoms of increasing economic difficulties of small farmers are seen in the N. S. S. data on the leasing out of land. For instance, it reveals that of the total area leased out, 61.38 per cent is leased out by those holding lands below 5.0 acres, which means that the small owners have found it difficult to continue in cultivation because their holdings are too small even to grow a bare subsistence.

A direct corollary of this situation is the dependence of small farmers on off-farm subsidiary occupations. The Rural Credit Survey found a close relationship between the size of landholding and the extent of dependence on subsidiary occupations. Again, in a study into the problems of low-income farmers in Kodinar Taluke (Gujarat), it was found that 83.0 per cent of the small farmers depended on off-farm labour, and a few on sale of subsidiary products. Similar observations have been made in the numerous unpublished village reports of the agro-economic research Centres and other studies.

Another important aspect of the small farm economy is the liquidation of physical assets or net disinvestment over a period of time. For instance, in the Gujarat Study, it was found that during 1948-53, a period of high prices of agricultural produce, small cultivators had sold away land to finance the acquisition of other assets like implements and livestock. Again, comprehensive data about investment and disinvestment was collected in the All India Rural Credit Survey and it was found that in almost all the districts except a few the small cultivators showed a net disinvestment position, while for the medium cultivators this was the position except in respect of a large majority of the districts.

The liquidation of assets or net disinvestment by small farmers only accelerates the process of their gradual alienation from the farming business and increases their dependence on borrowing and off-farm sources of income.

All these symptoms are only aspects of the basic problem, the uneconomic and unremunerative character of small scale cultivation. Since no comprehensive studies over two points on the relative performance of small cultivators in respect of agricultural output, income, capital investment, productivity per acre etc. are available, one has to depend only on these indirect symptoms of a basic malady.

However, recently resurvey investigations have been completed in several villages in different states which are expected to throw some light on the nature and extent of socio-economic changes in the farm economies of different groups of cultivators. The preliminary findings of one of these studies on the relative performance of the different size-groups of cultivators in respect of agricultural output over the years are shown in the Table.

Percentage changes in gross value of output, output per acre, and residual income (total and per acre) from cultivation (net of actually incurred expenses) at constant prices according to size of operational holdings in village Sohalpur Gara

Size-Group (acres)	p.c. Change in the gross value of output over	p.c. change in gross value of output per acre	p.c. change in residual income from cultivation	p.c. change in residual income per acre
1	2	3	4	5
Below 4.1	- 41.2	- 19.8	- 9.9	- 24.8
4.1- 8.2	- 4.1	- 2.3	+ 21.2	- 7.5
8.2-12.3	- 0.6	- 0.3	- 13.2	+ 1.8
12.3-16.5	+ 23.0	+ 12.9	+ 13.1	+ 9.1
16.5 & above	+ 6.6	+ 3.8	+ 34.2	+ 1.0
Average	+ 1.8	+ 1.0	+ 11.0	- 1.0

From these data, it is evident that during a brief period of 4 years, significant changes have taken place in the farm economies in different size-groups of cultivators, and the small cultivators have suffered a decline in gross value of output, (both total and per acre) as well as in residual income from cultivation (total and per acre). And the farmers of lands between 12.3 to 26.5 acres have achieved the maximum increase in gross output as well as residual income. These changes have altogether changed the relative position of small farmers in terms of even gross value of output and residual income per acre, and reduced them to the lowest ladder in the scale, as shown in the Table.

Changes in gross value of output and residual income from cultivation per acre during 1954-55 and 1958-59 according to the size of operational holdings in village Sohalpur Gara.

Size-Groups (acres)	Gross Value	Output per acre	Residual income per acre	
1	2	3	4	5
Below 4.1	203.3	167.1	166.05	124.80
4.1- 8.2	180.0	175.9	137.30	127.02
8.2-12.3	189.2	188.6	138.57	141.03
12.3-16.5	178.4	201.4	127.22	138.77
16.5 and above	175.6	182.2	129.98	131.22
Average	128.7	184.5	135.41	133.20

These data show that changes in opposite directions have taken place in different size-groups of operational holdings and have entirely changed their relative position. They pertain only to one village and are used here for mere illustration of the manure as to how different farms respond to the processes of a competitive market mechanism, and how the gap between the small and the large farmers widens under its impact.

The opposite process of increasing prosperity along with increasing economic ruination has its social symptoms as well. These are reflected in 'the conflict between the rural elite and the rural poor' which, according to an eminent sociologist, 'is bound to grow acute as the latter become increasingly conscious of the fact that they are not benefitting as much as they should from the various development programmes.' This conflict generates social tensions and intensifies caste feuds, mutual rivalries, and the struggle for economic and social power in the village. And these tensions are only the reflexes of a deeper economic process penetrating into the vital pores of our rural economy and society. The whisper about increasing inequalities of income and wealth and the cry about the rich getting richer and poor getting poorer also owe their genesis to the inevitable logic of this process.

For those who are shaping the course of the current agrarian revolution in India, it is necessary first to grasp this vast and complex process, before they can muster the strength and the will to cope with the problems generated in its development.

11

Role of Education

Basic Issues

The significance of education in modern societies cannot be overestimated. A literate and educated people are a prerequisite both for maintaining and further developing these societies. The crucial need of education for the people in various spheres of modern social life (economic, political, social, ethical and others) has been unanimously recognized. We will see why this need arises.

Fiscal Problems

In contrast to the multitude of self-sufficient village economies which mainly constituted the economic life of the pre-modern communities, the economy of a modern people has a national basis. Further even this national economy has been largely outmoded in recent decades and has become an integral part of the single world economy. The national economy, in fact, produces industrial, agrarian and other commodities, both for the national and international markets. Consequently, it is the world price movement of various commodities which finally determines the volume and the price of products in different production centres. An intelligent and correct understanding of the complex economic life of mankind as a whole therefore becomes necessary for all producers.

It was not so in pre-modern societies. In pre-British India, as observed earlier, the village farmer group produced just enough to meet the requirements of the village population and of the land revenue to be paid by the village collectively to the state. In post-British India the village farmer group has been producing for the local, national and even international market. If the village agriculturist is not to be a victim of the vicissitudes of the world market, he needs to be educated enough to follow the movement of national and world economies.

Education is necessary for the modern rural aggregate also for political and administrative reasons. Formerly, the state exercised nominal sovereignty over the village. Its administrative machinery did not penetrate and function in the village. The village panchayat and caste committees regulated the life of the people. After the modern society evolved, the village has become an integral part of the political and administrative machinery of a highly centralized state. Since the modern state appreciably shapes the economic, social, and cultural life of the people, it is indispensable for the rural people to study its mechanism. The rural man needs to know a minimum of law, governing judicial and administrative processes as well as powers of various state organs. Further, in recent decades, various political parties have sprung up in the rural area. These parties struggle among themselves to win the support of the rural people with a view to gaining control over the state. It is, therefore, also necessary for the rural people to study the programmes and policies of these political parties. Both these reasons make it obligatory for them to have education.

Education is essential for the rural people also for the broad social reason, viz., that all social relations between citizens are, in the modern society, governed by the principle of contract and not by status as in the former epoch. Contractual social relations are complex and multifold demanding from the citizen an understanding of the basic structure of the modern society and hence this need for education. The economic relations between citizens, the relations between the members of the family and other types of social relations, which in their totality form the complex variegated pattern of the modern society, are governed by laws based on the principle of contract. Only an educated citizen can have a comprehension of such a diversified system of contractual relations.

Factors at Work

There is another reason why the rural man must be an educated man. In the modern society the ethical life of the individual as well as of the sowety aggregate is increasingly being based on secular and humanist instead of on religious principles as in the medieval society. Equality of all men, individual liberty, development of human personality, reason as the determinant of human conduct-such are some of the principal conceptions which have been progressively determining the behaviour of the individual and the social aggregate. Modern education is absolutely necessary to comprehend these basic conceptions.

Cultural Factors

Education is also the prerequisite for the study and assimilation of the rich culture which has developed in the contemporary age. Human knowledge of the natural world has registered a phenomenal advance in modern times, giving man a greater mastery over nature. Similarly knowledge in the sphere of social life too has immensely grown, thereby enabling man to mould his collective social life more consciously. Further, there has been a tremendous advance in the field of artistic culture also. A part of this rich modern culture has even acquired the character of a world culture. Education is indispensable for assimilating this mighty world culture so vital for enriching the intellectual and emotional life of the individual and thereby increasing his capacity to contribute to the advance of society. The best part of modern culture lays strong emphasis on individual liberty and social co-operation both of which are so essential for the development of the individual's personality and powers and for social progress. The citizen who imbibes such a culture will feel an inevitable urge to work for the creation of a society free from social antagonism and discord and based on social solidarity and individual freedom.

For the agriculturist, education is, in addition, necessary for understanding of the advantages of the use of such advanced agricultural techniques as tractors, fertilizers, harvesters and thrashers.

It must be also noted that the modern society throws up

specific problems which only modern knowledge can successfully solve. For instance, the economic or political science embodied in Arthashastra by Chanakya cannot aid in solving the economic and political problems emerging from the soil of contemporary society. And modern education is the only means to acquire modern knowledge.

Just as old knowledge cannot assist in solving modern problems, educational methods of gaining old knowledge cannot help to assimilate modern knowledge. Modern science of pedagogy, modern methods of instruction and modern schools are required for imparting modern knowledge.

A shockingly large portion of the Indian rural population is submerged in gross ignorance and illiteracy. The problem of transforming tens of millions of those illiterate rural humans into educated and well-informed citizens is a problem of herculean proportion and still has to be resolved if the Indian society is to advance materially and culturally.

We will first delineate the main features of education in the pre-British Indian rural society based on subsistence economy.

Education in the agricultural, industrial, and other occupational arts was imparted to the members of the growing young generation not in schools but in the process of their direct empirical participation in those occupations under the guidance of family elders.

Social education or education in the arts of social behaviour and adaptations was imparted to them by the family and the caste as the social life of the village people mainly moved within the family and the caste matrix.

The growing young generation received its moral and intellectual education largely from the priests, the Kathakars and saints, and also, to some extent, from the family.

The multitude of secular and religious functions, festivals and celebrations, which the family, the caste, and the village community organized and in which the youngsters of the village participated, served as the school for the aesthetic education of those youngsters.

The world outlook inculcated by that education was fundamentally religious. It propagated the concept of the divine origin of the world and of God's free will determining all phenomena and happenings. In addition to one supreme God it also taught the belief in a pantheon of gods and spirits behind all phenomena, significant and insignificant. Eclipses and earthquakes, floods and epidemics, were not scientifically explained but were declared to be the result of the wrathful actions of malevolent gods and goddesses. For instance, the eclipse signified the temporary suppression of the Sun-God by the two demons, Rahas and Ketu. The earthquake was the consequence of the movement of Shesh Nag who supports the earth on its colossal hood. The eruption of small-pox was the result of the ire of the deity Balia Kaka who, therefore, had to be propitiated by a proper ritual. Education, then, also encouraged belief in animism in tree gods, mountain gods and river goddesses.

Thus the rural people of the pre-modern society had a religious unscientific conception of the world.

The history of the past Indian society taught to the young generation was largely mythology. It dealt with the superhuman feats of god-kings. Even gods participated in the terrestrial battles between these god-kings. Such a history could not give a consistent continuous account of the development of the social, economic and political life of the people in the past and explain all historical transformations by means of secular causes.

The social education adapted the individual to the exigencies of joint family, caste and village communal life. Since the social structure was authoritarian, the social education was authoritarian too in spirit. It exhorted the individual to completely subordinate himself to the joint family, the caste or the village community. It disciplined him in the service of these institutions. Such a social education could hardly serve individual liberty or help the deve-lopment of human personality.

All education including agricultural and craft education consisted of empirically acquired and hereditarily transmitted body of knowledge from the past. It was imparted to the young orally, mostly in the process of practice in arts, crafts and agriculture and participation in social life. There did not exist any technical institutes, musical and other art academies or schools of social sciences in the village. It was only in some distant urban centres that some educational and training institutions existed and functioned.

Impact with the west in general and Britain in particular and the resultant rise of modern society in India led to the spread of modern education among our people.

The new education was essentially secular and, on the whole liberal in spirit and content. This signified a shift from the religious and authoritarian to secular and liberal character of education. The spread of the modern education was, however, extremely slow and mainly restricted to middle and upper strata of the urban society. Very few villages had schools, and, even where they existed, the stark poverty of the rural people made it impossible for them to take advantage of the educational facility due to high cost. Further, since the modern education was introduced in India by the British mainly to meet the need of the personnel for their administrative machinery and economic enterprises, its liberal aims remained hazy or were even distorted. It did not set to itself the ideal of turning out citizens armed with modern knowledge who would use that knowledge for the untrammelled material and cultural advance of the nation to which they belonged. It was bereft of nationalist spirit and ideals. Nevertheless, it must be recognised that in spite of these serious flaws, the introduction of the new education brought the Indian people in contact with the liberal, democratic and rationalist ideologies of the modern west. Supersession of the pre-British education, authoritarian in spirit and largely superstitious in content, by the modern education, however defective, was an event of great significance in Indian history. Radhakrishnan's University Commission Report vividly depicts the achievements as well as the limitations of the system of modern education introduced during the British period.

The benefits of the modern education hardly extended to the rural India. The problem of education in the rural area was almost completely ignored by the British as is evidenced in the fact that, even after a hundred and fifty years of the British rule, 86 per cent of the total Indian population, including its advanced urban section, still remained illiterate.

A number of agencies worked for the spread of the modern education in India. The British Government, various foreign missionary bodies, Indian social reform organizations and subsequently political institutions like the Indian National Congress, were the chief among these agencies.

All these agencies, however, failed to achieve any appreciable result in the rural area.

The problem of rural education, it must be said, was not even thought out in all its complexity.

With the advent of national independence, the problem of rural education has assumed urgent importance and new significance. The free Indian people have set to themselves the task of building up of a democratic, progressive, national life, which surely cannot be achieved when tens of millions of rural people are illiterate, ignorant and superstitious.

Campaign against the mass illiteracy among the rural people is the urgent task to-day. Further, treasures of rich modern knowledge have to be brought within their reach if they are to be effective participants in the creative work of national reconstruction.

For successfully evolving a comprehensive and scientific programme of rural education a number of problems germane to it have to be resolved.

We enumerate these problems below

1. Objective of Education.
2. Structure of the Machinery of Education.
3. Technical and other Means for its Spread.
4. Finance and Personnel.

It is now recognized by eminent educationists that the present system of urban education lays unduly greater emphasis on the training of intellect than on the development of the physical, emotional, and moral aspects of the pupil's personality. Such education results in the one-sided and therefore defective development of the young generation. It fails to evolve an integral human being with an all-sided development of his personality.

The present system of urban education is further criticized on the ground that, during the long period of schooling which extends from childhood to almost adulthood, the role of general knowledge is over-emphasised. It is not related to concrete problems of real life. Consequently the educated youth, when he enters the arena of life after completing education, finds it difficult to grapple with the concrete problems of real life.

Various views have been advanced in the field of controversy over the question of education.

There are some who emphasise that education must have the liberal and humanist ideal before it. Others lay greater stress on the technical and practical aspects of education.

There are some who declare that the basic aim of education should be the development of the individual's personality. There are others who give greater importance to the cultivation of the virtues and qualities of an ideal citizen in the pupil.

There are some who desire secular education to be reinforced by religious training. There are others who sharply disagree with this view and uncompromisingly stand for purely secular education.

There is a group of educationists who are the exponents of a synthetic type of education which would help the development of all sides of the pupil's nature, intellectual, emotional, moral, and social, and help him to evolve into a synthetic man.

The view is gaining ground among a large number of social thinkers that the present education, which at the lower level, concentrates on the three R's, thereby concerns itself only with the development of the intellectual side of the pupil. They recommend that, instead of this, education should focus on three H's, i. e., education of hand, heart and head. This will guarantee, they observe, the all-sided development of the pupil. Such education will result into the emergence of citizens, physically healthy and strong, emotionally rich, intellectually alert and capable of social co-operation. They will be valuable assets to the society.

The new Constitution of the Indian Union has stated in its Preamble that it aims at creating a democratic society based on "Justice, social, economic and political; liberty of thought, expression, belief, faith and worship; equality of status and opportunity." Further it aims at promoting among all citizens "Fraternity, assuring the dignity of the individual and unity of the Nation."

It implies the creation of a society free from all forms of inequalities and exploitation and based on individual liberty and social solidarity and cooperation.

For the realization of such an objective, it is necessary that the conception and the programme of education should be in harmony with and be derived out of it.

In his University Education Report, Dr. Radhakrishanan has given an elaborate picture of the social ideal depicted in the Constitution and has further described how it should be paraphrased and expressed in terms of the educational ideal of the nation.

Reconstruction of the Indian society as a whole in the spirit of the social ideal embodied in the Constitution would imply also the reconstruction of the Indian rural society in the spirit of the same ideal. Rural education should be therefore adapted to the needs of creation of the new and higher type of rural society envisaged in the future.

The study of a society reveals that the prevailing system of education serves the needs and ideals of that society. The educational system of a society based on self-sufficient economy serves the needs and ideals of that society. Similarly the present educational system sub-serves the requirements of the existing capitalist society based on a competitive and market economy and its social ideals.

A new educational system will have to be evolved if a new society based on co-operative socio-economic relations is to be created. It will have to instill virtues of social solidarity and social co-operation in the members of the young generation, uproot anti-social individualism, infuse social passions, and build up the ability for social co-operation among them.

The type of rural society which is programmed for construction should determine the educational system to be elaborated for the rural people.

The rural sociologist has to give the most earnest attention to this fact while making suggestions for a new system of education for the rural people.

The success of an educational scheme like that of all schemes depends upon the machinery evolved for implementing that scheme. The scheme may be scientific and adapted realistically to social conditions and, further, the social ideal conceived by it may be noble, yet, if the appropriate machinery for its implementation is not forged, it will meet with failure.

The task of elaborating the organizational machinery for a scientific and comprehensive educational plan for millions of illiterate and ignorant villagers is a stupendous task. This is obvious when we consider that even the problem of creating a machinery for carrying out the minimum programme of the abolition of illiteracy among the rural people presents formidable obstacles.

The task raises a number of problems. What type of primary schools should be established for children? How will they be coordinated with such schools started for adult illiterates? In what manner will the primary schools be linked with secondary schools and the latter with higher educational institutions?

Further, should the schools in the rural area be open air or single room schools? Should they be specialized and differentiated or omnibus institutes? And, finally, how should the school time be adjusted to the exigencies of agricultural and artisan labour in which not only village adults but also youngsters participate?

The educational scheme will also raise such problems as those of the graded system of schools, suitable curricula to be evolved in the spirit of the social ideal in view, and the graded system of courses.

During the last two hundred years, humanity has made amazing progress in the domain of technology. It has invented railways, steamships, aeroplanes, telephone and telegraph, radio, cinema and other marvellous technical devices. These devices constitute the valuable material means of integrating humanity into a single unit as well as of building up of a rich unified economic and cultural life on a national and even international scale.

Formerly the school was practically the only effective lever of education. After those astonishing inventions, the school can be reinforced by other means also.

These modern means, it must be noted, have not yet been sufficiently utilised for educational and cultural purposes in our country.

We will enumerate below some of the principal among these means which along with the school, are available for the rapid advance of education and cultural enlightenment of our people:

(a) School.

(b) Library.

(c) Museum.

(d) Movie.

(e) Radio.

(f) Mobile Van.

(g) Gymnasiums and Sport Centres.

A maximum and simultaneous utilization of these means will undoubtedly accelerate the process of extension of education and culture among the rural people.

We will refer very briefly to the specific role of these various means.

(a) *School*: The school should remain the principal lever of education. It can serve as the medium of formal education, patterned and planned.

(b) *Library*: The library adequately equipped with books scientifically dealing with varied subjects; with newspapers and magazines of local, national and even international significance; and with charts and maps; can be a rich reservoir of variegated knowledge, social, political, technical, economic and cultural. It can also enable the villager to follow decisive national and international happenings. The art section of the library can help him to develop a refined aesthetic sense and artistic taste. The library, when properly made use of, will help him to broaden his outlook, enlarge his vision extend the frontiers of his knowledge and to visualise local developments as an integral part of one single organic world development. He will thereby steadily build up a national and even international consciousness.

The library is particularly necessary in the village to-day, because, due to its absence, a large number of even those few, who have become literate through elementary village school education, cannot maintain their ability to read and hence lapse into illiteracy. As in the case of a bodily organ, a capacity atrophies when it is not continuously exercised.

The programme of providing the library to the rural area raises a number of problems. A veritable legion of them will be required for tens of thousands of villages in our country. Further, a good section of the village library should comprise literature adapted to the specific psychology, lower cultural level, and requirements of life of the village people. The production of such literature will itself present a task of stupendous proportion. The problem of fixing its content will bring headache even to expert educationists.

(c) *Museum*: The role of the museum as a source of knowledge is not often sufficiently realized even by the educated man. The various studies prepared by the League of Nations in the past vividly demonstrate the great significance of the museum in the educational programme for the rural people. Even a museum with a local scope has a great value for the enlightenment of the villager. It can bring him rich information about the geography, the geology and the topography of the local territory, its flora and fauna, racial stocks inhabiting it, its arts and crafts as well as its past embodied in historical- records and relics. This would enable the villager to get a vivid composite picture of the life and culture of the local people of whom he is a part, in various stages of their development. It would thus help him to develop a historical sense and thereby recognize the causal connection between the past and the present. It would further deepen and vivify his imagination, enhance his sense of appreciation and strengthen his habit of observation. It would also deepen his interest in the social and natural worlds in which he lives. This would engender in him the urge to transform those worlds.

The museum will prove a valuable reinforcement to the school and library in the complex of means of disseminating education and culture among the rural people. It will not only improve the quality and quantity of education but will also, further, serve as a priceless additional source of material and factual data for preparing an authentic, multi-sided history of the people.

(d) *Movie*: It is very difficult to realize the hidden potentialities of the cinema, one of the most outstanding inventions of modern times, for creative social use. It can be a most powerful means of disseminating the modern protean culture among the people on a mass scale. It can be a classic weapon of mass education. It is one of the most effective means precisely because it enables hundreds of persons simultaneously to imbibe education and culture visually. In minimum of time the cinema can transmit maximum of instruction and cultural information. Further, since it operates through a succession of visual images interpreted through words, it accentuates interest in the educational and cultural content of those images. It is, in addition, the most economical method of spreading knowledge because it does not involve the necessity of engaging a large personnel of instructors.

This marvellous instrument has not still been utilized for

mass education in India. It should be adopted as rapidly as possible as a means for educating the rural population in the briefest possible time and also for making accessible to them the immense wealth of contemporary artistic and intellectual culture.

(e) *Radio*: Radio is another remarkable invention which, too, can reinforce the school as an auxiliary means of the education of the rural people. Ideally, each village should be equipped with a radio in the central place. Songs of great artists relayed by the radio will not only have recreational and emotionally nourishing value for the villager but will also develop his aesthetic faculty. Radio will further keep him acquainted with day-to-day events, both national and international. Further, talks given on radio do various themes by eminent experts and specialists will bring valuable knowledge to the village people.

(f) *Mobile Van*: Mobile vans, equipped with loudspeakers, radio, films, libraries and cultural objects, will greatly accelerate the spread of knowledge among the rural population. They can travel from village to village and bring enlightenment at the very door of the rural people. This would draw even its inert section, which lacks sufficient enthusiasm to visit schools or libraries into the orbit of modern culture.

(g) *Gymnasiums and Sport Centres*: The role of gymnasiums and sport centres as valuable means of physical culture and recreation should not be underestimated. They help to build up a physically sturdy and vivacious rural people. Further, by drawing the people in the sphere of vital and pleasant collective activities, they develop such qualities as social solidarity, co-operative habits, and social discipline among them. This is recognized by educationists and sociologists all over the world. The technique both of physical culture and sport has appreciably grown in quantity and quality in modern times due to the great advance of general technique. The modern gymnasiums are equipped with more complex and varied instruments than those of the previous societies. In the world of sport too, new games like cricket, lawn and table tennis, badminton, hockey and others have been added to the old ones.

Further, in former times, gymnastics and sports were isolated local activities only. In contrast to this, in modern times they have acquired a national and even international scope as is proved by national and international contests which are organized to-day. Not only are modern games and sports more specialized, differentiated and consciously planned but they have also become a permanent feature of the life of the society. This is unlike in former times when games and sports were only episodic phenomena mainly associated as subsidiaries with important social and religious functions.

It must, however, be noted that modern games, which have been practically transplanted from the West, have not still penetrated the rural area. This is primarily due to their expensive character.

Indigenous games and gymnastics bequeathed from pre-modern India still exist in the rural area.

One of the tasks confronting the rural educationist is to evolve a synthetic physical and sport culture which would be a creative amalgam of the best elements of pre-modern and modern physical and sport cultures.

The establishment of gymnasiums and sport centres, conceived in the spirit of such a scheme of synthetic physical and sport culture, in villages should be a part of the educational programme for the rural people.

This in brief is a survey of the role of various means, available in the modern age, for carrying out a comprehensive scheme of education and culture for the rural people. The problem is complex and the task colossal. However, the solution of this problem is vitally necessary for evolving a generation of sturdy people equipped with modern knowledge who alone can be the architect of a rural society based upon democratic and cooperative socio-economic relations and pulsating with rich cultural life.

For accomplishing this signal task it is necessary to abandon not only the old conception of rural education but also of the machinery to spread it. It is not only necessary to create schools and libraries in the rural area but also to establish museums, cinemas exhibiting educational films, radio sets relaying topical news and gymnasiums and sport centres, and, further, to organize a numerous fleet of mobile vans equipped with libraries, films and loudspeakers constantly engaged in their peripatetic educational and cultural campaign.

The principal prerequisites for a successful fulfilment of the programme of rural education and culture outlined before are first, the mobilization of the necessary finances and secondly, the creation of the personnel to man the gigantic venture.

The financial resources at the disposal of a nation for implementing progressive plans in various spheres of life, in final analysis, depend on the productive power of the social economy which, in its turn, is determined by the natural resources of the country, the technique of production in industry and agriculture, and above all, by the character of the social economy within which the production process is carried on. The extant social economy may help or hinder the free and rapid development of the productive forces of a society. The rural sociologist has, therefore, to be interested in the economic system prevailing in a country, study it, and decide whether it requires to be modified or even overhauled in the interests of the economic advance of the people and the resultant expansion of their material wealth. Only then the community can set apart finance requisite for the realization of comprehensive reform or reconstruction programmes including that of the rural education. Material prosperity and social and cultural advance of a people are indissolubly bound up. Culture is the spiritual perfume of the social economy.

The problem of teaching and directing personnel is another baffling problem. An enormous number of cadres of instructors, who have imbibed modern culture and who are, further, fired with social passion, will be needed for fulfilling the comprehensive educational plan.

Only when all the above mentioned factors-a comprehensive scientific educational and cultural plan, a properly elaborated organizational machinery, various modern technical devices, a large personnel trained in modern knowledge and, finally, adequate financial resources-are created, it is possible to liquidate illiteracy among the rural people and also to bring treasures of modern knowledge and culture to them.

The problem of the rural education-its scope, methods, means, agencies, finances and personnel-is one of the most vital problems confronting the student of rural society in India.

12
Teaching Methods

According to Secondary Education Commission "Even the best curriculum and the most perfect syllabus remains dead unless quickened into life by the right methods of teaching and the right kind of teachers." Method is the means of teaching predetermined ends. It forms the most important link in the total teaching-learning chain with the goals and purposes on the one hand and results and values on the other. Method is the middle link connecting in the objectives with its value. Method determines the quality of result.

All decisions regarding teaching procedures in civics should be governed by the objectives of teaching. The objectives are the specific goals or purposes of a particular unit as well as the nature of the content area of the unit. These would largely determine the methods to be used in teaching or dealing with the unit. In order to achieve the objectives of teaching civics, methods are needed to expose the pupils to knowledge and experiences helpful in the development of understanding, critical thinking, practical skills and interests. The procedures adopted should also provide training in constructive thinking, reasoning and critical judgment. The goal expectations in the teaching of civics involve deeper and extensive participation of students in learning. Hence lecture or merely question answer method would not be adequate. If comprehensive objectives of teaching civics are to be realised in students, there should be child exposed to a variety of learning experiences involving book learning, observation, interviewing, surveying, interpreting, reviewing, recording, reporting and evaluating. The need to make him an enlightened, discriminating, dynamic, productive and democratic citizen would make it imperative to provide him learning experiences geared to that end.

The civics teacher must be conversant with the theory and practices of different methods of teaching the subject due to mainly, two reasons :

There is no royal road to successful learning. The teacher should be able to use a permutation and combination of methods, devices, and techniques to make the subject interesting, vital and living. He may use lecture or discussion method or a combination of these two, to lend colour to class-teaching. The teacher should be conversant with a variety of methods of teaching civics.

Avoiding monotony: If a teacher uses the same methods-lecture or text-book, project, discussion or socialised recitation in every circumstance it becomes monotonous. In the past few decades a tremendous increase in equipment, materials, means and teaching procedures has been witnessed to provide variety and colour to civics teaching. Children should be exposed to varied experiences to create and maintain their interest and avoid monotony.

No single method is the best for all situations, and with all teachers and pupils. The method of teaching civics should emerge out of the abundance of information and skill of the teacher and should harmonise with the content to be taught. This requires every teacher of civics to be familiar with the different means for reckoning the desired ends.

Producing change in behaviour: Arranged on an individual as well as group basis, it should provide a group of related experiences and activities specially designed to produce certain changes in terms of knowledge; understanding, habits, attitudes and skills of the students.

Creative expression: It should give scope for the creative expression of the child's individuality.

Arousing interest: Rather than be a mechanical device for passing on facts and figures it should arouse a large range of interests in the minds of the students.

Shift in emphasis: It should shift emphasis from verbalism and memorisation to learning through purposeful, concrete and realistic situations.

Self study and knowledge: It should train the students in the techniques of self-study and the methods of acquiring knowledge through personal effort or intuition.

Stimulating: It should stimulate the desire for further study and exploration.

Awakening insight: It should awaken an insight in the materials and techniques used by a successful civics teacher. It should enable students to know the varied interpretations of events and clash of characters.

Corresponding to the different aims of teaching civics there are the following different methods of teaching civics which the teachers may use according to the needs of a situation.

Story telling is one of the most important methods of teaching civics. Stories of great men and women, story of early man, stories of famous rulers, reformers, writers, saints, discoverers and scientists, stories of ideal citizens, all should be told to the children in the primary classes. Narration is an art which aims at presenting to the pupils ordered sequence of events in such a way that their minds are able to reconstruct these happenings and live in imagination through the experiences recounted, either as spectators or possibly as participators. As an actor and speaker, the teacher's capacity can make the lessons lively and interesting to the pupils. They can almost visualise the events and personalities described before their eyes.

For lending colour to personalities and events varied types of stories as myths, legends, moral fables and true historical tales can be used. The type of stories and the manner of their narration will vary with the age of children.

Upto class V, the method of teaching civics should be mainly the story method. Stories and anecdotes enliven the subject matter. Telling of related stories will make the subject matter interesting and lively, even while using other methods as Lecture or Conversation Method or even Discussion and Problem Method.

Satisfies curiosity: Children have an inborn curiosity to learn about various objects and people. The educator can take advantage of this curiosity to tell the children many things through the medium of the story.

Interesting: There are very few people who object to listening to stories. Children in particular enjoy being told stories and hence a story can be used as an interesting medium of education.

Assists memory: It is always easier to remember a subject one finds interesting. Hence, things taught by a story are remembered more easily.

Entertaining: For children, education must also be entertaining, and this is possible only through story telling. This makes the child enjoy his education.

Inspiring. By the use of selected, good and psychological stories much can be done for developing the child's personality and character because stories are stimulating and inspiring.

Development of character: Moral education cannot be given in sermons. It is better, and more effective to tell inspiring stories to the child so that he is presented with a good example which he may strive to follow.

In order to take advantage of the technique of story-telling, it is essential to present it psychologically, and, in any case, story-telling is an art, albeit an art which can be acquired through practice. The more important factors in successful story-telling are the following

Identification with the story: The more the teacher can forget himself in telling the story, the better it will be. But this is possible only when he himself finds the story interesting. For this reason, it is advisable that the educator should tell only those stories which first interest him.

Sufficient knowledge: Only that story can be powerful and impressive which the educator remembers in all its details. But the story must be told in the educator's own words. It should never be read out, because this is the surest way of boring the audience.

Dramatic presentation: In presenting the story, the educator should enact the various expressions and emotions-described in the story and carry out the actions and gestures which are a part of it. This creates concrete picture in the child's mind and helps him to remember the story.

Adequate language: The language used in telling the story should be simple and within the comprehension of the audience.

Interesting style: The style of story-telling should be natural, life-like, interesting and varied.

Systematic presentation: A systematic presentation and proper ordering of sequences is absolutely essential. If the educator forgets some part and returns to it later on, after having described some future event, the educands are likely to lose the thread and become irritated. Hence, the educator must remember the sequences of events very clearly.

Confirming-to the mental level: Different kinds of stories interest children of different ages. Very young children are usually interested in stories of magic and adventure, stories which are awe-inspiring. Adolescents find such stories disgusting. But in all such stories, action should be the main element, although the stories are to be selected according to the age group of the audience.

Purposeful: In telling the story, the educator must always keep in mind its purpose. If this is not done, then the purpose will remain unfulfiled.

Necessary atmosphere: In order to tell the story, it is necessary to have a calm and peaceful environment. From the - psychological standpoint, the right environment for story telling is one of curiosity and expectation.

Apart from these suggestions which should be kept in mind, one should consult books on psychology in order to learn the art of storytelling. The educator must critically analyze his own style, language, acting, etc., in order to eliminate the errors he finds.

Story telling is an art. Every teacher, particularly every civics teacher, should know this art, with rich imagination, accurate and wide knowledge of the past and a rich collection of stories to be able to use them when the situation demands.

Lecture is the oldest procedure of teaching civics through imparting authentic, systematic and effective information about events and trends.

To motivate: While starting the study of a new unit or topic, the teacher may present the outstanding aspect effectively in a lecture. He may refer to some of the significant persons, events and problems and thus arouse the curiosity of the pupils.

To clarify: In the study of a unit, problem or topic, when the pupils are troubled by the same difficulty, lecture can be given to save time. A few minute's lecturing can help to clarify matters and thus save valuable time in the situations calling for review, for new synthesis, for an interpretation, or for the establishment of hitherto unrecognised associations.

To review: By summarising the main points of a unit or topic through lecture, the teacher can very well guide the pupils and indicate some of the important and significant details.

To expand contents: Pupils are interested to know beyond the text-book. They are interested in the teacher's reading, in his travels and in his experiences. This is possible if the teacher manages to give a lecture punctuated with interesting anecdotes, stories, personal experiences and chatty descriptions. Thus, lecture is one of the best ways of presenting additional materials.

As no text-book, however comprehensive it may be, gives the latest and most up-to-date information about these topics lecture, method can prove particularly useful in dealing with units concerning United Nations, Emergence of Asia, Africa, and Latin America, Developing Countries, the Contemporary World and India, International Peace and Cooperation, etc.

Interesting: A well-prepared and well delivered lecture can make civics teaching interesting. The spoken word is frequently far more effective than the printed one. By tones, gestures and facial expressions the teacher can indicate the exact shade of meaning that he wishes to convey, while delivering a lecture. By shifting his position, by impersonating characters, by changing his voice and by using simple devices, he can deliver his message effectively and impart life and blood, colour and vividness to the lifeless and colourless printed material.

Teacher-taught contact: Lecture gives the teacher an opportunity to come into immediate contact with the pupils to see and know whether the pupils are appreciating what he says. He can repeat the message or change the approach and thus manage to carry the pupils along with him.

Listening and Noting: Lecture gives the pupils training in listening and taking rapid notes.

Saving time: Lecture ensures adequate preparation by the teacher. Greater enthusiasm and interest on the part of the teacher is bound to be felt by the pupils as this enthusiasm is somewhat contagious.

Stimulation: Good lectures stimulate brighter pupils. They are prompted to put in more work.

Substitution of the teacher for the pupil: If the teacher is in the habit of giving frequent lectures, he secures valuable experience, but the pupils are deprived of their chance to similar experience. As learning is participating in the learning process, the pupils need the opportunity to talk, to ask questions.

Therefore it is advisable for the teacher to resort to an occasional and informal use of this method.

Reducing opportunity to learn: As readymade 'cooked' material is presented to the pupil the lecture reduces the opportunity for the pupils to learn by doing.

Monotony: Lecture may create a deadening monotony. Only an exceptional teacher can stimulate and keep up the interest of the students continuously.

Choosing the occasion: The teacher should choose the occasion for the lecture with great care. Some of the best occasions for the use of this method are the opening of a unit or topic, presentation of additional material, summarising of an extensive topic, clarification of a complex problem, elaboration of a current event. The teacher may give a hint about some topic or unit to be developed in some later lecture so that the pupils, may be led to anticipate the lecture with eagerness.

Synopsis: The teacher should prepare a synopsis of the lecture and give it to the pupils to save the former from pointless digression. It will help the pupils to pay undivided attention to the lecture.

Careful delivery: The teacher must speak clearly and slowly so that the pupils are able to keep pace with him. He should talk to the students rather than lecture to a class. Rise and fall in his voice is necessary to lay emphasis on a point and also to attract the pupils. Frequent natural changes of positions help the speaker to feel at ease and to ensure an equal opportunity to hear to every member of the class.

Humour: Lecture should be enlivened by analogies, comparisons, illustrations and anecdotes bearing upon the topic. Aids such as pictures, films, film strips, slides, diagrams, etc., should be used to make the lecture interesting.

Testing: Lecture should be followed by a written test to measure the success or otherwise of the lecture. If the pupils have learnt well, the lecture is successful, if not, the teacher can revise his methods.

This is a popular method of teaching civics. In it the teacher puts the questions to the pupils, while the answers given by the pupils are supplemented and elaborated by him. By asking questions, the relevant experiences in the memory of the students come to the surface while the familiar and known associations help in learning and granting the unfamiliar and the unknown. The pupils readjust the old for acquiring new knowledge. The old and the new get integrated and the process of learning becomes simpler and easier.

To motivate the pupils and create a felt need for learning something new or solve some new problem sometimes, the teacher himself puts questions. Initially questions are asked directly about such past experiences of the pupils which are relevant to the present lesson, in a manner that the present topic appears to the pupils as a problem in whose solution they would be naturally interested. These are generally developmental questions. In the presentation stage both the narrative and developmental questions are used in seeking the solution to the problem developed during the preparation or introduction stage.

Deepening insight: It develops the pupil's insight into the lesson and leads to the understanding and comprehension of the subject matter presented.

Application: In the recapitulation or application stage, questions are asked to find out the grasp of the subject matter or to help the pupils apply the knowledge granted to new situations. Thus, learning in consolidated and insight deepened.

The question-answer is a good method of teaching civics as it ensures active participation of the pupils. It should be supported by visual aids like pictures, charts, films, filmstrips, etc., and devices like dramatization in different forms, sustaining the interest of the pupils.

Direct experiences are more effective in the process of learning. They are retained for a longer period of time. They are rich, full-bodied experiences, purposeful experiences seen, handled, tasted, touched, felt and smelled. They are the unabridged version of life. A trip to the actual site, say a monument, a fort, a temple, an institution, provide the most first-hand experiences. As they are real; children can see them, hear them, ask questions about them and examine them. Such experiences are most edifying and highly conducive to learning. They are a motivating force for further enquiry. Immediate surroundings and community afford many opportunities for observation. Tangible, visible and describable concrete data on cultural, social and political facts and relationships prove invaluable for teaching civics. These lend vitality to the subject-matter of civics. Hence observation method is particularly useful in teaching civics.

Observations under the careful guidance of civics teacher provide ample opportunities for the pupils for asking questions, gathering data and pooling information. Visits to Panchayat and District or Municipal Board in session clarify ideas about local self government.

Field trips: Field trips may be undertaken for securing information, changing attitudes, awakening interests, developing appreciation, promoting ideas and enjoying new experiences. Used to initiate a unit of study ; they may be a part of the core of it or they may give it the finishing touch.

Community surveys: Community surveys foster-comprehensive understanding of community structure and processes in their everyday operation, interaction and complexity. They stimulate insight into community problems and trends influenced by past conditions, present developments and future prospects.

Community service projects: These involve individual activity of an integrated, mental, physical, emotional and spiritual nature resulting in genuine educational value to the pupil as well as significant social value to society.

Observation resources: These vary from community to community. If the teacher is resourceful and class enthusiastic and clever, they can prepare a catalogue of the available resources for proper and detailed study. Proper procedure should be followed for the observation of the resources to achieve maximum benefit for the pupils.

In it the teacher puts the question to the pupils while the answers given by the pupils lead to the development of the lesson to be presented. The teacher supplements and elaborates the answers of the pupils from time to time. By asking questions, the relevant past experiences come to the fore and the familiar and known associations help in learning and grasping the unfamiliar and unknown. For acquiring the new knowledge, the pupils readjust the old and the new and the process of learning civics gets simplified.

Sometimes, the teacher puts questions to the pupils to motivate them and create a felt need for the solution of a problem: Initially, questions are asked directly about past experiences of the pupils relevant to the present lesson, in a fashion that the present lesson appears to them as a problem in whose solution they would be naturally interested. These are generally developmental questions. Both the narrative and developmental questions are used in seeking the solution to the problem developed during the preparation stage. They develop pupils' insight into the lesson and lead to the learning of the subject-matter presented. Learning is consolidated and insight deepened in the application stage when questions are asked to help pupils apply the knowledge gained to new situations.

The Conversational method or Question-Answer method is quite a good method of teaching civics. It should be supported by visual aids like pictures, charts, models, films, filmstrips and devices like dramatization in different forms. This makes learning of civics an interesting experience for the pupils.

Some teachers use note-dictation as one of the methods of teaching civics for the following reasons

Absence of suitable text-books: The absence of suitable text-books is one of the reasons for the use of this method by most of civics teachers. Some topics are magnified beyond proportion in text-books because they have some individual appeal for the author, while others receive scanty treatment. The language of the text-books is tough as they are written by university and college teachers who neither have experience of teaching youngsters nor are teachers conversant with their psychological needs. This makes the reading material tough and beyond the comprehension of average students. Teachers start dictating notes to get speedy results.

Pressure of work: A civics teacher is often overburdened with work. Expected to take at least thirty-three periods a week, he does not get enough time for thorough preparation. He is generally allotted some period towards the fag-end of the day when most of the pupils are already tired due to strenuous work put in the preceding periods. In such exacting subjects as Mathematics, English, etc., the teacher starts dictating notes to avoid the distraction of attention on the part of students due to exhaustion, and to keep them engaged.

Shortage of time: The curriculum in civics is overcrowded. To finish the course in time, the Civics teacher looks for a short-cut-dictation of notes.

External examination: Teachers dictate notes of important and expected questions to get good results in external examination.

Inadequate power of expression: Civics teachers lacking the power of expression can neither narrate nor lecture well. They resort to note-dictation and are saved the trouble of making preparation for narration or lecture.

Detailed notes on important topics: Some teachers prefer to give detailed notes on important topics only, viz., on topics such as international peace and cooperation, local self government, etc. The notes are given, after the teacher has already discussed the topics in the class.

In the form of substance: After explaining the topic in detail some teachers give notes in the form of substance on the black-board. They, sometimes, also require the pupils to prepare the lesson in advance at home. Pupils are asked to copy the substance from the black-board.

Question answer form: Some teachers prefer to give notes in the question-answer form selecting important and expected questions and dictating their answers.

1. Note dictation is a malady eating into the vitals of civics teaching. The dictated notes do not give any training in the use of critical powers, which is one of the important aims of teaching civics. A pupil takes the matter dictated by the teacher as gospel truth and crams it without testing the relevance of the material.

2. This method is based on the mistaken notion that instruction is a process of memorisation and civics teaching is synonymous with the memorisation of facts communicated by the teacher.

3. Pupils start disregarding the text-books. They do not develop the habit of consulting reference books. They fail to develop proper insight into the subject.

While teaching civics, it is essential to make the pupils think and express, consult all possible works on the subject and prepare their own notes.

Discussion is one of the most valuable methods of teaching civics. It is said that "Two heads are better than one" but, when a number of heads combine to solve a problem, wonderful results are achieved.

A problem, an issue, a situation about which there is a difference of opinion, is most suitable for discussion method of teaching civics. Ideas are initiated, opinions exchanged, accompanied by a search for its factual basis. Speech is free and responsible. Values are created, the participants are engaged in a process of competitive cooperation. Agreement is the declared purpose of discussion which is, an ordered process of collective decision making. If agreement is not reached, discussion has the value of clarifying and sharpening the nature of agreement.

As a method of teaching civics, discussion may be used for the following purposes:

1. To lay plans for new work ;
2. To make decisions concerning future action ;
3. To share information ;
4. To obtain and gain respect for various points of view ;
5. To clarify ideas ;
6. To inspire interest ; and
7. To evaluate progress.

In the case of Problems

(i) Locating and defining problems of common interest and significance ;

(ii) Working together to find ways of solving the problems ;

(iii) Allocating responsibilities for the solutions suggested ; and

(iv) Evaluating the effectiveness of the suggested solutions and their implementations.

In the case of plans for projects and programmes:

(i) Deciding on the programme and the particulars such as date, time and place.

(ii) Enumerating the jobs to be done in organising the programme;

(iii) Allocating duties to the members of the group ; and

(iv) Evaluating the results.

Discussion may be classified as a classroom discussion, a debate, a symposium, a panel discussion or brain storming, etc.

It is a programme in which two or more students present arguments holding contradictory opinions on a particular problem. They are given an opportunity to rebut the opposite side. The rest of the class is encouraged to ask questions from the debaters or engage in a brief discussion with them. A debate has a moderator. In order to get significant results, the teacher should work both with the debaters and the class. Some useful topics for debate in Civics Teaching may be :

1. Democracy is the best form of government.
2. For forms of government let fools contest, that which is governed least is best.
3. Democracy in India is more formal than real.
4. Preventive detention of citizens by the government deprives them of their fundamental rights.
5. In a backward democracy, fundamental rights are of no use, etc.

In symposium the participants present their views to the audience about various aspects of a selected problem or topic through speeches or paper reading. In the words of Struck, "We think of a symposium as a group of comments, either spoken or written, which portray contrasting or at least different points of view." The chief objective of the symposium is to clarify thought upon controversial questions. The general audience listens to the discussions. Each person forms his own conclusions concerning the validity or value of the points of view presented. The ideal number of pupil participants in a symposium is four or five.

Symposia may be arranged on such topics as :

1. Local self Government
2. Panchayat as village government
3. Gandhi and his thoughts
4. Rights and Duties of a citizen
5. Democracy as the best form of government.
6. Declaration of assets and liabilities of the Ministers, etc.

It is a discussion among a selected group of four to six persons, large enough for variety and small enough for purposeful deliberations. The participants are usually eminent in their fields, they present various points of view before an audience which joins in the discussion subsequently. The purpose of panel discussion is to get important facts from different angles, to stimulate thinking and lay a basis for wide participation. No speeches are made by the members or by the leader. Only informal conversations take place.

In a panel discussion, one can follow either the rotation system where each member expresses his opinion in turn or the members may speak briefly as the thought comes to them one after the other.

The panel discussion provides a natural setting in which people have the opportunity to ask questions, to evaluate replies and to contribute constructively.

1. The role of Panchayats in rural development
2. Democracy can no longer solve the problems of underdeveloped countries.
3. "The President represents the nation but does not rule the nation. He is the symbol of the nation."

4. "An active king, whose opinions were a matter of public concern, is unthinkable within the framework of our (England's) constitution"-Laski.

5. "The Parliamentary system produces a stronger government for (a) members of the Executive and Legislatures are overlapping and (b) the heads of the government control the legislature"- K.M. Munshi, etc., etc.

In this method of discussion the brains of the participants are stimulated to create a storm of ideas and provide suggestions regarding the topic without any deliberation to find whether or not they are meaningful and purposeful. The principle behind this method is that when the brain is let go thus without social inhibitions, it would be able to give expression to some of the most useful and practical suggestions. "Students could do a lot to strengthen the cooperative movement" is quite a good topic for brain storming.

Planning: Discussion method can produce the desired results only if the teacher and student representatives do considerable planning. It requires a well-directed procedure.

Preparation: For thorough preparation for the discussion, the teacher should read wide and deep enough purposefully and critically and prepare the material conscientiously. Points to be discussed should be arranged logically, written on the chalk board for guidance. The problem to be discussed should be a felt problem.

Conduct of discussion: While conducting the discussion, the teacher should see that it is disciplined. The arrangement of seats should ensure face-to-face talk. As the strength of the discussion is obtained from the information and viewpoint of all members of the group, all contribute to its progress. It is a thinking together process which should not be dominated by one or more members of the group. The teacher must see that every member of the group participates. He should encourage sincere questions and comments. The discussion must be geared to the realization of specific objectives and development of proper skills and methods.

A relaxed and informal climate: It is essential to obtain desirable results to be achieved. The discussion should be truly a cooperative experience, not a competitive quarrel. Discouraging attack upon persons the teacher should seek to bring the participants to focus their comments on the proposition not the person. A discussion should be objective-oriented. Questions should be skilful and direction sound. A happy rapport should be established between the teacher and the taught.

Evaluation: Discussion must conclude in certain achievements such as expanding information or lessening or removing prejudices, changing attitudes or ideals, increasing the range of his interest, altering his ideas concerning national and international policies, or causing him to become a more active citizen.

Useful both for the juniors and seniors: On the lower level, children learn to take turns, listen attentively, act cooperatively, speak distinctly, stand and sit correctly, respect the ideas of others, share interests, ask pertinent questions, utilize simple information and comprehend the problem before the group. On the upper level, they plan and discuss problems with the entire group and in smaller units. A group learns together and presents important information, makes suggestions, shares responsibility, comprehends the topic, evaluates the findings and summarises results.

Clarification and sharpening of the issues: As new ground is discovered both for agreement and disagreement old ideas and values may be replaced by new ones.

Crystallisation of thinking and identification of concepts: Thus, their knowledge of civics becomes clear.

Knowing and understanding: The difference in perspective need not result in disaster.

Discovering what he did not know: What he has overlooked and wherein he is mistaken. He may find out what he knows and with what surety he knows it.

Giving knowledge a round trip: Discussion is not a one way affair of the teacher. It engenders more reflection than the question and answer recitation. Of all the methods of teaching social studies, it is farthest from rote learning. In place of cajolary, threat, coercion or propaganda, it employs reasonable persuasion.

Representing a type of intellectual team-work: Resting on the philosophy and principle that the pooled knowledge, ideas and feelings of several persons have greater merit than those of a single individual, discussion is valuable as a team work.

Tolerance: Discussion engenders toleration for views which are at variance from those one holds.

Self-evaluation: Discussion activates thinking along the lines of self-evaluation helpful in establishing an attitude of looking forward to progress and growth.

Discovery of talents: Discussion can help the teacher in discovering students who have a potential for becoming genuine leaders.

Assignment Method

This method is advocated for the teaching of civics in higher classes. In it the whole of the syllabus is split into significant topics, each topic is sub-divided into assignments. The pupils are required to prepare the assignments in writing as written assignments help in organisation of knowledge, assimilation of facts and better preparation for examinations.

Preparatory assignments: These assignments are meant for the purpose of circulation. The pupils are prepared for the work which is to follow on the next day. This pilot work enables the teacher to lead the class with ease and understanding.

Study assignments: Study assignment can be problem solving assignments, assignments on making and handling tools, assignments on picture reading, assignments for the preparation of a topic in the light of references provided.

Revisional assignments: These assignments are given for (a) providing drill to the work done by the students, and (b) for checking their retention and reproduction of facts, incidents, etc,.

of the topic and (c) for checking the understanding of the topic. They are worked out in advance according to the specific objectives of the subject-matter being tested.

Remedial assignments: Devised in the light of pupil's reactions to the three types of assignments mentioned above, the purpose of these assignments is to remove weak points and clear misunderstandings.

Preparation: In this step, efforts are made for developing the pupil's interest in writing, the assignment. Broad heads are outlined under which the assignment is to be written. The necessary information are given including the reference, etc., which would help the pupils in working out the assignment. This work should be completed in one period.

Writing: The pupils may write the assignment at home. Writing in the class under the supervision of the teacher, they should be allowed the facilities to consult books and ask questions whenever necessary. This may take more than one class period.

Selection of pairs for mutual corrections: The pupils are given a list of the types of probable errors which may occur in writing civics assignments to help them in correction work. Common errors may be : omission of vital facts, wrong statement of facts, statement of irrelevant facts, failure to bring out causal relationships, etc. The pupils are to point out all these.

Correction by pupils: The pupils are asked to correct their assignments at home.

Correction of sample assignment scripts by the teacher.

Preparation of common list of errors.

Discussion of the list in a correction class: The common errors committed by the pupils are discussed in a correction class to check their recurrence.

Knowledge of interests: It enables the teacher to know the interests of his pupils. He discovers the specific abilities of the individual pupil to be developed and used for their own good.

Foreseeing difficulties: The teacher foresees the difficulties which the students may have to face in the learning of the topic. He guides the pupils by putting thought-provoking questions in his assignments. The questions and guidance to study a topic prepares the pupils to face the difficulties boldly.

Suitable for pupils of different ability levels: Gifted, average and slow.

Project Method

The most concrete of all types of activity methods, Project Method provides learning experiences suited to individual differences.

Meaning: Project is an activity willingly undertaken by the pupils for the solution of a felt problem. It leads to learning as prescribed in the curriculum. It is a concrete activity directed towards the learning of a significant skill or process. It can be taken to include any activity like dramatics, pageants, making models, drawing maps and charts, collecting pictures, preparing scrap books, going on historical tours and exhibitions, preparation of civics wall newspaper, organisation of debates, etc.

Activity: The project should involve mental or motor activity.

Purpose: It should be purposeful; a felt need of the pupils.

Experiences: It should provide varied type of experiences to the pupils such as manipulative, concrete, mental, etc,

Reality: It should provide real experiences.

Freedom: The pupils should be free to undertake the different activities connected with the project.

Utility: The project should be useful.

Providing a situation: In a suitable situation the pupils feel a spontaneous craving for carrying out a useful activity. The teacher discovers the interests, needs, tastes and aptitudes of the pupils through conversation, discussion, exhibition of pictures, models, etc. Telling a story or taking the pupils out on a field trip initiates them to the world of projects. Exposed to so many situations they are in a position to determine the selection of the project. Opportunities should be given to express their own ideas and to have discussions among themselves, as well as with the teacher. The situations or problems to provide to the pupils, should preferably be social to provide better social training.

Choosing and purposing: One of the important duties of the teacher is to guide the pupils to choose a good project. To quote Dr. Kilpatrik "The part of the pupil and part of the teacher in most of the school work depends largely on who does the purposing. It is practically the whole thing." However the most important thing about a project is its purposing part. To get quick and good results, the teacher may have however the temptation of making the choice of the project himself. This way violates the most important principle of the method, as the final selection of the project should be made by the pupils. Self-choice and self-imposition enable the pupils to work whole-heartedly and energetically. They are stimulated to better planning, thorough execution and successful completion of the project. The teachers guidance to pupil-effort should in no way hinder the development of the pupils. The final choice of the project must be made by the pupils. The project "must enlist the whole-hearted enlistment of the student."

The teacher has to see that the projects chosen satisfy a real felt need of the children and also have educative potentialities. He should expose the pros and cons of the project, let the children reconsider their decision. He should scrupulously resist the temptation of imposing his own ideas on the pupils as they seldom take interest in an activity thrust upon them.

After the choice of the project the pupils may write in their note-book the reasons for their choice which will help them to collect their ideas regarding the choice.

Planning: Planning of the project should be done by the pupils under the guidance of the teacher. The teacher should draw the attention of the pupils to the necessity of the good plan. Discussion should be held in which the pupils and the teacher should be free to express opinions and give suggestions. After taking stock of the resources and limitations of various plans, a plan is drawn up. It requires time and consideration before a really good plan can be made. The whole plan should be written down by the pupils in their notebooks.

The teacher should prepare two or three possible plans in his own mind so as to be ready with replies and all kinds of help to the pupils.

Execution: When the plan of the project is ready, pupils should be encouraged to start work on it. They should distribute the various parts among themselves according to individual interests and capacities. The teacher should see that every pupil is assigned some work and contributes something towards the successful completion of the project. He should not give too much help to speed up the work.

Evaluation: Through evaluation or appraisal of the work pupils find out their shortcomings and good points. After the execution step, the pupils review their work to ensure that nothing has been omitted and that the work has been carried out in accordance with the plan laid down. The mistakes committed are noted to serve as eye-openers for the future. Useful experiences and successes are reviewed to serve as good examples. The pupils critically appraise their work.

Recording: As impressions left unrecorded are likely to be wiped away from memory pupils should be encouraged to maintain a complete record of all activities in the project book connected with the project ; the discussions held, proposals advanced and accepted, duties assigned, books and journals consulted, information sought for, work undertaken, difficulties felt and experiences gained and short and long-term gains obtained. Self-appraisal, along with important guidelines and future references, should be noted down. Well prepared project books may be awarded prizes.

1. Story of Transportation through the Ages
2. The Indian Renaissance
3. The Big World, etc.

4. Our Town
5. Nationalist Movement in India
6. Achievement of Independence
7. The Socialist Movement
8. UNO and Its Achievements.

Conforming psychological laws of learning: Project method provides the most natural conditions of learning. Pupil remembers the principles learnt for a longer time.

Freedom: Project method is a method of self-direction. The pupil learns to improvise, to invent, to experiment, to find knowledge in all ways possible, to translate the knowledge into action until the need is met developing the creative mind.

Maturation: The project method provides the sort of learning material that suits a particular stage of mental development. While the more mature pupils are likely to go for the abstract and difficult features of the task in hand, the simple elements will be left to the others.

Social benefits: As separate groups take responsibility for making their own contributions which are subsequently pooled and become the class effort, the method results in social benefits.

Training for social adjustment: Project method aims at developing in the pupils the capacity to adapt themselves to their environment, to make use of whatever is available and to meet a situation resourcefully.

Saves from insincerity and superficiality: In carrying out their purpose the pupils learn and do because they understand the value of what they learn and do.

Training for a democratic way of life: Project method encourages children to co-operate, to think and act together for a common goal. Teaching students to be responsible, it gives them freedom within the framework of co-operative democracy.

Learning through practical problems: Project method

encourages pupils to achieve a deeper insight into principles through actually seeing them in operation.

Growth. Both the student and the teacher grow through this method Stimulated and encouraged in his exploration of many materials the student ultimately approaches other areas of learning in a similar manner. The teacher grows in his understanding of a child's creative development.

Evaluation: An intrinsic standard of evaluation is set up in project method. The pupils learn to evaluate their own work. This self evaluation shows the mistakes and *Holistic satisfaction* makes for rapid progress and true learning.

Holistic satisfaction: The pupil gets the satisfaction of completing the whole of task. Organised according to the project method, work is divided into definite tasks to be completed by the child who sees before him a definite unit of work and gains the pleasure of a completed task. By dividing work into a series of projects, the child can finish it in a reasonable time and then have something definite to show for his work. While making learning more interesting, project makes it more effective. Pupils get joy and pride in the finished product of their labours.

1. The practical difficulties of covering a syllabus rule out the project method as the basis of teaching in most schools. Children taught by the project method often show astonishing knowledge of details in odd things revealing depths of real ignorance outside the projects.

2. At a later stage of education, it is not so easy to formulate projects having a satisfactory degree of width and comprehensiveness.

3. There is grew difficulty in ensuring any kind of systematic progress in instruction.

4. Very highly qualified teachers are required for success in this method. These teachers should be zealous and well-prepared.

Problem Method

The problem-solving approach to learning in civics is one of training children in the technique of discovery. More than learning the formalized procedures for the solution of problems it is more than analytical thinking that proceeds a step at a time. Development of effectiveness in intuitive thinking, it is learning to utilise adequate modes of thought. It is learning that art of predictive reasoning, of manipulating knowledge to make it fit new tasks. It is developing a style of problem solving that will serve for most of the difficulties in life. By generalising what they have learned about the solving of intellectual problems in civics, children solve their problems of social living efficiently and effectively.

In contrast to the project method, in problem method emphasis is laid on the mental solution reached rather than on a practical accomplishment. The major purpose of the problem method is to afford training for the pupil and reforming their opinion and future attitudes.

1. Discovering, considering, discussing, selecting and starting the specific problem or question.
2. Collecting, organising, comparing and judging significant information in the light of the defined problem.
3. Exploring the problem and framing some possible solutions.
4. Drawing preliminary conclusions for further exploration and study.
5. Evaluating findings and establishing a conclusion.
6. Considering the summarization with the possibility of further study.

Intellectually challenging: The problem should stimulate critical thinking, evoke a desire to seek cause and effect relationships, and to discover reasons as well as information. It should open up opportunities for formulating and testing generalisations.

Touching the lives of majority of the children: Within the realm of their past experiences the problems should have an impact upon the children.

Centering on a basic human activity: Illuminating man's effort to meet his basic human activities the problem should shed light on the role of basic human activities in community life.

Practical problem: To assure meaningful development of the problem, there should be an adequate number of opportunities available in the community. The range of instructional resources should be sufficient to meet the varying duties of children.

New and expanding interests: The problem should lead to new and expanding interests among the pupils not only in the development of the problem itself but also in a variety of the side interests it stimulates.

Sequence of learning: Experiences undertaken to solve problems and answer questions result in a sequence of learnings. To solve a specific problem the facts and information have to be marshalled leading to concepts, undertakings, attitudes and skills, which pave the way for generalisations for civics which help achieve elementary school objectives.

Realistic method: Problem-solving is a realistic method for presenting the experience that will face the pupil throughout his career. It gives him a chance to think, to judge, to evaluate, to compare and select what is best. He is challenged to bring to bear all his information and experience in such a problem, arousing his interest and awakening his curiosity as to how it can be done.

Pupil's objective: The problem furnishes an objective of the pupil because he can easily see its significance and the importance of securing its solution.

Logical way of thinking: This method points out a logical way of thinking to the pupils. They can see the necessity and sequence of following each step properly.

Evaluation and reorganisation: The pupils learn to track down information quickly and efficiently, to evaluate, to think, to deduce the truth from different viewpoints, to tell what is real and what is propaganda, to organise ideas and draw conclusions.

Adjustment: The problem can be adjusted to groups and to individuals to promote the proper amount of adaptation without sacrificing the social values that arise from co-operative understanding.

Initiative and responsibility: The problem tends to develop initiative and responsibility. The process is not a task which is assigned, but an inevitable requirement of the solution.

Open-mindedness and tolerance: These traits develop because the pupils see many sides to a problem and listen to many points of view. Their horizon of thinking is widened. They learn to think critically and independently and to struggle for solutions to selected problems.

Proper relationship: Good and harmonious relations are established and promoted between teacher and pupil. The pupil feels free from arbitrarily imposed tasks of the teacher and learns to appreciate the guidance of the teacher. Thus, a foundation is laid for good and happy relations between teacher and taught leading to the success of the teaching-learning process.

Adjustment to needs: In a small unit or a long term assignment the problem can be adjusted according to the needs.

Problem Method too has certain limitations

Monotony: According to Maurice P Moffatt this method will become monotonous if used too frequently. Therefore, it can not be used as the sole method.

Social pertinence: The problem method is in danger of implying a social pertinence and value that it very seldom achieves.

Over estimation: Problem solving in the classroom means solution of simple problems, just to give training to the pupils. But the solution of simple problems may easily lead the pupil to think that he has acquired a technique applicable to complex social problems as well as to classroom exercises.

Too advanced: Edger Bruce Wesley believes that the problem method may lead to the selection of trivial and untimely topics, and in some instances to those that generate more feeling and emotion than thought. This may be avoided if the teacher is very cautious in selecting the problems. As Wesley writes, 'The problem method may become a seminar method that is too advanced for the pupils."

Intellectual change to the pupils: In problem method the problems are largely intellectual in their nature, constant use of which may lead to too little attention to activities.

Socialised Recitation method can be used in civics for the introduction of a topic and for studying a problem. It eliminates the limitations of traditional and formal classroom teaching. Group thinking is developed, the classroom becomes a unit of dynamic group life ; the pupils have a sense of freedom as no one is repressed. He develops reflective thinking, supplements previous knowledge, has creative expression, develops desirable social attitudes by practicing in a large variety of socialised situations, and having opportunities for practice in the techniques of cooperative thinking.

Techniques of socialised recitation method: (1) Seminar, (2) Workshop, (3) Symposium (4) Panel discussion (5) Brains Trust.

Committee meeting: It can be a sort of committee meeting in which the members decide on an agenda, express their ideas freely, share their information willingly and eventually come to some conclusion about an issue or a problem.

Class discussion: The whole class may carry on the discussion with teacher as the discussion leader.

Under a chairman: The class elects a chairman to guide the discussion and discussion takes the form of socialised recitation.

Parliament: The class may be organised as a parliamentary group with a president, a vice-president and other special office bearers.

Procedure involved in the method: 1. Planning, 2. Conducting, 3. Reporting, 4. Evaluating.

Training for participation in social environment: It provides with opportunities for participation to the pupils with ease and freedom in conversation, the readiness to mix in friendly groups and the ability to work in co-operation for the interest of the class as a whole.

Ensures increased learning: The democratic procedure in determining classroom activities results in increased learning.

Development of leadership qualities: Opportunities are provided to the pupils for participation in a number of socialised situations and get a chance for development of leadership traits.

Democracy in action: It develops a faith in the ability of pupils to work cooperatively in the solution of problems. The combined intelligence of all members of this group proves greater than the sum of their separate insights. Co-operative thinking produces better decisions than those rendered by individuals.

Practice in correct parliamentary procedure

1. Socialised recitation is time-consuming, permits a few pupils to dominate the discussion, produces monotony, is difficult to organise and manage and permits wandering from the topic.
2. Arthur C. Bining and David H. Bining write, "One great danger in the use of the method resides in the likelihood that the lesson will be socialised in name only. In other words, we shall have the form but not the substance... the procedure may become mechanical and pupils respond not through any social urge but through habit or desire to please the teacher. Under such procedure, the method has less value than the old type recitation."
3. Socialised recitation is wasteful of time. It is not conducive to an adequate mastery of the subject-matter of social studies.

Suggestions

1. It should centre round a topic which is important from the pupil's point of view.
2. The teacher should prepare everything.
3. During the period of socialised recitation, a friendly atmosphere must prevail.

4. The teacher should have good control.
5. It should never be used to promote the spread of prejudice.

Source Method

1. To develop critical thinking by using the sources and weighing the evidence.
2. To form their own independent judgement through a critical analysis of sources.
3. To develop elementary skills of collecting data, sifting the relevant data, organising them and interpreting them.
4. To create proper atmosphere so as to make the people and events of bygone times more real.
5. To stimulate the imagination of the students for reconstructing the past.
6. To develop and promote interest in the study of social studies in the right perspective.

Lower stage: Dr. Keatings has pointed out that original sources can be used for creating atmosphere in the lower forms. Such a use of the sources does not necessitate any great exposition.

Secondary stage: The pupils should be encouraged to collect, examine and correlate the facts and even to compare and rationalise different conflicting accounts of characters. The exercise, to begin with, should be fairly simple and graded in difficulty.

Pre-lesson use of sources: Sources can be used to motivate the pupils for a particular lesson.

Mid-lesson use of sources: The use of sources can be made for developing the lesson.

Post-lesson use of sources: Sources can be used by the teacher after he finishes the lesson. Interesting and useful extracts from the original or secondary sources may be given to the students and they may be asked to write answers to some questions on their basis.

Advantages

1. It develops a sense of vividness and reality.
2. It can satisfy the curiosity among children on the question- "how do we know this?"
3. The original sources serve as an effective means for creating a right type of atmosphere.
4. The use of sources provides certain useful mental exercises such as right thinking and imagination, comparing and analysing, drawing inferences, self-expression and discussion.
5. The original sources can be used to illustrate more important points in support of an oral lesson or to supplement the one-sided picture of historical, political, economic and social accounts.
6. The method initiates the pupils in research.
7. Though the method is most suitable for the pupils of higher classes, it can be used with advantage by the pupils of primary classes also.

Limitations

1. It is not always possible for the teacher of schools to have easy access to original sources.
2. Use of sources is not easy for the teachers.
3. The method is too complex and technical.
4. The sources available are in many languages and scripts covering a period of more than three thousand years.
5. There is also the difficult problem of sifting the suitable evidences from a multiplicity of sources.

Unit Method

This method is of foreign origin quite popular in the United States of America. Gestalt's psychological theories have played a vital role in its development. It is proposed to present the subject matter for teaching as a whole. In the words of Henry C. Morrison: "Unit is a comprehensive and significant aspect of the environment, of an organised science and an art. This is intended to make the teaching easy and convenient. For the convenience of teaching, a subject matter is divided into certain units".

Morrison has laid down the following five steps of a unit: -

Exploration: The students are prepared for a new unit. An attempt is made to explore.their past knowledge.

Presentation: Through lecture and narration the teacher tries to present an outline of the unit to be presented before the students.

Assimilation: The students try to own and acquire the information that is provided to them.

Recording: The students try to organise the information that they have assimilated.

Recitation: The students try to express in form of a lecture or action that they have acquired.

1. It creates interests in the pupils for the subject.
2. It is based on the idea of giving whole knowledge to the pupils and tries to remove the shyness of the pupils.
3. The pupils are taught to draw up plans of action, which is helpful for their future life.
4. It is based on individual differences and develops the habit of self-study.
5. The pupils are taught the lesson of carrying out their duties sincerely and shouldering the responsibilities properly.
6. It develops the qualities of sympathy, love, tolerance, leadership, discipline, etc.

Limitations

1. It is not useful for all subjects.
2. It does not train the students in the art of appreciation.

3. It is a very expensive method consuming a lot of time.
4. It lays stress on imparting knowledge of the whole to the students, so either the pupils acquire a whole knowledge or do not acquire any knowledge at all.
5. It may degenerate into a mechanical method.

Laboratory Method

Civics is a social science. So some scholars are of the view that the teaching of Civics should be conducted in a laboratory, equipped with materials, connected with the subject matter of Civics. The pupils should be encouraged to acquire knowledge independently. As soon as pupils enter the laboratory they should think that they are the future citizens of India.

1. A room with space for seating of 30 to 40 boys
2. A good number of chairs and desks.
3. Blackboard preferably painted green.
4. Arrangement for models, pictures, maps, sketches, charts, lists and such other things.
5. Bulletin board
6. Almirahs and book-shelves.
7. Books that are lodged should deal with Civics.
8. Films and slides.
9. Radio and, a television set. In poor countries television shall be extremely expensive.
10. Magazines, Dictionaries, Encyclopaedias, etc.
11. Other teaching aids.

Role of the teacher: The teacher determines the whole programme. He draws up the entire outline of the work. He gives an idea of the programme to the pupils with the help of available sources. He determines the time, during which the work is to be completed. The pupils have to finish the work within that prescribed period. If a pupil finishes the work beforehand, then he is allotted some other work.

There is a progress report for every student in which are entered details of the work done by him.

Though this method is expensive, but it helps the students to take to independent teaching. Individuality and activity are the essentials of this method of teaching.

Dramatic Method

Based on the theory of- 'Play', attempt is made to get the subject matter enacted or dramatised with the help of the students who take interest in dramatising the subject-matter.

The working of the Parliament or Zila Parishads may be dramatised with the help of the students.

1. It brings about a development of the mental faculties.
2. Interest is created in the students about the subject that has to be taught.
3. The subject-matter of Civics is made interesting and intelligible.
4. It creates a sense of self-confidence and self-importance.
5. It leads to development of social and moral qualities. Pupils try to liveup to the ideals of the great men whose role they play.

Requirements

1. The teacher should be well aware of the techniques of drama. He should also know the art of writing dialogues.
2. He should have the capacity to select the dramatic material.
3. He should be acquainted with the qualities of simplicity and authenticity that are the requisites of dramatic procedure.
4. He should have the capacity to mould his personality accordingly, as and when required.

13

Teaching Approaches

Organisation of the subject-matter in Civics teaching is essential in order to teach it in an effective and coherent manner.

Different Approaches

The following approaches may be adopted for organising the subject-matter of civics

1. Concentric Approach
2. Topical Approach
3. Unit Approach.

Concentric Approach

According to this approach, children in the primary classes begin to develop simple generalisations about man carrying on his everyday activities. As they progress through the middle and high classes students work with more and more difficult arrangement of information, and, deepen and reshape the dimensions of their generalisations about these activities. By the time they complete the secondary stage, they refine the same generalisations many times, using increasingly more abstract levels of thought at each higher echelon of learning. In civics teaching an attempt is made to design a sequential arrangement of experiences that will produce a spiral of cumulative learning. Areas of study at each level are treated holistically Whatever is taught to the child is a whole in itself though scope for additions should be made with the addition of understanding and maturity. For instance, boys and girls should know India's freedom struggle. In the primary classes, the information about this unit will be imparted through some of the more important leaders. In the middle stage, the information will be imparted through events – the Indian National Congress, partition of Bengal, the Gandhian era – Civil Disobedience, the INA, Quit India Movement etc. In the secondary stage, the pupils will, learn to compare and contrast the freedom movement in our country with other countries of the world. They should know about the United Nations and its role in international peace. In the primary classes, they will know something about the importance of cooperations among nations, work of UNICEF, WHO; UNESCO, India in the U.N. In the middle classes again, information will be provided about the need for cooperation, co-existence, the United Nations, etc. In the secondary stage, more information will be imparted about international peace and cooperation and the role of India in the United Nations and the world. Thus, as the child advances in age and understanding, he can think in more abstract terms. Learning is continuous and unbroken through the primary and secondary stages. The learning sequence progresses from the simplest unit to the most detailed in gradual stages.

Thus, concentric approach is devising a strategy that fosters continuous, unbroken learning of the subject-matter of civics through the primary, middle and secondary stages.

In this approach, while the path is narrower, the way is simpler ; the pupil gets somewhere and will not easily forget his journey. As he is interested from the very beginning, it is easy to proceed from the known to the unknown.

Use of this approach will make civics a subject of immediate and real interest. For the average pupil, it will be the basis of an abiding interest. For the more intellectual, it will be the basis on which higher studies can be built.

This approach is criticised on many grounds :

(i) This approach is psychologically unsound as the same facts are repeated again and again. Being devoid of freshness and novelty the presentation inevitably fails to rouse curiosity and a sense of wonder in the pupils.

(ii) In this approach, it is difficult, if not impossible, to give a clear picture of a problem vivid with detail. Hurried and passing references will not be of help in understanding complex problems.

(iii) It is difficult to develop time and space sense in the pupil's in this approach.

(iv) In this approach the joy of discovery, the freshness of events, the adventures and achievements of great personalities, the atmosphere of an age or era, the constitutional landmarks are denied to the children in a strictly concentric approach to civics. A sense of boredom and dullness is inevitable because they have gone through the whole course more than once. They develop a sense of familiarity without the fullness of knowledge.

This criticism can be met by making the repetition interesting by following a different approach and a fresh point of view in different stages.

Topical Approach

In this approach, certain topics of study suitable for the age, ability and interest of children make up the whole syllabus. Each topic stands by itself and all the topics are connected together by the teacher with the help of individual lessons called 'link' lessons. For the children of the age group 13 + and above, topical approach is quite worthwhile.

According to the topical approach, the curriculum maker takes particular topics as the central theme of work in civics at different levels of instruction. The nature of the topics vary in accordance with the age, ability and interests of the children. In the primary classes, the child may start the study of the developments of means of transport. In the middle classes, they may be introduced to more important and more difficult topics such as the history of government. The development of the topics is traced; the topic supplies the central theme from which subsidiary investigations can radiate as far as pupil's time and intelligence allow. Several events are logically and intelligently related.

By a careful selection and detailed study of the topics, opportunities can be provided to the students- for an intensive study of a particular problem. Instead of repeating the content a number of times the teacher can discuss all the aspects of a problem and give an overall view of that particular problem.

(i) This approach provides a solution for dealing with a vast material in a logical and rational fashion. It helps the pupils to understand the facts in their developmental setting. This is the only approach by which civics could be studied through considerable stretches of lines without grossly overloading the syllabus establishing at least a foothold in ancient societies, while at the same time, maintaining a connection with them here and now.

(ii) The topical approach can be adapted according to the age, ability and aptitude of the children. This flexibility is of special significance when we think of projects on topics pertaining to' transport and communication, government, etc.

(iii) The study of civics through this approach imparts a sense of purpose to the pupils. They are clear about what they are studying.

(iv) The topical approach enables the teacher to control the subject-matter and adapt it to the varying needs of the students. As there is a definite problem before the pupils the consequent study shows an intelligible objective, *i.e.*, understanding the problem in all its facets.

If the topics are selected wisely, and the treatment is interesting, the approach can prove useful in teaching civics in all the stages- primary, middle and secondary.

Unit Approach

Of the various ways of organising material in civics courses, the unit approach predominates in popular usage. The grouping of related lessons into about ten to twenty or more major topics, provides a tangible aid both in planning instruction and in comprehending the scope of the course of civics.

Dictionary of education. Unit, "is an organisation of various activities, experiences and types of learning around a central problem or purpose, develops cooperatively by a group of pupils under teacher leadership ; involves planning, execution of plans, and evaluation of results."

I. Hanna, N. Hageman and G. Potter. 'A unit can be defined as purposeful learning experience focused upon behaviour of the learner and enable him to adjust to a life situation more effectively."

E. S. Johnson. "Unit is a segment of experience which is cut out for study ; within it, method is employed. It is my understanding that every unit is a *project.* It is a project in the sense that one projects inquiry into it. Furthermore, every unit has a *topic, theme or central tendency* or whatever name you choose to call it, otherwise it could have no unity. Every unit is a *contract in* the sense that the student enters upon a contract or obligation to study how the things, which it contains, are related, how they work, how cause and effect are identified and related, and how a conclusion is reached. Every unit is also a *problem:* a problem of significance and meaning in some unknown or less than thoroughly known phase of human experience."

John Jarolimek. "A unit is a means of organising materials for instructional purposes which utilizes significant subject-matter content, involves pupils in learning activities through active participation intellectually and physically and modifies the pupil's behaviour to the extent that he is able to cope with new problems and situations more competently."

Experience: It is purposeful learning experience, having significant content, comprehensive enough to have scope and unity.

Involvement: It involves pupils in learning activities through active participation intellectually and physically.

Development: It develops certain information, understandings, attitudes, interests and skills to enable the pupils to cope with new problems and situations more competently.

Resource unit. It is a teacher's guide to planning and action, a blue-print of suggestions and resources for developing a theme, problem or topic. Regardless of former structure, it includes the following elements

(i) Statement of objectives related to a theme

(ii) Problem or topic

(iii) An approach or initiation

(iv) Content or subject-matter basic to the area of study

(v) Direct and related experiences

(vi) Organising and summarising experiences

(vii) Evaluation of learnings, and

(viii) A collection of instructional resources.

Teaching unit. It is used to describe the development of a unit of work in the class-room. Referred to as the unit in action, it focuses on implementation, learning activities and processes that take place as the unit develops. The areas of learning and the sequences in it may or may not be prescribed. However, the needs, the maturity level and the background experiences of a particular group of children set the boundaries of the teaching unit and determine its direction.

A resource unit contains an organised collection of teaching ideas and suggestions built around a large topic of significance while the teaching unit contains definite plans for teaching a specific group of children under a given set of circumstances.

Topical: It should deal with a sizable topic.

Appropriate: In terms of the child's understandings, interests and capabilities it should be of appropriate difficulty. A variety of activities, materials and modes of expression are essential for meeting individual needs so that each child gets opportunities to make worthy contributions to the achievement of group purposes.

Variety of material: It should allow the use of a variety of materials and activities like community resources, audio-visual materials, dramatic play and excursions, map-making, chart making, planning, discussing and evaluating.

***Reading material*:** It should allow use of sufficient amount of book and other reading materials.

Suitable to the maturation level of the children: Units should be of shorter duration in the primary classes. In middle and high school classes than those in the primary classes the units may last a few days to a week or two. Higher class children may engage in a single unit for several weeks and continue to find themselves in a challenging, interesting situation.

Evolutionary or functional: It should be based upon the principle of a process. Whatever the field or aspect, it must move towards something to show development or evolution.

Connected with past experiences: It should emerge out of the children's past experiences and lead to broader interests, an integrated learning experience and the continuity of the child's learning.

Creative: It should provide opportunities for creative experience like expression in art, dramatic play, poems, stories, songs, etc.

Objectives: Objectives may be clearly stated, in categories like 'knowledge', 'understandings', 'skills', 'attitudes', 'interests'. They must be achievable and make the teacher conscious of the process of teaching.

The theme: It enables the teacher to get a clear background of the whole unit and focus the attention of the teacher on the main points of teaching.

***Subject-matter*:** It should be selected with care and arranged in proper order and sequence.

***Pupil's activities*:** It suggests the learning aspects of the educative process. The teacher may suggest some of the activities essential for learning civics. These may be of varied types such as activities in the class-room, outside the class-room, individual activities, group activities, etc.

References: References for the guidance of teacher's need should be given from books from their libraries along with a list of films and film strips.

Teaching aids: Different types of teaching aids may be utilized for the proper teaching of a unit.

Teacher's remarks: *These* should be serving as guidelines for others in the implementation of units in other classes. These may include suggestions regarding the total number of periods necessary for the unit, and other points which may prove helpful to other teachers.

***Suitability*:** In the words of Jarolimek, "The extension of knowledge and the development of skills, abilities and attitudes are all possible outcomes of good units". Well suited for the growth and development of the abilities and skills attendant to democratic behaviour, ideals and processes Unit, afford limitless possibilities for the development of critical thinking, problem-solving, planning, consideration for others, responsible habits of work, listening, discussing, reporting and experimenting.

***Facilitation*:** The organization of experiences and materials into units facilitates the child's learning significant relationships, concepts and processes. Acts learned in their proper context are remembered longer.

Adaptation: Because of its flexibility the unit provides facility in adopting instruction to individual differences of children. It rejects the notion of fixed, uniform standard of achievement. It substitutes the concepts of continued progress and growth for individual children. Unit planning focuses attention on the individual child, his chief concerns, problems and interests Standards of achievement are kept at a high level. They are also different for each child. The structure of the units facilitates meeting the educational needs of individual children.

Need satisfaction: As distinct from the requirements of the content the needs of the learner are given top consideration providing for varied experiences, activities and opportunities for the development of the child.

Focusing attention: Focusing attention upon significant results the unit avoids the confusion- and discouragement from long attention to insignificant details.

Useful division: As it is impossible to study every thing at once, Unit is a logically useful division cutting out a field or phase of study.

Proper organisation of the curriculum is required for achieving the aims and values of the teaching of Civics. Teachers have to look towards the various informations and the subject material, whose organisation may lead to the achievement of the aims and objectives. Though this is a difficult task, it is on the basis of which, the subject material or the content material of the civics may be organised.

Flexibility: Man is a dynamic being with activity as an essential part of his personality. He continues to progress higher and higher. He has to struggle hard with the circumstances to face the difficulties of life. As he has to adjust himself as well he requires elasticity or flexibility. It is through flexibility that he is able to establish his superiority over other beings. Through struggle with the circumstances he gains certain experiences which are given place in the curriculum. This is helpful in acquiring further knowledge. When the present experiences are correlated and connected with the past experiences, it is easy to acquire further knowledge. If the link that is established is weak, one cannot make the knowledge stable and permanent. Therefore, it is the duty of every person, interested in education, to preserve the experiences of the past. The values of the past provide a foundation to the child, to build his own super-structures of the values. Therefore the past experiences are given a place in the curriculum. This can be done by the curriculum framed on the principle of flexibility.

Activity: Educationists believe that 4 H's should find a place in the curriculum: Health, Head, Hands and Heart. A coordination should be established between the hands and the mind. It would enable the children to act intelligently. Child is active by nature. His path of activity and agility should be free from difficulties. The organisation and selection of the subject material of Civics should be based on activity. Such events, instances and topics of Civics that lead to the activity in the child should be included in the curriculum. The curriculum should be so organised that it may bring about activity in the children.

Utility: Ours is a world of selectivity. In regard to subject material and activity we follow the principle of pick and choose. Subject material of Civics which fulfils our educational needs shall be useful.

Whitehead has classified the educational life into three stages- (1) Romance, (2) Precision, and (3) Generalisation. Here precision is nothing but utility. Selection of the subject material of civics should be based on precision and utility. Material that is not precise and useful should not find a place in the teaching of Civics. With the development of various mental powers, the child is able to discriminate between useful and useless, welcoming what is useful and discarding what is not useful. If the content material of teaching civics is not based on the principle of utility, it shall not attract the students towards the study.

***Formality and cultural heritage*:** In India, each individual is proud of his or her cultural heritage. Indians try to preserve the culture handed over to them by their forefathers. Along with it we also try to enrich it. This can be done by including the teaching of civics in the curriculum. Civics should be taught through the subject material that helps preservation of culture and its enrichment. This may be done only if the subject-matter is selected on the basis of the principle of formality.

***Interest*:** Interest, aptitude and other mental faculties play a vital role in the child's education. Hence attempt is made to base the entire education on the interest of the children. Subject material selected should be of interest to the students. The teaching of Civics should be so organised that it is interesting to the educands. If the content material is not based on interest, children shall not be inclined to study it. Modern education is child-centred. Therefore, to organise the subject material of the civics, one must keep his eye on the interest of the child. The selection and organisation of the subject material should be according to the nature of the child.

Principle of selectivity: A teacher cannot teach each and everything in the curriculum. He has to follow the principle of pick and choose. Things that are helpful for the betterment of the society and bring about the preservation of the social values and cultural standards are given place in the curriculum of civics. The content material has social and political problems. The material should be in tune with the intelligence and mental power of the students. .

Concentric growth: According to this principle the teacher should proceed 'from known to unknown' and 'from concrete to abstract'. First of all, those facts should be presented before the child that are already known to him. Then facts unknown to him may be presented. While teaching Civics, first the problems dealing with the local aspect of citizenship should be presented before the children. Then should be presented the national and international problems appertaining citizenship.

Widening circle: Initially a child lives in the family. As he grows first he comes in contact with his neighbourhood, then in contact with the town, the state, the country and the entire world. The knowledge and the teaching of Civics should begin with the knowledge of the family. The teacher should try to present the ideals of citizenship before him as it affects his family. He should gradually broaden this circle of knowledge to arrive at citizenship of the world or world citizenship.

In constructing curriculum or laying down the subject material of teaching Civics the teacher faces the problem of organisation of the facts. These should be so organised that the students may acquire and assimilate them thoroughly. Following principles have been laid down as principles of organisation of the facts

Integration: The selected content material of teaching of Civics should be integrated and co-ordinated with the curriculum of Economics, History, Geography and other branches of social studies to enable the students to think that various subjects are interdependent and coordinated. They should be given a thorough knowledge of other subjects.

To be systematic and well-ordered the integration should be

so organised, that the content material, that a student studies in one class, should not be repeated in his next class. The teacher should remember that in higher class the student should get higher knowledge about a thing that he has studied in the lower class. This shall make the knowledge of the students systematised and organised. A systematic integration will help the students to learn the subject material easily and thoroughly. With such a process of integration he shall have a thorough knowledge of the subject.

Solid or concrete circumstances: While organising the content material of teaching civics the circumstances and the conditions in which the child lives, should form the foundation to help the child to grasp the subject material easily and quickly.

Individual interests and aptitude: The organisation of the content material of civics should be based on the interests, aptitude and mental faculties of the children. If it is organised to suit the interests and the aptitude of the children, it shall be useful and helpful for them.

Co-ordination of the knowledge of one subject with other subjects: In the scientific way of education the content material of the Civics should be so organised that it is co-ordinated with the knowledge of other subjects.

Following are the various stages of education according to the Secondary Education Commission:

Primary stage. This includes classes I, II, III, IV and V in which the students of the age group of 6-11 years come to receive education.

Junior High School or Pre-secondary stage of education. This includes classes VI, VII and VIII in which the students of the age group of 11-14 years receive education.

Secondary stage of education. It includes classes IX, X, XI and XII. Class XII is not included in the secondary stage of education.

University stage of education. It includes the teaching of BA., B.Sc., B.Com., MA., MPA., M.Sc., M. Com., etc., and also research work.

Presentation of subject-material of civics is concerned only with the first three stages of education.

Principles of the presentation of the subject-matter: Following are the basic principles that the civics teacher has to bear in mind while presenting the subject-matter of civics before the students of the first three stages of education :

Matter. The matter presented should be factual and intelligible.

Individual differences. The teacher should try to present the subject-matter with an eye on age, mental growth, needs, interests and aptitudes of the students.

Practice. As theoretical presentation of the subject-matter alone is not enough for a civics teacher, stress should be laid on the practical importance of the knowledge.

Teacher's conduct. As children are prone to imitation in the earlier stages, the teacher of civics should present material before the students in such a way that they may do such things that are good for civics education and the work in the class. This means that the conduct of the civics teacher should form an ideal for the students.

Co-ordination. It is the essence of teaching of Civics. The teacher should try to correlate the subject-matter of Civics with life to help the student to use the subject-matter in their practical life.

Scientific method. In order to follow the scientific method of teaching, the teacher should try to proceed from simple to complex and from concrete to abstract.

Children of 6 to 11 years of age group are taught at this stage. As they are fresh from the family life, an attempt should be made to conduct their life in such a way that they may develop the social qualities, which shall be helpful for their future life.

Curiosity is the basic instinct at this stage of life. Children of this stage are very fond of listening to stories as they have a lot of curiosity. The teacher should base his presentation of the subject-material on the basis of curiosity. He should utilise this instinct of the students and their fondness for listening to stories, in presenting the subject-matter in the form of stories. The teaching should be through the story method.

Activity. The story may develop the activity of the students.

Interests and Mental age. The story should be in accordance with the interests and mental age of the children.

Nature of story. The story may be historical as well as imaginary.

Ideals. Every story shall present one or the other ideal of Civics.

Precautions in presentation of material

(i) The teacher should not use the text-book very much at this stage of education. Books utilised should be profusely illustrated.

(ii) *Simple and Natural.* The nature of the story should be simple. The teacher should to narrate it in a natural manner and at a speed that the students may follow it. Short sentences should be used.

(iii) *Practical.* The students should be given practical education as far as possible.

(iv) *Development of Civic Qualities.* Civic 'qualities should be developed in the students through stories. An attempt should be made to develop those qualities and habits in the students that may be helpful in their practical life.

(v) *Discipline.* The training of the discipline may be imparted to the students through drill method or exercise.

Use of the Black-board. At this stage black-board should be used for explaining the pronunciation of the names to the students. Too much use of black-board shall not be useful. The teacher should write out very legibly on the black-board. If the teacher writes in a good hand witing it shall encourage the students to imitate it and also improve their hand-writing. The students should be given the training of expressing their ideas. Excursion, trips and tours shall also be helpful to impart the training in civic virtues.

Use of Dialogues. In attempting to teach the principles of Civics through dialogues, these should be very short but interesting in the lower classes. The dialogues may be of one to two minutes of duration. These should not be carried out for more than 10 to 15 minutes.

Use of charts, maps, pictures, models, etc. These teaching aids make the lesson interesting while teaching Civics. The teacher should use these things in the class room. He may also encourage the students to copy these things. Only essential things should be taught to the students at this stage of education, as far as possible.

At this stage of education the students of the age group of 11 to 14 years are taught, who are slightly grown up children. They are not very much fond of listening to stories. They are actually heading towards maturity and adolescence. They no more live in the world of imagination. At this stage, they start using their power of thinking and reasoning. Therefore, fairy tales cannot be interesting for them.

Hence, the teacher should change his course of action and method of teaching. He should keep an eye on the developed brain, vocabulary and the knowledge of the students. The subject-matter should be presented to them in a practical manner.

Story method. Story method can be used at this stage but it should not be of the type that is used at the primary stage of education. The story should be of slightly developed nature so that it may develop certain civic qualities in the students.

Other methods. Observation, narration, question-answer, project and dramatic methods may be employed at this stage of teaching civics.

Tour and excursions. The teacher should take the students out on tours and excursions and make them see the working of Municipalities, Corporations, Panchayats, Zila Parishads, etc.

Text-books. It is useful to employ text-books at this stage. These text-books should not be read out in the class. They should be used by the students at home for revising the lessons that they have learnt in the class room.

Material for Reading

Supplementary reading material may also be used by the students.

Other Areas

The students should also be encouraged to take to practical works. These should be directed towards ideals of teaching of Civics.

Black-board. As compared to the primary stage of education black-board should be used more at this stage. The teacher should draw sketches, maps, graphs, etc., on the black-board. He should explain the topics to the students with the help of these tools. The students should also be encouraged to come and write on the black-board.

Models, charts, maps etc. All these tools should be used at this stage of education to strengthen the experience of the children. The students should be encouraged to draw these tools themselves.

Radio and Films. Radio and films may also be used at this stage of education.

Home work. Home work should begin at this stage of education. The teacher should ask the students to do some home work. He should himself examine the home work with interest. If the teacher is interested in the home work the students shall also be interested in it. Most of the teaching should be oral though written work must start at this stage.

At this stage of education the teacher has to deal with adolescents, in whom the power of reasoning, thinking, arriving at decisions, etc., have developed. Their physical development is fast and considerable. The teacher should take the interests, aptitudes and the talents of the students into consideration. He should organise his teaching, with an eye on these elements.

Besides the physical development Self-Regarding Sentiment develops, at this stage of education. The teacher should not insult the students. On the other hand, they should be encouraged to do things in a way that they receive appreciation from the members of the society.

Moral development takes place by this time. Vocabulary also grows rich. The teacher should utilise these developments for the benefit of teaching Civics.

This is called the Age of Organisation'. The various talents and faculties of the children start organising themselves. The teacher should arrange his teaching with an eye on this aspect of the personality.

Use of Text-books. Text-books should be compulsorily used at this stage. The students should be encouraged to repeat and revise their class room lessons at home with the help of the text-books. They should be encouraged to prepare notes with the help of the text-books. The teacher should ask them to write out answers of certain questions, which may encourage and awaken their mental powers.

Self-study. The students should be trained in the art of self-study. They should be asked to go to Library and select out good books themselves. The teacher should help them in this task.

Discussions. At this stage students should be encouraged to take part in discussions and debates. Such discussions may be organised in the class room. Discussions and debates will improve the power of thinking, reasoning, etc.

The students should be encouraged to undertake tasks of responsibility in the school. They should be encouraged to form voluntary student bodies and take part in student's Government. These organisations should be so directed that they take up healthy activities to generate and strengthen the civic qualities of the students and prepare them for their future life.

Use of Black-board. Black-board should be used sparingly. The teacher should put down substances and other short notes, while students should be encouraged to develop that substance in the form of essays, etc.

Teaching aids. **Models, charts, maps, etc, should be used to make the lessons interesting. Tape recorders, radios, films, newspapers, magazines, etc., may be used to add to the knowledge of the Civics. The teacher can make his subject material interesting with the help of these things.**

At this stage of life, as students are very fond of roaming about, excursions to places of civic importance will add to their interest and knowledge of Civics. They should also be acquainted with the current events of social, political, religious and moral importance. They should be encouraged to take active interest in gathering information about all aspects of life. An attempt should be made to make civics teaching practical as far it is possible.

14

Teaching Techniques

Devices and Maxims

In the process of teaching civics, the teacher has to resort to the use of certain *techniques, devices* and *maxims* to facilitate and promote learning.

Techniques: A technique means a method of performance, manipulation, everything concerned with the mechanical part of an artistic performance. "A time-honoured method of imparting knowledge to pupils is connected with oral teaching." Important techniques of teaching civics are explanation, narration and description.

Devices: Devices are "certain external forms or modes which the instruction may from time to time assume." Devised or designed these different modes of presentation are *questioning-answering, illustration, home work, the use of library, and text-books, notes- assignments, - supervised* study, etc. These devices or modes of presentation and teaching are used to foster the development of knowledge and attitudes among pupils.

Maxims: The maxims are general principles serving as rules or guides. Well-known maxims of methodical procedure useful to the teacher, are proceeding from the known to the unknown, simple to the complex, indefinite to the definite, concrete to the abstract, particular to the general, psychological to logical, empirical to rational, etc.

Different Techniques

Techniques of civics teaching do not have their individual capacity. They are a part and parcel of the method of teaching. They are ways of teaching Civics to the students at different stages. An additional help to the methods of teaching, they are employed for making the teaching more effective and interesting. To quote Prof. M.P Moffat, 'All techniques should be in line with the democratic process and relate to the goals desired in the study of the topic. Techniques are employed for getting the learning under way with guidance from the teacher. They should be selected as a means of serving the best purpose of a particular line with the resultant growth for the individual."

(1) Question-answer technique

(2) Illustration

(3) Home Work

(4) Notes

(5) Assignment

(6) Supervised Study

Question-answer Technique

Questions have a very important place in the teaching of Civics. By questioning, the students may be kept attentive and active. The teacher can also test if he has succeeded in imparting the knowledge to the students.

It can also be safely tested whether the students have actually acquired the knowledge of the subject taught.

Questioning technique or the Question-answer technique can bring about the following achievements:

Awakening interest and curiosity of the students.

Encouraging the students to finish their work, within a prescribed period of time.

Developing the various mental powers of the students, namely : reasoning, thinking, imagination, etc.

Encouraging the students to take to research and discovery of new things.

Helping the students to present their various problems so that their solution may be brought about.

Helping in testing the knowledge of the students.

Questions may be of various types such as the following

(i) Questions that awaken and develop memory

(ii) Reasoning questions

(iii) Organising questions

(iv) Informative questions

(v) Evaluating questions

(vi) Comparative questions

(vii) Analytic questions

(viii) Thought-provoking questions

(ix) Interpretative questions

(x) Judicative questions.

The difficulty of this technique lies in asking of the appropriate questions. Though even the biggest fool can ask an unanswerable question, the question asked in the classroom must have some educative value. Asking such questions is no less than an art. This art, which is one aspect of the technique, is acquired through continuous practice. What is really required is complete awareness of the purpose of asking a particular question. The educator himself must possess the following abilities in order to phrase his questions skillfully:-

Accurate and comprehensive knowledge of the subject: In order to ask appropriate questions, the educator must have comprehensive knowledge of the subject, as otherwise the questions are likely to be useless. It is only this knowledge which tells the educator the questions he must ask in order to teach something.

Ability to analyse the subject: The teacher's ability in asking questions depends upon his ability to analyse the subject matter and to locate the areas of difficulty inherent in it.

Knowledge of the educand: Before embarking on questions, the educator must have knowledge of the educand's psychology so that the questions may conform to the latter's mental level, abilities and motivation.

Experience: Much of the facility, variety and accuracy of the questions depend upon the educator's experience.

Mental ability and decisiveness: In order to ask the right questions, the educator himself must have mental ability and the power to arrive at a decision quickly.

Power of expression: Linguistic ability is essential in asking questions. The educator must also have experience in modulating his voice properly.

The various reasons for asking questions are the following :

Motivation: Through questions motivation is created in the educand by arousing his curiosity, focusing his attention and awakening his interest.

Knowledge relating to the educand: The object of many questions is to find out the educand's problems, attitudes, aptitudes, knowledge, etc. Hence, one of the objectives of asking such questions is to provide the teacher with adequate knowledge concerning the educand.

Relating to old knowledge: Another reason for asking questions is to relate the new knowledge given to the educand to the old knowledge he has received. This helps the educand to assimilate the new information.

Locating difficulties: The only way of finding out the student's difficulties in learning a subject is to ask him questions. This is essential, because without removing difficulties, teaching cannot be effective.

Test of knowledge: One set of questions can be specially devised to test the knowledge that the individual educand has grasped so far. It is believed that greater accuracy in the answer of one educand than of another, indicates a better grasp of what is being taught. In our own examination system, questions are asked for this purpose.

Cooperation and active participation of educands: If the lecture on any subject is interrupted frequently to ask questions to the educands, they are compelled to attend to what is being said and perforce to remember it also. Hence, educands are asked to answer questions in order to ensure their active participation in teaching.

Means of development: Asking questions can also be the means of the intellectual and social development of the child. Social development depends on asking questions and receiving answers, because this increases mutual contact. If educands are permitted to ask questions freely, it helps in their free development.

Localising around the basic lesson: Another objective of asking questions is to localise or concentrate the subject matter around the basic subject. It sometimes happens that the educator wanders from the subject he is teaching. In such a situation the question asked by the educator or the educands once again focus his attention on the subject matter.

Practice and repetition: Another reason for asking questions is to allow the educand to apply his knowledge. In answering questions, the educand has to make use of the information he has acquired and this helps him in retaining it.

Practice and repetition: Yet another aim of asking questions is to repeat the subject, matter and give the educands practice. The text books prescribed for various levels of education are equipped with a set of questions at the end of each chapter. These questions are intended to provide practice and repetition. That is why these questions are frequently entitled 'questions for practice'.

Encouragement to thinking and observation: Sometimes the questions are deliberately framed in such a way that the answers to them cannot be found either in the educator's lecture or in any text book. In order to answer them the educand has to depend upon his observation of things, objects, individuals and surroundings which form part of his environment. He is also compelled to think about such things. Such questions have particular importance when they are used to encourage independent thinking and originality of ideas. Educands with a greater degree of creativity rarely need such stimulus for they are in the habit of observing things of life and thinking about them.

Increase in self-confidence: This method has the advantage of adding to, the educand's self-confidence because when he answers questions successfully, he realizes that he has understood and learnt the lesson.

It is clear from the foregoing account that this method of asking and answering questions is valuable both for the educator and the educand. It is not essential that a particular question must have only one specific reason behind it. It may be motivated by a number of reasons, even a few of which have not been included in the preceding account.

Apart from the aims and the language of the question, the manner in which it is asked is also significant. If the manner of questioning is faulty, the question will not fulfil the purpose for which it was asked. Hence, in asking questions, the teacher must remember the following points:

Seriousness: Questions should always be asked seriously. It is improper to laugh, show anger or smile when asking questions.

Attracting attention: Questions should be asked to arrest the educand's attention when it shows signs of wandering away from the subject being taught.

Proper frequency: The frequency of questions should be so managed that they should not be too far apart in order to avoid lassitude or disinterest and not so close together as to give the educand no time to think at all.

Proper interval: The interval between questions can be determined by the complexity of the subject matter and the intelligence of the educands.

Proper distribution: Questions should be distributed over the entire lecture so that students are compelled to attend to each part of it.

Entire class: Questions should be asked to the entire class so that every individual is forced to exercise his mind.

No side issues: Questions should not be prefaced with side issues, they should be clearly stated so as to avoid wastage of time.

No repetition: Questions should not be repeated as a matter of habit. If this is done, educands do not pay attention to it the first time, confident that it will be repeated. It should only be repeated as an exception, not as a general rule.

Neither too simple nor too difficult: The subject matter of the question should conform to the knowledge and intelligence level of the educand, neither too simple, nor too difficult. If the questions are too simple, they will not require any mental effort, while excessively difficult questions will cause excessive strain on the educand's mental faculty, without achieving the desired result.

Varied form and language: The form and language of the questions should be varied in order to bring in variety and avoid monotony and disinterest.

Collective thinking: Even if the question has been satisfactorily answered by the first educand, the educator must continue to ask the same question to the other educands so that all the aspects are clarified by the thinking of all the educands.

Encouragement: The question should be accompanied by repeated comments which encourage the students to answer the question. This builds up the confidence of the educands and makes them feel that they can answer the question if they try.

Proper language and subject matter: The language and subject matter of the question should be determined beforehand. If the educator repeats the same question in different words, it creates the impression that either the educator has no self-confidence or that he has made no preparation. In both the cases the impact on the educand is undesirable.

It is clear, therefore, from the above description, that the questions should be carefully, asked, keeping in mind the language, the style, purpose, etc.

In this technique of asking and answering questions, the answers are just as important as the questions. On the one hand, it is essential that the questions should be presented in the best possible way, and on the other, it is equally important that educands should be trained to answer questions properly. In the modern examination system, the educand's character, ability, mode of thinking, knowledge, in fact, everything is judged by the answers that he provides to the questions asked in the examination. Hence, the educator must train the educand to give the right kind of answer, and in order to do this, he himself must be aware of the qualities a good answer must possess. The following are these qualities:

Appropriateness: The first quality of a good answer is that it must answer the question without going into long and purposeless digressions. But the answer can be appropriate only when the educand's ideas are clear. Lack of clarity in ideas communicates itself to the answer and makes the answer inappropriate.

***Completeness*:** When the answer is complete, it helps the audience or the reader understand the subject. Hence the words used in the answer must convey the same sense to the listener that they convey to the user, the sense in which the latter has used them. Incomplete answers should not be accepted. The teacher must insist upon the educand's completing his sentences and providing a complete answer.

Linguistic qualities: Language is the medium in which answers are given and in order to make language intelligible it is necessary to follow certain rules of grammar. Hence, the language of the answer should be grammatically correct. Besides, it must also be simple and clear, because there is no virtue in using difficult language. The only purpose in answering a question is that the answer should provide the information which is being called for. And since language is a medium of expressing ideas, the educand must be trained in the correct use of language so that he can express his ideas with clarity and precision. As far as possible, the language of the answer should be pure not mixed with a large number of obsolete or uncommon words or foreign expressions. Again, the educand should be taught to avoid hyperbolic language because his aim is not to impress the listener with his command over the language. But the use of long and crude words should also be avoided, and in answering questions economy of expression should be exercised. Verbosity, again, is no virtue.

Order: The answer must also have properly ordered parts, the arrangement being determined by the order of the various parts of the question. If the answer is not properly ordered, it cannot be said to be good or accurate.

Quickness: When questions are being asked verbally, there is some value in the answer which is made rapidly and quickly. If the educand takes unnaturally long time in answering the question, this detracts from the merit of the answer.

Proper tone: The proper tone also plays a vital role in the answering of questions, because an unusually high tone has a bad effect on the listeners. Hence, there is no need for the educand to shout his answer, just as much as there is not any need to speak in an inaudible whisper. The educator should train the pupils to answer questions in an even and balanced tone of voice.

Illustration Technique

In the illustration technique of teaching, a subject is explained by providing examples of facts or experience of which the educands are already aware. In this technique is implicit the principle of proceeding from the known to the unknown. Very often concrete illustrations and examples are used to explain some abstract idea or theory. In this is implied a progress from the concrete to the abstract. In the same way many known facts are cited as example to help the educand to understand facts of which he is as yet unaware. The principle underlying this situation is the progress from the known to the unknown. In each case, the real aim in providing an illustration is to create an association, the right background for presenting new knowledge. This method of teaching has many advantages, among which are the following:

Overcoming difficulties: Illustrations and examples help to overcome the difficulties faced by the educand in understanding the subject. Thus, his ideas are clarified and he is enabled to understand something which had eluded his comprehension.

Assists in elaboration: Illustration help in the explanation and elaboration of abstract concepts and many scientific principles, because verbal explanation becomes more concrete so that the complex subject is somewhat simplified. For this reason, teaching by illustration is considered essential for the teaching of many sciences.

Encourages interest and curiosity: Illustration tends to increase the educand's interest in the subject and to enhance his curiosity to know more about it. In the absence of interesting illustration, the teaching of science becomes drab and monotonous. Illustrations also provide the correct distraction for the student so that the process of learning becomes interesting and compelling.

Helps memorizing: Illustrations not only help in teaching and understanding but also in memorizing or retaining subject. It helps recall because concrete facts are easier to memorize and recognise than abstract ideas.

Assists observation and experimentation: The presence of numerous illustrations during a lesson sharpens the educand's observation. Besides, the teaching of many sciences is done through experiments which serve as illustrations.

1. Non-verbal, natural, objective or concrete illustrations
2. Verbal illustrations.

Under the first category we have :

(i) Analogies,

(ii) Comparisons,

(iii) Similes,

(iv) Word pictures, etc.

This depends upon :

(i) The nature of the subject

(ii) The level of pupil's development.

Lower the classes, the more profitable will be concrete illustrations. As the child grows and his intellectual level rises, one can use pictures, diagrams, sketches, graphs, etc. Verbal illustrations such as analogies and similes, etc, should be used with children with a higher level of intelligence. They should be used with pupils at the secondary and higher secondary stage.

Simple: Use simple illustrations. They should be easily understood without any need of comments and explanations.

Relevant: Use illustrations which are relevant to the topic.

Best: Do not use too many illustrations in a single lesson. Only a few and best should be used to illustrate a lesson.

Proper occasion: Use illustrations at the proper time during the course of the lesson. Do not lay out a number of illustrations on the table before the class, just in the beginning of the lesson.

Illustrations are a good antidote to verbalism. Wisely selected, exhibited with timing and intelligently and tactfully used, illustrations prove a great asset to teaching civics.

This is another technique which can prove helpful in teaching civics to the students of secondary and higher secondary classes.

Home-work gives opportunity to pupils to plan and perform their work independent of the guidance and help of the teacher. Pupil's ability improves by the better use of books and resources outside school. It stimulates voluntary effort in the pupil to follow up the study of topics or units that appeal to his interest and accustom him to revise and consolidate the work done in the school.

In civics, home work may take many forms. Students may supplement class-notes with brief notes from or reference to text-books, standard books upon the topic or unit. They may prepare detailed notes from specialist sources. Essays may be given as homework, either as answers in examination or more exhaustive accounts.

Home-work may also be in the form of projects. The pupils should work on the projects, keep up diaries, scrap books and news cutting from books.

The teacher may also set simple problems from work books or assign multiple-choice questions. The students may be asked to prepare charts, graphs, posters, maps, etc, connected with different topics of civics.

While using home-work as a technique in teaching civics, the teacher should try to set a task interesting in itself and making intellectual demands on the pupils. Home-work should not be made too hard or too long. More time will be spent on it if the work is interesting.

Carefully organised, intelligently assigned, properly understood and regularly checked Home-work is invaluable in the teaching of civics.

There are few things the teacher of civics can do for his pupils which will be of greater practical use to them than to teach them how to take notes. Notes-taking is useful in education and life. The pupils need to take notes both from the lessons or lectures they listen to and the books and periodicals they read. Notes provide a permanent record and afford easy reference.

To be permanent, the notes are to be well-written and well set out. Pupils should be asked to rewrite the class lessons to give them proper shape. To serve the purpose of affording quick reference, notes need to be well set out under headings and sub-headings and sub-sub-headings.

Preparation of notes should be a work of the student. Dictation of notes is not a desirable practice though there is no harm if quotations and some of the definitions are dictated. Notes should be the unique product of the mind of the teacher and the mind of the taught.

The teacher should give guidance to the pupils in the art of note-taking by writing on the Black board the numbered or lettered headings and sub-headings of what he intends to talk about during the lesson. This will lay down guidelines and the students can develop their own notes under the headings. The essay type material should not be given under the headings. It is to be analysed into separate numbered or lettered points.

Right from the earlier classes the pupils should be guided in the preparation of notes. At the early stage, the teacher may give a skeleton framework for a lesson and ask the pupils to write a few sentences of their own under each heading. Later, the pupils may be put to work on making detailed notes according to a provided scheme of headings. They may be encouraged to go in for some collateral reading. It is advisable to suggest the sources from which the required material is to be collected. The pupils should be encouraged to prepare their own notes about such complicated topics which call for greater display of their wits, critical and reasoning faculties as Five Year Plans, India and the World, India as a nation, State and National Government, Democracy in India, etc. More importance should be attached to the way in which the notes are organised such as their page headings, cross references and table of contents. Checking the notes prepared by pupils the teacher will be in a position to put his finger on the pulse of the pupils in matters of extra reading.

Assignment is a very useful device of teaching civics, particularly to the pupils in secondary and higher secondary classes. Some significant topic or sub-topic is assigned to the pupil for preparation, study, revision or remedial work. The pupils are required to prepare the assignments in writing. Written assignments help in organisation of knowledge, assimilation of facts and better preparation for examinations.

Preparatory assignments: This preliminary pilot work is meant to prepare the pupils for the work to follow on the next day. It enables the teacher to lead the class with ease and understanding.

Study assignments: The study assignments vary with individuals- each according to his need and each according to his capacity. These can be- Problem-solving Assignments, Assignments on making charges, graphs, tables etc., assignments for the preparation of a topic in the light of references provided, assignments for listing points in favour or against a given argument, reading valid conclusions from statistical or visual data, etc.

Revisional assignment: These assignments are given for

(a) providing drill to the work done by the students,

(b) checking their retention and reproduction of the facts of the topic or unit, and

(c) checking the understanding of the topic.

Keeping in view the specific objectives of the subject-matter being tested, these assignments need to be worked out in advance.

Remedial assignments: Devised in the light of pupil's reactions to the three types of assignments mentioned above these assignments remove weak points and clear misunderstandings.

The civics teacher should bear in mind the following points in making assignments:

Motivating pupil effort: Students need good reasons for doing things. As they want to see the pertinence of the assigned work to their concerns, problems and needs, it is necessary for the teacher to relate the assigned work to the pupil's present needs and stimulate related interests.

Related to purpose: Assignments must be pertinent to the goals of instruction. The teacher should help students understand the learning objectives and recognize the relationship of assignments to them.

Challenge, not punishment: Assignments can be challenging if they are meaningful and promote student involvement. Assignment should never be given by the teacher as punishment.

Provide for individual differences: As students differ in interests, aptitudes and abilities, some provision for individual differences is desirable. An assignment is too difficult for some and too easy for others. The civics teacher should divide the class into subgroups and provide appropriate assignments for different groups. Differentiated assignments should be made, the quantity and quality of work expected for various grades may be indicated and the student may be allowed to choose and work towards the grade he wishes.

Co-operatively made: Both the teacher and the taught should to be actively involved in assignment. The student is doing the work for his own benefit. He should have an opportunity to contribute to the sort of assignment he is supposed to work on.

Not to be lightly tossed of as the final bell sounds: A vital part of teaching assignments require serious consideration and thoughtful planning. If well planned, the assignments can promote serious learning.

Assignment is a useful device of teaching civics. It helps the teacher know the interests of the pupils and to foresee the difficulties which the students may have to face in the learning of the topic. The teacher can guide the pupils by putting thought-provoking questions in his assignments. The guidance to read or to study a topic prepares the pupils to face the difficulties.

Supervised study is one more useful device of teaching civics. While the people work at their desks on the assignment given to them, the teacher supervises them. When the pupils find a difficulty they cannot overcome, they ask the teacher for direction and assistance. The teacher is always available at the pupils desks, watching the pupils do their work, continually on the alert for any wrong procedures that they may follow. He is always ready to direct and help them. Maxwell and Kilzer have aptly defined supervised study as the effective direction and oversight of the silent and laboratory activities of pupils. Supervised study is a directed study procedure. The pupils learn certain skills essential to successful use and understanding of civics content under the supervision of the teacher. As the teacher gets an opportunity of observing the pupils from a close quarter he can be of considerable help in more ways than one. Pupils benefit from his attention. This brings to the situation that knowledge of each pupil is accumulated from observation. He can detect a pupil's habits, efficiency of study skills and degree of progress. At the spot guidance proves very useful. As the errors are corrected at once pupil's time is saved enabling the teacher to redirect his efforts.

Democratic relations: Supervised study encourages democratic human relations. Pupils learn to share materials, to wait their turn and to understand their own difficulties. This develops a sympathetic attitude towards the difficulties of others. Aware of individual differences, teachers become guides.

Guidance: As the teacher supervises each pupil, who proceeds slowly, he goes into effective learning experience guided by teacher's questions or suggestions to overcome difficulties. The discontented pupil can be given a more satisfying interpretation. The pupil who works more rapidly and requires a greater challenge to use his ability can be further motivated to put in his best.

Effective use of learning material: As the teacher constantly supervises materials like books, reference books, charts, maps, etc, these can be used more efficiently. The pupils learn the specific types of information available in various reference books.

Developing better pupil-teacher relations: Instead of being a hard task master the teacher is a helper and a guide displaying sympathy and understanding. Able to understand the pupil and his difficulties he is in a position to spur him on to greater effort.

Critical thinking and discrimination: The supervised study is useful in establishing habits of critical thinking and discrimination in evaluating ideas and in objective investigation of facts on the part of pupils. It encourages the pupil to compare facts and to evaluate their sources. He learns to withhold his opinion until enough evidence is available to justify a conclusion. Thus, pupils learn to examine the material critically which is a valuable experience.

From the known to the unknown: The most natural way of teaching a lesson in civics is to proceed from something that the pupils already know to the facts they do not know. Old knowledge serves as a hook on which the new can be hanged. To make the new knowledge acceptable, the civics teacher must try to win over some part of the child's past experience to act as host on which ideas, sensations and impressions can be apperceived or assimilated. An attempt has to be made to remind the pupils of what they already know so as to be ready to pin the new knowledge on it. The civics teacher must search diligently to find which of pupils experiences have been such that by recalling them, he is likely to ensure a ready welcome for the new knowledge.

In teaching a lesson on India and the United Nations, the teacher may ask the pupils to describe the organs of the UNO and the various attempts made by it to bring peace in the world and then introduce the pupils to the contribution of India in UNO.

From the simple to the complex: The civics teacher should divide the lesson in such a manner that the ideas which are easier to understand are used as a starting point and the difficult ones follow in the proper order during the lesson. 'Simplicity' and 'complexity' should be determined from the pupil's point of view. While teaching any topics of civics, the teacher should begin with the most striking and prominent features of a topic, and then continue to add further details. While teaching a lesson on Social and Economic Reconstruction to the VIII class students, he shall tell that what is needed to be done is removal of poverty, checking increase in population, meeting the problem of unemployment, etc. He should analyse each issue and discuss it in detail.

From the indefinite to the definite: While vagueness characterises the early ideas of the pupils, the aim of teaching is to make ideas clear and precise. This can be done by making pupils interested in the lesson, and take an active part in learning. Good teaching of civics necessitates that every definition, concept, idea discussed in the lesson stands out clearly in the pupil's mind. The use of pictures, charts, graphs, films, filmstrips, analogies, comparisons, etc., should be frequently made to clarify ideas and make them definite.

From the concrete to the abstract: The civics teacher should try to teach his subject in a psychological way. He should be careful about the suitable arrangement of the subject-matter and the child's nature. He should be fully conversant with the requirements of the syllabus and understand the pupil's interests, needs, reactions and mental make-up. There should be psychological selection of the matter to be presented. Then he can logically arrange the matter into sequences and steps. The civics teacher should proceed from the concrete to the abstract, from the simple to the complex, from the known to the unknown. In really good lessons on civics, pupils are gradually made to learn difficult facts in a very easy manner.

From empirical to rational: Empirical knowledge is based on observation and first-hand experience while rational knowledge implies abstraction and argumentative approach. The child has the rational basis for any knowledge much after he has experienced it in his day-to-day life. In civics teaching, Local Self Government would make better sense, if it were taught in the practical context of everyday life, instead of in the format of abstract theory.

15

Pace of Progress

Now, we attempt to make a sociological analysis of the Community Development Projects which have been sponsored by the Govern-ment of the Indian Union to assist the reconstruction of the agrarian economy and the rural society.

The Planning Commission in its First Five-Year Plan has described the Community Development Projects as the method through which Five-Year Plan seeks to initiate a process of transformation of the social and economic life of the villages. It is, according to an U.N.O. report, `designed to promote better living for the whole community with the active participation and, if possible, on the initiative of the Community, but if this initiative is not forthcoming, by the same use of techniques for arousing it and stimulating it in order to secure its active and enthusiastic response. The Community Development Projects are of vital importance, according to Pandit Nehru, not so much for the material achievements that they would bring about, but much more so, because they seem to build up the community and the individual and to make the latter the builder of his own village centres and of India in the larger sense.'

The word 'Community Development' itself is a novel nomenclature in India. As the Report of the Team for the Study of the Community Projects and National Extension Service (popularly known as the Balwantrai Committee Report) states, 'We have so far used such terms as rural development, constructive work, adult education and rural uplift to denote certain of its aspects. The word "Community" has, for the past many decades, denoted religious or caste groups or, in some instance, economic groups not necessarily living in one locality; but with the inauguration of the community development programme in this country, it is intended to apply it to the concept of the village community as a whole, cutting across caste, religious and economic differences. It is a programme which emphasises that the interest in the development of the locality is necessarily and unavoidably common to all the people living there. It is sociologically significant to note that to renovate the agrarian economy and the rural society through the active participation of millions of villagers, the sponsors of this movement could not find an appropriate term in any of the State languages of India to symbolize this vast process. We will examine the postulates underlying this new connotation of the term " Community " subsequently.

Factors at Work

The Community Development Projects emerged as a result of inspiration from the following earlier experiments

(i) Intensive rural development activities carried out at Sevagram and the Sarvodaya centres in the Bombay State; (ii) The Firka Development Schemes in Madras; (iii) Experiments to build up community centres for Refugees at Nilokheri and other places; (iv) And more particularly from the Pilot Projects at Etavah and Gorakhpur in the U.P. under the inspiration of Albert Meyers.

This idea also arose out of a realization that various efforts made by the Government departments such as Agriculture, Animal Husbandry, Co-operation, Health, Education and others which were carried on separately, should be co-ordinated to make them more effective. Further, according to the sponsors of the movement, this programme was launched with a view to changing the very philosophical basis of rural reconstruction. Most of the other institutions approached the village and rural reconstruction work in a philanthropic spirit. The Community Development Movement 'wants to create a psychological change in the villagers... It aims at inculcating in the villagers new desires, new incentives, new techniques, and a new confidence so that this vast reservoir of human resources may be used for the growing economic development of the country'.

The Community Development Programme was inaugurated on October 2, 1952. Fifty-five Community Projects were launched. Each Project Area comprised about 300 villages, covering an area of 450 to 500 sq. miles, i.e., about 1,50,000 acres with a population of about 2,00,000 persons. A project area was divided into three Development Blocks of hundred villages, each with a population of about 65,000 persons. Each Block was divided into about twenty groups, each containing five villages. Each group of villages was being served by a Gram-Sevak (the village level worker). Of the five villages, one generally became the headquarters of the Gram-Sevak.

The programme launched in 1952 was extended to wider areas at the end of the First Five-Year Plan. There 603 National Extension Service Blocks, and 553 Community Development Blocks covering 1,57,000 villages and a population of 88.8 million persons were created. Nearly one out of every three villages in India was brought within the orbit of this Programme.

The Second Five-Year Plan proposed to bring every village in India under this scheme, 40 per cent of the area being brought under a more intensive development scheme. In all 3,800 additional Extension Service Blocks will be set up, 1,120 of these being converted into Community Project Blocks. The ambitious scheme has, however, been subsequently modified.

The Community Development Programme is broadly divided into three phases, viz., the National Extension phase, the Intensive Community Development Project phase and the post-Intensive Development phase. Of course, it is not laid down that everywhere the first two phases must follow each other, the National Extension phase in some areas having been skipped over to usher in the Intensive Community Development Project phase. Usually, the period of the first and the second phase is to last for three years each.

In the first phase, the areas selected are subjected to the method of providing services on the ordinary rural development pattern with a lesser Governmental expenditure. In the intensive phase, the blocks selected are subjected to more composite and more intensive development schemes with larger Governmental expenditure. In the post-Intensive phase, it is presumed that the basis for self-perpetuation of the process initiated during the earlier phases has been created and the need for special Government expenses reduced. Slowly the areas are left in the charge of the Departments for the development.

In 1952-53 series of community projects, the provision per block was Rs. 22 lakhs for a period of three years. This was reduced to Rs. 15 lakhs for the 1953-54 series. The present provision for the N.E.S. stage of three years is Rs. 4 lakhs and for the Community Development stage is Rs. 8 lakhs, making up a total of Rs. 12 lakhs for six years. In other words, the annual expenditure per Block was reduced first from Rs. 7.3 lakhs to Rs. 5 lakhs and now to Rs. 2 lakhs.

An imposing list of activities has been prepared by the sponsors of the Community Development Projects. They include various items connected with the following eight categories of undertakings

(1) Agriculture and related matters; (2) Communications; (3) Education; (4) Health; (5) Training; (6) Social Welfare; (7) Supplementary Employment; and (8) Housing.

The fourth Evaluation Report of 1957 adopted different criteria for classifying activities undertaken by the Community Development Projects. They divided the programmes of activities into the following major categories: (1) Constructional programmes; (2) Irrigational programmes; (3) Agricultural programmes; and (4) Institutional and other programmes. The detailed list of the various activities undertaken under each of these programmes is as under:

Constructional programmes: 'Kutcha' roads, 'Pucca' roads, culverts, drains, pavement of streets, school buildings, community centre buildings, dispensary buildings, houses for the Harijans and drinking water sources.

Irrigation programmes; Wells, pumping sets, tube wells and tanks.

Agricultural programmes: Reclamation, soil conservation, consolidation of holdings, improved seeds, manure and fertilizer, pesticides, improved methods of cultivation and improved implements.

Institutional and other programmes: Youth Clubs, Women's Organisations, Community Centres, 'Vikas Mandals,' co-operative societies, distribution stores, maternity centres, dispensaries, veterinary dispensaries, key village centres, panchayats, adult literacy centres, primary schools, 'dai' training centres, cottage industries, production-cum-training centres, demonstration plots, soakage pits, smokeless 'chulha'.

An elaborate organization has been created to implement Community Development Projects; it is known as the Community Project Administration. Originally functioning under the Planning Commission, it is now under the charge of the newly created Ministry of Community Development.

The entire administration is composed of four major types-the Central administration, the State administration, the District organization and the Project administration. The power and the control flow from top to bottom making it a hierarchic bureaucratic organization. At every level there is an Executive Officer, functioning with the aid of a Development Committee and helped by an Advisory Board. At the Centre, there is an Administrator, at the State level there is a Development Commissioner, at the District level there is a District Development Officer of Collector's grade and at the Project level a Project Level Officer equipped with a staff of some 125 supervisors and village level workers.

The Development

We will now survey the achievements of this programme. It is extremely difficult to give a total quantitative assessment of these achievements for a number of reasons. First, to the best of present writer's knowledge, such overall data have not been compiled. Second, it is not very easy to separate the achievements of the Community Development Projects from those brought about by other agencies. Some observers have pointed out that a number of activities attributed to the Community Development Project movement should, in fact, be credited to other agencies. We shall, however, accept for the purposes of evaluation, the achievement data in regard to constructional, irrigational, agricultural, institutional and other activities as collected by the Fourth Report of the Programme Evaluation Organization. It is a data carefully collected from seventeen Project units from different States studied by the Project Evaluation Organization.

The impact of the Community Development Projects has been subjected to analysis and evaluation by a number of scholars and organizations. Prof. Wilson, Prof. Carl Taylor, Prof. Oscar Lewis, Prof. Opler and his team, Prof. Dube, Prof. Mandelbaum and many others have attempted to assess the nature of the impact of the Community Development Projects on the life of the rural people. The Programme Evaluation Organization has also been doing assessment continuously and their Reports are valuable documents. The Bench Mark Surveys also provide insight into the working of the Community Projects. The popularly known Balwantrai Committee Report on the subject is one of the latest authoritative evaluation. Prof. Dube's India's Changing Villages is the latest comprehensive and systematic analysis of Community Projects, although based on a very intensive examination of only two different types of villages in U.P. it will be very difficult indeed to adequately indicate here the main findings of these studies and reports separately. However, a certain general pattern of evaluation emerges which deserves our careful attention.

Various Trends

It should be noted at the very outset that all the scholars and organisations who have evaluated the Community Development Projects, fundamentally accept the major postulates of the economic policy of the Government of India and of the Five-Year Plans. Further, all these evaluators have assumed that the Community Development Movement is both desirable and appropriate as a technique of reconstructing the agrarian economy and society of India. Not one of them has even raised a single query or attempted to critically examine the major postulates of the Movement. It is, therefore, necessary to make explicit the major assumptions taken for granted by others. As Prof. Carl Taylor remarks: " The whole concept and plan of Community Development-Extension Programme is that local self-help village groups will mobilize their natural and human resources for local improvements of all kinds and all technical agencies of Government will aid them in this undertaking." It implies, according to him (i) initiative of people in both formulating and executing the programmes. (ii) therefore the schemes of generating and organizing a large number of voluntary associations almost of primary group nature and also a wide variety of local institutions, (iii) reliance upon group work techniques, (iv) active participation of people in all the stages of implementation, resulting in local leadership, (v) governmental administrative machinery which acts as an assisting body. The personnel of the administrative machinery, at all levels, should not merely be equipped with administrative and other technical skills but must be fairly well-versed in social skills of evoking voluntary association and community participation.

The philosophy under-laying this Movement, in the context of the Indian agrarian society, therefore, implicitly accepts the following major sociological assumptions: (i) the individuals, sections, groups and strata forming the Village Community have a large number of common interests, sufficiently strong to bind them together; (ii) the interests of the various groups and classes within the village are both sufficiently like and common to create general enthusiasm as well as a feeling of development for all; (iii) the interests of the different sections of the community are not irreconciliably conflicting; (iv) the State is a super-class, impartial, non-partisan association and that the major policies of the Government are of such a nature that they do not further sharpen the inequalities between the existing social groups; (v) people's initiative and enthusiasm and active participation are possible in the extant village communities because they have common interests.

None of the scholars or the committees have critically inquired as to whether these assumptions about both the Village Communities in India and the Indian State and its governmental policies are valid or not.

However, we will review at present only the major findings of these scholars and committees regarding the operation of

Community Development Projects and their impact upon the life of the rural people.

Prof. Taylor and most of the scholars feel that the Government machinery, though staffed by intelligent, hard-working and conscientious persons, has not still assimilated the true spirit underlying the entire programme. The Community Development-Extension Programme is operated more as an executive assignment. According to Prof. Taylor, the administration of the programme is predominantly based on aid from and reliance on the Government. The initiative of the people is still lacking. The Government machinery relies more on propaganda and spectacular results rather than on group work and voluntary creative participation. According to Prof. Taylor, a certain amount of active governmental participation was inevitable in a country like India during the earlier phases of the movement. But if that earlier phase was not crossed over and if the movement did not elicit active participation and initiative from the people, the very basis of the Community Development Programme would crumble. The danger has been slowly raising its head.

Prof. S. C. Dube also comes to the same conclusion. "Planning so far appears to be from the top down ... It is necessary to examine the implications and results of the present trends in planning. Because of the unique curbs on Projects autonomy its officials hesitated to demonstrate much initiative. What was worse they tended on the official level to accept orders from above, i.e., from the State headquarters, without question or comment, and this despite pronounced private reservations. As an outcome of this trend the officials were oriented less towards the village people, and more towards the pleasing of their official superiors." And further, "A large number of Project-sponsored activities are directed along the lines of traditional government `drives' rather than according to the proved principles of extension work. Visible accomplishments under such pressure and stimulation and completion of physical targets are greatly valued, and too little attention is given to the question of finding out if the movement is really acquiring roots in the village society." According to Prof. Dube, government servants function as bureaucrats and have not become agents of change with an active social service mentality.

The Balwantrai Committee Report is critical of the structural foundation of the Community Administration. According to the Report:

"admittedly, one of the least successful aspects of the C.D. and N.E.S. work is its attempt to evoke popular initiative. We have found that few of the local bodies at a level higher than the village panchayat have shown any enthusiasm or interest in this work; and even the panchayats have not come into the fields to any appreciable extent. An attempt has been made to harness local initiative through the formation of *ad hoc* bodies mostly with the nominated personnel and invariably advisory in character. These bodies have so far given no indication of durable strength nor the leadership necessary to provide the motive force for continuing the improvement of economic and social condition in rural areas. So long as we do not discover or create a representative and democratic institution which will supply the `local interest, supervision and care necessary to ensure that expenditure of money upon local objects conforms with the needs and wishes of the locality,' invest it with adequate power and assign to it appropriate finances, we will never be able to evoke local interest and excite local initiative in the field of development."

The report suggests that the elected Village Panchayat at village level and an elected Panchayat Samiti at the block level act as agencies to execute the Community Development Programme and the present Block level and Village level bureaucratic machinery be wound up.

In short the major criticism offered by scholars and Evaluating Committees boils down to the following major points: (i) its bureaucratic nature; (ii) absence of elective principle at any level in the machinery; (iii) decisions taken at the top and communicated below, almost like executive fiats; (iv) considerable confusion in the overall administration of the country, expressed in the relationship between the Project Administration and other Government departments; (v) considerable confusion and conflict with regard to powers and duties, and relative position and seniority within the staff of different departments as a result of their being interlocked with the Project Administration;

(vi) duplication of work for a section of the administrative personnel and resultant overworking and the problem of divided loyalty towards functions; (vii) absence of social service mentality; and (viii) lack of social work skills among the staff.

In regard to the actual achievement of the Projects, within the cluster of villages operated by a Gram-sevak, his headquarters-village receives more benefits. Further, it has been found that bigger villages get greater benefits. Similarly, commercial belts receive more facilities than the non-commercial agrarian belts. As the Evaluation Report points out

"There is wide disparity in the distribution of the achievement and therefore of the benefits of the community project programmes. This disparity exists as between different blocks in the project areas. Within the blocks it exists as between the H.Q. villages of Gram-sevaks, the villages easily accessible to them, and the villages not so easily accessible. Within the villages, it exists as between cultivators and non-cultivators; and within the cultivating classes, it exists as between cultivators of bigger holdings and larger financial resources and those of smaller holdings and lesser financial resources. This is a matter of serious concern not only in terms of regional and social justice but also in terms of the political consequences that may ensue in the context of the increasing awakening among the people."

Though this disparity of benefits is recognised, none of the scholars or evaluation organizations has made a systematic analysis of its consequences; its ecological repercussions are not even seen by them. The Indian rural society is undergoing transformation under the impact of numerous forces today. Government's programmes of industrialization electrification, land reforms, major irrigation works, export and import plans, taxation, commercialization and monetization of various sectors of economic life, and unification of the country through development of means of communication, are producing important changes in the agrarian areas also. The impact of urbanization and industriali-sation upon the pattern of rural life are being studied by a number of scholars. Unfortunately, however, none of the evaluators has analysed the impact of the Community Develop-ment Project upon the rural life from this wider perspective. Nor have these evaluators indicated the significance of this uneven growth of various regions, blocks, and villages.

The advantages of the improvement, as pointed out by the Community Evaluation Reports, are taken by larger cultivators. As Prof. Dube points out

"Although the ideal of the Community Development Project was to work for the many-sided development of the entire community, from the foregoing account of its work ...it is clear that its significant and best organized activities were confined to the field of agricultural extension and consequently the group of agriculturists benefitted the most from them. A closer analysis of the agricultural extension work itself reveals that nearly 70 per cent of its benefits went to the elite group and to the more affluent and influential agriculturists. The gains to poorer agriculturists were considerably smaller .... For the economic development of this group, as well as for that of the artisans and agricultural labourers, no programmes were initiated by the Project."

Similar observations are made by all Project Evaluation Reports as well as by scholars like Mandelbaum. This impact of the Community Development Project is fraught with serious consequences. It sharpens the gulf between the rich and the poor cultivators. It makes artisans and agricultural labourers relatively more handicapped than the cultivators and therefore generates greater inequality and wider chasm between the affluent farmers, the agrarian capitalist class on one hand and the poorer strata, composed of poor peasants, artisans and agricultural labourers on the other. It implies that in the context of the economy which produces for market and profit, the poor farmers and other strata are made weaker in their competitive strength against the richer strata.

The organizations for rural change are dominated by the upper sections of the rural population. As pointed out by the Programme Evaluation Report, " When one considers the pattern of membership in village organizations, be they Co-operative Societies, Vikas Mandals, Gram Panchayats or Nyaya Panchayats, one clearly finds that the membership is confined to the large cultivators and that the smaller cultivators as well as landless agricultural labourers, have practically no stake in the organizations of the village." As Prof. Dube has pointed out

"The Community Development Project sought the co-operation of the existing village institutions such as the village panchayat and the adalati panchayat schools and co-operative societies. Persons holding offices in these bodies or otherwise prominent in the activities were regarded as ` Village Leader', and the development officials made a special effort to work closely with them. Some others who had contacts with politicians and officials were also included in this category and were consulted in matters connected with the project .... Thus a group of village people having contacts with the world of officials and politicians largely came to be viewed as the local agents of change .... The first mistake was in assuming that these people were the leaders .... Because of their association with the officials and the urban ways of life these leaders as a group had come to possess a special status within the community, but the average villager did not trust them without reservations. Some of the common stereotypes regarding government officials applied in a modified form to these village officials who were recognised as having a semi-government status .... Among others included in the category of ` traditional leaders' were the important and influential people in the village. Naturally most of them were from the dominant landowning group. In identifying power and status with leadership, an important and emerging aspect of group dynamics was ignored .... The undue emphasis in working with ` traditional leaders' was construed by villagers as an effort on the part of the Government to maintain a status quo in the internal power rela-tions within the village communities and indirectly as a step to support the domination of the landowning groups."

The same conclusion is drawn by almost all the evaluators. This reliance on the upper stratum of the village population by the Government has sociological significance which cannot be underestimated. Nay it has serious social implication in terms of the dynamics of rural society. It implies not merely a hold over the economic resources in that area by a small upper class, but also a hold over the political, social and cultural life of the community. It further means that in agrarian area, as a result of the functioning of the community development programmes, a stratum becomes strengthened economically and politically, and utilizes various institutions for its own end. It also means that in agrarian area, the Community Development Projects are creating an institutional and associational matrix wherein the Government buttresses the economically dominant classes, and in their turn, the economically dominant classes strengthen the power of the present rulers of the State. This development has dangerous significance for the all-round development of the rural society and also for the unprivileged strata of the agrarian area which constitute the bulk of the rural people. It is very unfortunate that the implication of this developmental tendency in terms of class polarization in agrarian area, and the role of the state as an agency of the upper stratum is not fully appreciated.

Almost all the evaluators have recognized that the contributions to be made by the village people are felt very burdensome by the lower sections of the people. Shramdan is the technique by which masses were asked to make contribution to the Community Development. Prof. Dube's observations on Shramdan as a voluntary movement of village self-help deserves attention

"From a close observation and analysis of four Shramdan drives ...certain points emerge that explain differences in reactions to Shramdan. The village elite, as well as the upper status groups have, on the whole, welcomed the Shramdan drives, and through them the construction and repairs of roads. They gained from it in two ways. First, the repaired and newly built roads facilitated the transport of their sugarcane and grain. Secondly, in these drives they could assert their position of leadership and prestige in the village .... because of their status they assumed supervisory roles in this work, and left the hardest and less desirable part of the job to be done by the people of the lower status and lower income groups. Even this token participation won the praise and acclaim of the officials and outside political leaders. The poorer groups, on the other hand, had no practical and visible gain from these projects. Few among them owned bullock carts, and most of them did not have large quantities of sugarcane or wheat to be transported to the urban markets. Their work did not win much praise from outsiders. All that they got often was a formal acknowledgement from the lower officials and some village leaders. They not only had to work hard, but they also lost the wages for the day, which they otherwise might have earned. This explains why many of them viewed this thing as a revival of *begar*, a practice under which influential landowners and government officials compelled the poorer people to work without wages or at nominal wages and which is now prohibited by law."

New associations have been launched or some of the old associations performing those functions have been claimed to be revitalized. Youth clubs, women's organizations, community centres, schools, libraries, adult education classes and social education centres form the predominant type of institutions. These organizations have emerged only in a very few areas. Excepting some institutions like Bhajan Mandalis or Akhadas at some places, very few institutions have taken roots in the villages. A large number of these institutions are operating more as paper organizations. Almost all the evaluators have indicated the failure of this section of the Community Development Programme.

Almost all critics including Taylor, Wilson, the Balwantrai Committee, Dube and V. K. R. V. Rao indicate these trends. They criticise one aspect of the programme or the other. They suggest some symptomatic remedies to cure the ills. Prof. Taylor wants thousands of trained officers, equipped with social skills to make this programme a success. The Balwantrai Committee makes certain proposals for making Village Panchayats and Panchayat Samitis the instruments for operating the Community Development Programmes. It also wants to abolish two-phased division in the form of N.E.S. and C.D. with unequal financial allocations and creation of six-year unit with larger financial allocation. Further, it wants the C.D. Programme to concentrate more on select items like increase in production rather than cultural improvements. According to them, there is nothing wrong with the major premise of the Community Development Projects, nor is there any fundamental fallacy in the postulates of the Five-Year Plans. According to these evaluators, the failure of the C.D. Projects in essence is due to one or more of the following factors: ignorance, lack of will on the part of the personnel, faulty organizational principles, fatalism of the vast bulk of the people, lack of technical and social skills, or wrong choice in selection of items. According to Prof. Dube, the main obstacles are: " (i) the general apathy of a considerable part of the village population, (ii) suspicion and distrust of officials and outsiders; (iii) failure on the part of the Project to evolve effective and adequate media of communications; (iv) tradition and cultural factors."

Are these costly projects, which do not fulfil their proclaimed major objectives, worth continuing? Are they not becoming agencies which do not merely defeat the very purpose for which they are ostensibly launched, but are actually playing the harmful role of strengthening the richer strata in the agrarian society?

In spite of the fact that considerable factual material has been collected which indicates the class structure of the agrarian society, and which also points out how the agrarian proletariat, a large number of uneconomic holders, and an enormous group of ruined artisans constitute the bulk of the rural community, none of these evaluators confronts the question, viz., how can a programme which essentially supports the upper strata of the rural population and which primarily benefits this minority in strengthening it institutionally, be called a Community Develop-ment Programme? The very name, to say the least, is deceptive.

Sociologically, the Community Development Programme is not merely proving futile in its acclaimed goals, but is becoming harmful.

Social Organisation

The large-scale development plans which are now under way in India are, in the main plans for technological and economic change. As these plans become realised, they cannot but have effect on social organization and be affected by it. Such reciprocal influence is now being felt in various spheres of Indian society. Certain broad trends of this interaction can be stated, as they are seen in the joint family, in caste structure, in village organization and in relation between villagers and government.

The joint family has long been the common form of family organization in India, sanctified in scripture and sanctioned in secular law. It consists typically of a set of men, related as fathers and sons, or brothers, together with their wives and children. The several nuclear families thus grouped together form a single unit of consumers and often also a single producing unit. The property of all is held in common under the trusteeship of the senior male; every male child is entitled to a share of the joint family property. All in the joint family are fed from a single kitchen and receive money from the family purse. Among cultivators, all in the joint family work together for the family's crop.

Formation and fission go on now as they have before but the regular tendency is toward smaller joint families. Many factors are involved in this, among them the increased chances for a man to earn a living as an individual rather than as one of a joint family team, and the decreased willingness to be subservient to the head of the family or to pool both effort and income. An added impetus toward splitting the larger joint families has come about in those areas where land reform measures have been introduced.

A common feature of these measures is to set a limit to the amount of land which any family may own. Hence in these circumstances the men of a large joint family hasten to split up into nuclear families when such reform measures are brought about lest they be restricted to a holding uneconomical for a large family group. With formal separation there tends to be separation in fact also, at least in so far as the joint family is a producing unit. But in many cases the larger family group is a much more efficient producing unit than is the small family group. This is especially true where continuous work is required, as where ripening crops must be watched against animal and human predators and when field labour must be quickly mobilized and intensively worked, as at harvest. The larger joint family is also more apt than the smaller to be able to raise the capital necessary for implements and animals. Thus one rather unforeseen, though by no means inevitable, consequence of land reform may be a hastening of the push toward smaller families with some consequent decline in agricultural efficiency.

Caste structure has close ties with village economics. In the classical system of relations among castes in a village, the *jajmani* system, the various non-cultivating castes provided specialised services for the cultivators and received foodstuffs in return. The economic interdependence is strictly regulated by social and religious patterns which both keep the caste groups segregated in certain respects and require communication and interchange in other respects. Caste ranking and economic status were, and for many villages still are, closely linked. Caste rank is particularly manifest through ritual symbols: a group which was economically well off could acquire ritual hallmark to raise its relative position in the hierarchy.

The results of the development programmes of the last century in the fields of transportation and communication, in the spread of Western education, in the frequent switch from subsistence crops to cash crops, have all had consequences on village caste relations. But the criteria of ritual rank are not greatly changed the eating of meat and the performance of menial services are still stigmas of lower rank and ritual rank remains a main concern in the village. While there may be some relaxation of the taboos on interdining among castes there is no easing of the prohibition of intermarriage.

As the newer development programmes take effect there often is some levelling of economic differences among the villagers. The less high castes, newly advantaged, jockey for higher ritual rank and may attempt to use their new political franchise to gain both economic and ritual prerogatives for their caste.

One exception to the levelling effect of the newer development programmes must be noted. The lowest caste, those who are mainly landless labourers, often gain nothing at all from the irrigation projects and the redistribution of land. They have nothing to begin with, nothing which can be improved, no means of getting an economic start and so they remain economically as well as socially disadvantaged. The gap between them and the other villagers frequently widens rather than diminishes on account of development projects.

The changing nature of caste has effect on village social organization and on agricultural output. The social and economic systems were both relatively stable over many centuries partly because they reinforced each other. Now that both are being modified though still closely connected, changes in one may accelerate changes in the other. Thus the *jajmani* system of traditional, personal, exchange relations is being replaced by contractual, impersonal, pecuniary relations. Many cultivators who could summon sudden aid if quickly needed from among their traditional associates of other castes now can hire labour only if they have the cash. This process is a familiar one and has been going on in India for a century or more. But in recent years the full effect of the change is being widely felt.

As the rights and obligations of one village caste to another tend to lapse, so does the whole village drift away from the ceremonial order within which these reciprocal patterns were organized and reinforced. The traditional caste system provides for a division of labour, the traditional ceremonial order stipulates how and when the various divisions co-operate and are rewarded. With the loosening of the system of economic cooperation under religious auspices there is not usually available as effective a plan of village co-operation under purely economic or political auspices, and agricultural output may decline for this reason.

Governmental agencies, of both the central and the state administrations, have attempted to encourage the growth of a new social organization in the village which would be able to cope with modern problems and could make the transition from the old order to some new procedure. Legislation has been passed in some provinces and funds provided to enable village councils, panchayats, to be formed and to function. In name, these are the same as the traditional councils which have for centuries adjudicated disputes among villagers. In manner of composition, in function, they are very different. The members of the new panchayat must be elected, must electioneer; in the old, they were accorded place by universal respect and could hardly keep that respect if they pressed their claims. The old councils were arbitrary, conserving agencies whose prime function was to smooth over or settle village friction. The new panchayats are supposed to be innovating, organizing bodies working for changes rather than conserving solidarity.

Where they have been installed, the new panchayats seem generally to be off to a shaky start. There is some tendency for them to become the battle-ground of village factionalism. Factionalism has long been a frequent disrupter of joint village action. The traditional ceremonial order provides opportunities for the healing of factional breaks by mandatory co-operation towards common ceremonial goals. With the passing of the old ceremonial order, there is not the same rejoining of those whom factional disputes have rent asunder. And village elections may become little more than ways of crystallizing each opposing and non-cooperating faction. In some villages the new panchayat is less a forum for factionalism than it is an empty form set up for the satisfaction of visiting officials. In such villages the older panchayat continues to function much as it has before.

But as a social form, it is not felt adequate by many villagers to deal with the new economic and technological influences-the procuring of irrigation water or of fertilisers, for example-and these influences reach even to relatively remote villages. Hence there is widely in Indian villages today a process of social change from the traditional forms and orders to some other forms. The newer forms may not be those proposed by legislators and planners but they are also not, it seems probable, a mere recasting of the older social system.

We have made sweeping generalisations regarding rural life and its problems. We have depicted village life as if the pattern was similar in all parts of the country. We have ignored the facts of alien invasions, different governments, varying religions and multiple levels of culture, as if they had little or no effect on our rural life. It is true that all parts of the country were not equally touched by social upheavals, invasions or conquests, but today we are becoming more and more aware of specific differences in different parts of the country. We know, however, the basic similarities in all villages and the personalities of villages as well. We know the common problems, and we also know the rough and ready prescriptions for our rural ills. What is needed in rural studies, today, is the shaping of effective scientific techniques of rural analysis to understand the problems of rural life in their wider contexts.

The status structure of our villages is in a fluid state. While still clinging to the traditional ways of eking out an income, the villager is today experiencing the impact of technology and competitive economy. Land is not in abundance, while the size of the family is on the increase. The artisan castes, no longer can secure a minimum level of living, out of their traditional occupation in the village and from the *jajmans* whom they still cater to. They either migrate to centres of greater opportunities, or live a precarious existence. More people today are in the grip of the money-lender than ever before and co-operative societies cannot as yet size up the want and poverty of the villages. The channels of rural finance have changed their course. The abolition of the zamindari has dimmed the halo around the heads of the high caste men. They are nervous about losing their rights-which they have enjoyed from time immemorial-and they are not prepared to give in without a struggle. Fighting tooth and nail they are trying to maintain their hold on the village. If they have lost some rights, they still have wealth, and that means power. Why should they not use their wealth in new ways to strengthen their position of importance? So that many of them have adopted money-lending as their profession, which till now was the much-maligned monopoly of the village-Bania. The breakdown of the status relations has deprived the artisan elements of the village of concessions in kind which helped now and then to relieve their chronic distress. They still yoke themselves to the village economy but they have been caught in deep furrows.

The relationship of status factors to the acceptance of innovations in dress, food and farm practices is important in the context of social change. A number of investigations carried out in various parts of the world on farm practices, for example, 'have highlighted farm-ownership, education, income, size of the farm and social participation as being associated with the adoption of improved farm practices.' Contacts with urban centres, and improved communications are helping adoption of innovations.

Leaders in community affairs are not useful in dissemination of new farm practices. On the other hand innovators are not likely to be leaders in community affairs. This is an area of study that must be given due consideration in planning and action research.

We are apt to isolate village leadership in its traditional setting. In the Indian villages of the past, leaders were born, but now in the new setup it is not so. The frequency of leadership from sections or castes other than the dominant one, requires evaluation. Goods, today, are not necessarily delivered through the traditional leaders. The new leaders may not even be from the status groups, neither have they jumped into the scene by the spin of the coin. The social awareness of the people is the medium which fashions new leadership.

We have simplified the social structure of our country by equating it with the magic word 'caste'. Caste is no doubt a complex structure, but it is also a dynamic one. Three significant periods in caste history are worth mentioning. Caste as it was in the time of Manu, a fluid structure, flexible and mobile; vertical as well as horizontal features characterised caste as is understood in the context of anuloma and pratiloma marriages, i.e., marriages prescribed and those forbidden. This was the formulative period of the caste constitution. Caste in the medieval period became rigid and stereotyped. The rigidity encouraged fission, but circumscribed the chances of fusion. The challenge of the rigid caste system was met by religious revivalism in which sectarian and other types of castes emerged to accommodate deviants and aspirants after social status. A critical evaluation of the caste structure at this period would show the caste system as a cross between 'feudalism' and, the 'schism of the soul' to use a Toynbean phrase. Today caste-structure is fighting a battle of survival, as it were, and is mobilising forces and factors, that were once dormant or unintegrated. The saving factors are the not-too-clear lines of demarcation among the castes, between the higher and intermediate and between the latter and lower castes. The intermediate castes most of whom are artisans, usually bridge the disparities between the two ends of the caste ladder. The new trend in caste dynamics today, is a concerted move on the part of the backward and socially non-privileged castes to rearrange themselves on a horizontal plane instead of pressing their claims for accommodation in the hierarchical ladder. The hitherto voiceless castes are becoming articulate, even vocal, and are not prepared to accept the status differentials. The new orientation in the attitude of the non-privileged castes has already made social distance ineffective in many ways. If the trend continues, and it is likely to continue, it certainly augurs well for the future of the Indian caste structure.

16
New Trends

In the earlier phases of the development of Anthropology, tribal societies of far-off lands, isolated from the main links of modern civilisation, were the subject-matter of its study. This led to a rather unfortunate assumption on the part of common man that Anthropology is the study of tribes. But "Anthropologists are no longer concerned primarily, or even mainly, with the study of tribal cultures; in increasing numbers they are now operating nearer home in village communities where they have discovered challenging possibilities of theoretical and applied social science research." (Dube, 1958.) Basically Anthropology studies Man—and He should be studied at all levels of cultural development. Keeping this aim in view, Anthropology has extended its frontiers to include not only the rural studies, but also urban societies, determination of national character, and analysis of complex cultures. "Today all over the world, Anthropology has embraced the whole human society." (Ishwaran, 1960:5.) It studies "just every thing human". (Redfield, 1956.)

The tools of research that were sharpened in the microcosms of little tribes could be used for the study of the "village" communities, easily and most effectively, with only slight modifications, and quite in consonance with the techniques of other social sciences. The concept of "Ideal Folk-society" developed by Redfield was tried out in analysing the cultures of Latin America, but there it was found almost non-operational. While re-examining it Redfield thought that there was nothing wrong in the concept itself. The communities that one wanted to fit into the conceptual framework were remote in several of the characteristic traits from the ideal type. The later studies proved that the folk societies tend to lose increasingly their basic traits when they come into contact with other advanced cultures. Folk societies, thus, gradually transform themselves into village communities and isolate themselves from the ideal types, say, the one constructed by Redfield. As a result of the processes of culture-contact it is today hardly possible to get any pure, unaffected, and completely isolated "primitive" community. The culture-contact gives rise to a continuum, technically known as the "Folk-Urban continuum". The intermediate category between the two polar types presents the "peasant society" or the village-community.

Thus, the processes of change initiated and accelerated by contact have opened new vistas of study. They presented new problems of analysis and research methodology. It was apparent that the holistic approach that could be successfully employed in the study of isolated and remotely situated small tribal communities was not possible here. The 'whole' of the village community was not complete. It was a part of a wider 'whole' of a greater society. In order to apprehend the village in its totality, it was deemed essential to take cognizance of extraneous forces and factors that affect the life-ways and work-ways of the community.

In the past few years, the programmes of directed and planned change in the underdeveloped countries have immensely increased the possibilities of modifying the form and structure of the village communities. It was therefore considered desirable to record the existing structure of the rural society which would later help the evaluation of the impacts of the development programmes of planned culture change. Some "challenging possibilities" of applied social science research were easily discernible and they provided enough incentive to the social scientist to undertake such studies.

In the Indian context, there is one more factor. Indian society is caste-structured. Knowledge about caste was nothing but "Book-view" and the "Upper caste-view" (Srinivas, 1955). What type of caste organisation is prevalent today? Which of the frontiers have had the largest impact of changes, and in which part of the country or which section of the society (rural or urban)? These were some of the pressing problems of theoretical interest and practical significance which demanded a more thorough and intimate enquiry in specific and limited fields in the different parts of the country.

In brief, following factors may be listed which have facilitated inclusion of a new dimension of study in Anthropology:-

1. Attempts to redefine Anthropology as the Science of man at all levels of cultural development;
2. Recognition of the fact that simple, isolated tribal folks are only an ideal construct and that culture-contact has already broken their isolation. Some writers go to the extent of saying that "they were never isolated";
3. The fact that the majority of world population is rural and it demands attention for systematic study;
4. Attraction toward research possibilities of the new field of study;
5. Facilities for research in terms of proximity, easy accessibility and therefore involving comparatively lesser expenditure than in the study of Tribes;
6. Need for the systematic and scientific study of Indian social structure as it exists today to provide authentic, factual material for the posterity, to reconstruct the past, and to enable the planner in his formulation of plans and projects;
7. Need for the study of changing situation in the village communities brought about by external agencies directly or indirectly, planned or non-directed; and
8. Applicability of the traditional anthropological methods of research to the analysis of rural society.

Economists and Sociologists have been engaged in the study of rural society and it could be said that the entrance of Anthropology in this field is an encroachment or an undesirable intrusion upon others' fields. But this is rather an overstatement. Neither Economics nor even Sociology attempts to intensively study any particular village community. Whatever is being written on rural society is only an outcome of the shuffling of data obtainable from official records like the Patwari Registers, census reports, etc. They give their generalised statements for the country as a whole without caring to go into the intricate details which lay hidden and remain unnoticed to the superficial observers. "Survey research of the extensive type does yield certain data that conform to the rigid tests of validity and reliability but its coverage must of necessity be limited. In its very nature it cannot explore the depths and covert aspects of behaviour ...." (Dube, 1958:2.) To the advantage of the planner they can yield general data but the analysis of human factors is beyond their scope. Thus, although the field is common, methods and techniques of study are different. Keeping this difference of techniques in view, if Rural Sociology has to be differentiated from anthropological studies of village communities, it is proposed that the generalised analysis on national level based on books and statistics be designated as Rural Sociology and the intensive study of particular village communities based on anthropological techniques of research be known as Rural Anthropology. Fortunately in India there is no need for such a distinction. Both Sociologists and Anthropologists are jointly exploring the Village Community with a largely common methodology. Rural India provides a good meeting ground for the two disciplines. This effective communication is indeed a healthy trend and one should welcome this happy "merging".

The year 1955 was of immense significance for Indian anthropology and sociology. In that year, for the first time four books and several papers on Indian Village were published. These studies were made by Indian as well as American and British social scientists. Dube's Indian Village, Majumdar's Rural Profiles (ed.), Marriot's Village India (ed.), and Srinivas' India's Villages (ed.) were the major publications of the year. The same year a conference was also held under the Chairmanship of Dr. (Mrs.) Irawati Karve at Madras, in which Professor Robert Redfield also participated. The much-discussed concept of Sanskritisation proposed by Srinivas in Religion & Society in Coorg was reiterated by him who thought the discussions had reinforced his belief in its validity. The proceedings of the conference have been published in a book entitled Society in India. Later, Twice Born (Carstairs;

1957), India's Changing Villages (Dube, 1958), Caste and Communication in an Indian Village (Majumdar, 1958), Caste and the Economic Frontier (Bailey, 1957) and Village Life in Northern India (Lewis, 1958) were added to the Library of Indian rural studies. Albert Mayer's book Pilot Project, India (1958) summarises the main achievements of the Etawah Project. An Introduction to Rural Sociology in India, an anthology edited by A. R. Desai, appeared in a revised and enlarged version in the year 1959. Recently Adrian Mayer's work "Caste and Kinship in Central India (1960) has come out. Besides these major publications, several research papers based on field work in rural areas have appeared in various journals. The yearly sessions of the Indian Sociological Conference have also included discussions on varied and important problems of Rural Analysis. University departments of Anthropology and Sociology have been and are undertaking various projects for conducting researches in the rural areas. The Research Programmes Committee of the Planning Commission, Government of India, is also promoting rural research through such centres.

The study of Indian Rural Society has helped in developing certain analytical categories. Srinivas has pointed toward a social process, which he christened as Sanskritisation, through which the lower castes try to bring about changes in their life-ways to obtain greater ritual purity, and thereby attain a higher status in the ritual hierarchy of castes. He has also analysed the process of Westernisation which simultaneously operates in a society. N. Prasad has tried to elaborate the concept and suggested the term Kulinisation for the same. Majumdar through Desanskritisation suggests a reverse process by which the Brahman castes also try to identify in some matters with other castes. Ishwaran considers the concept of Sanskritisation as "misleading" and asserts "A thorough understanding of the Hindu culture could only be had by referring to Brahmanisation but not sanskritisation. (1960:9.) Chauhan (1959) while suggesting the limitations of the concepts of sanskritisation and Westernisation mentions the other processes which are simultaneously at work. Efforts have also been made to analyse the hierarchical aspects of caste and the factors leading towards the dominance of a caste. The very concept of caste has been reexamined in an effort to make it more precise, less open-textured so to say. Marriott discovered the processes of Universa-lisation and Parochialisation (1955) which explain the complexity of Indian civilisation and the communication channels that exist between the Great and Little traditions of the country. To avoid the limitations of the polar distinctions, Dubey is busy in conceptualising the total realm of Tradition into a five-fold division. According to him, "In our study of Indian Village communities ...it may be useful to consider the contextual classical and local traditions as well the regional (culture-area), western (ideological-technological), and emergent national (nativistic-reinterpretational-adaptive) traditions." (1958:10.)

Main Issues

The most significant problem which has attracted the attention of a number of social scientists is that of the representativeness of a village. Can a village represent the whole nation? It could be said that as every one who is a resident of India is Indian so also is every village in India an Indian village. But the problem is not so simple. Every village has a distinct "personality" of its own. It has its distinctive structure, network of kinship-affiliations, caste-composition and dominance, and leadership patterns. The south Indian village is different in many respects from a north Indian village. Even in north or south India no specific homogeneity in the village organisation is to be discovered. In Marriott's Kishangarhi, "Marriage... is oriented to flow in a single direction only." There is no possibility of "marriage by exchange" there. But in Rajasthan this practice is observed and is locally known as "Anta Santa". The system of Seem Seemna Bhaichara found in villages around Delhi is peculiarity of this region alone. In the villages of Mahakaushal, it was found that it is the parents who will touch the feet of their daughter as a mark of respect. Similarly the brothers would respect their sisters irrespective of age-considerations. The elder sisters, in the same vein, touch the feet of their younger sisters. But in Rajasthan, it is always the daughters who would touch the feet of their parents. Similarly the younger sister has to bow down to her elder siblings. These instances prove that while in Mahakaushal sex of the child or the sibling has an important role to play in commanding respect, in Rajasthan it is not so relevant as the factor of Age is. To give another example, the Telis are oil pressers and traditional confectioners in Mewar. Their `pakka' preparations are acceptable even to high caste Brahmans. But in Mahakaushal the idea of Telis being confectioners will be abhorred. In Mewar, the role of midwifery is traditionally assigned to the Barber woman (Nain). In Mahakaushal two different castes have their role at the time of delivery. The Basor woman performs the surgical operation, and after the preliminary purificatory rites, the Nai-woman takes over. Similarly, differences in dialects, in dressing-patterns, in details of ritual observances, in kinship terminology and usages and in the economic sphere could be located. In such situations, when a village in the neighbourhood of Delhi is compared with that of Mexico, the utility of such a comparison is uncertain and the representativeness of the compared villages very much open to question. From this point of view the very title of the book viz., Village Life in Northern India is dubious.

In spite of all these considerations one moot question still remains: Is the significance of a village study confined only to the village studies or can the results of the research be used for a wider area? To put it in other words, whether the village represents its own confines or a region (or area) bigger than that? In the fifth session of the Indian Sociological Conference held at Lucknow (1960) Brij Raj Chauhan raised the same question in a different manner. According to him, the question as "to what extent any village in India can be considered as representative of the country ... can lead to four facts

1. Any village selected at random represents the nation;
2. There are various types of villages in the country and one village may represent other villages of its own type;
3. A village happened to be studied may be only selectively representative with reference to the item selected for study;
4. It may be possible to find a representative village for the country.

On the basis of Census of India – 1951, Chauhan created a Hindupur village. In terms of size of the village, sex-ratio, distance from a city, and availability of modern means of transport (bus and rail) Hindupur represents the Indian village. "Hindupur is the name given to the village that is 18 miles from the rail, 6 miles from pucca road, 4 miles from Kachcha road and 33 miles from a city. With 269 males and 260 females it is inhabited by 529 persons." When some of the Indian villages reported on in Anthropological literature were compared with this "Ideal type" or, Average Type of Hindupur, the following facts emerged in regard to the size of the village.

1. All the villages so compared "fall above the category of small villages thereby excluding 68% of the villages in India";
2. Villages of Mohana (Majumdar), Namhalli (Beals), Kishangarhi (Marriott), Kasandra (Steed) and Rani-khera (Lewis) having a population between 575 and 1,100 "are fairly near the mark of Hindupur and these villages represent 18.5% of the villages in India".
3. Rampura (Srinivas) and Madhopur (Cohn) of the population of 1,523 and 1,852 respectively, "represent 10% of villages".
4. Shamirpet (Dube) village of the size of 2,454 represents only 3.5% of the villages in India.

Similarly these eight villages were compared with Hindupur on the remaining three counts.

Here it is necessary to mention that Hindupur is Chauhan's own creation. He "has not visited this village and in fact does not know whether such a village exists at all". This is the magic of Census figures and statistical computations. Chauhan, however, believes that " for every region perhaps a picture of villages like Uttarpur, Madhyapur, Bangpur, Rajput, etc., will aid in furthering our knowledge and ignorance (sic) with regard to the efficacy of studies of single village communities for making nationwide conclusions."

The Response

Social scientists have reacted differently towards this effort of constructing an Ideal type in terms of limited factors, based on methods of statistical computations alone. There are certain theoretical difficulties in accepting Hindupur as a representative Indian village. The selection of the four factors on the basis of which this Ideal village was invented has been governed by the considerations of convenience and personal preference. The village as a socio-cultural entity cannot be deduced from quantophrenic rhapsodies. Possibly Asiapur (Asian village) and Vishwapur (universal village) can also be constructed as ideal types for Asia and the world in the same manner as Bangpur for Bengal and Hindupur for India. It is quite possible that the ideal village of Australia or Iraq may have closer identity with Hindupur or Rajpur. In that situation what would remain specifically Indian in Hindupur to justify the prefix "Hind"?

Secondly, where the suggestion for making 'purs' for Rajasthan, Madhya Pradesh etc. is offered, probably it is overlooked that the provinces are organised for administrative purposes and their boundaries are defined mainly geographically. But cultural boundaries do not necessarily coincide with the geographical.

It also appears that Chauhan wants to conceive of Indian Village as a concept. It has happened in the history of Anthropology earlier also; it is implicit in the effort of persons like Tylor, Morgan and Frazer to make anthropology the study of culture and not of cultures. Relevant data suitable enough to be fitted into the scheme of the cultural construct were collected from different cultures "torn out of their cultural context with little reference to their meaning". They were all in search of an ideal pattern of culture which, in extremist hands, split up into the schools of evolutionism and diffusionism. The number of village studies done so far in India is quite meagre and not quite adequate to yield nation-wide generalisations." In order to avoid a mechanical and overly schematic approach to the study of regional similarities and differences in the country, it is most desirable to continue with the anthropological tradition of single village studies." (Dube, 1958: 3.)

However, if we want to understand Indian village as a concept, we have to get hold of those points of comparison which are significant and distinctive of Indian culture. The factors that are analysed in establishing Hindupur as the Indian village do not give any idea of village as a culture-bearing entity. Their Indianness is accidental, and by no means refers to the specificities of our villages.

In spite of all this, the Hindupur proposal has certainly provided stimulation and food for thought. Perhaps, it serves to point out that thinking in terms of the Indian village, or talking about the nationwide representative character of a single village is fruitless. Statistical calculations alone cannot offer any answer. Although Shamirpet, Rampura, Mohana, Ranikhera, Namhalli, Kasandra, Kishangarhi, etc. are different in more ways than one, from the Ideal type Hindupur, they nevertheless represent the tradition of Indian villages in many respects. In every village in India, there is something which distinguishes it from the villages of 'the other countries of the world. If the two village studies of different countries are to be examined, at least this could easily be said that both these villages do not belong to the same country or culture. It, therefore, is implicit that each village has a certain measure of representativeness; the difference may be a matter of degree in which, and the area that it represents.

And moreover, representativeness is always relative. When Man is related to the Animal Kingdom he is supposed to have those characteristics which are found even in a protozoan. But the similarity in the characteristics would go on increasing as he is classified as a vertebrate, a mammal, an eutherian, a primate and ultimately a Homosapien. He would be having all the characteristics of his species and, therefore, would truly represent it. But nonetheless he also represents other subdivisions to which he belongs in degrees that go on reducing as he departs from his station in the scheme. In the same way the village would represent in many respects its own region, then its province, then the nation, the continent and the world.

Representativeness should be based on similarities of cultural traits and complexes, and aspects of social organisation. Size of the village, distance from the city etc., should be given a secondary importance. It is apparent that proximity to the city in terms of communication may not be coexistent with physical distance. It should not be difficult for the social scientist to assign relative significance to sociological contexts over biological and geographical ones. Thus, caste-system, concepts of ritual purity and pollution, agriculture, hereditary occupational-specialization, temple worship and polytheistic beliefs may be some of the factors on which the representative type may be constructed. Of course, this would necessitate undertaking of more village studies and developing an elaborate methodology of comparative approach. The villages and institutions of the same and of different culture-areas will have to be investigated in order to assess the range of similarities and differences.

The following hypotheses are proposed for determining the representativeness of an Indian Village:-

1. The language (or dialect) of a village can most adequately represent the linguistic area to which it belongs;
2. The ritual hierarchy of castes in a village could be representative of the culture-area or sub-culture-area to which the village belongs. However, it has to be remembered that it would only represent the ritual hierarchy of those castes which are found in the village.
3. In the same sub-cultural and the linguistic-area, social behaviour, ritual belief, customs and traditions, peculiarities of economic organisation, dressing and decoration patterns would tend to be similar;
4. From the point of view of caste-dominance, there could be wide-range differences between the village and the region. The caste which is regionally dominant may not necessarily have the same degree of influence and dominance in all the villages of the region;
5. Along with regional similarities in a social institution found to be present in all the villages of a given region, local variations are also associated. The complete understanding of the structure and functioning of that institution is only

possible when all its variations and ramifications are recorded. This requires the study of the institution in more than one village. In such a situation, the very fact of the presence of an institution in the village is not sufficient to justify its regional representativeness.

If, on the basis of these and other similar hypotheses, new researches are directed the regional ideal types could possibly be formulated. Once the problem of regional representation is solved, we shall be better equipped for the national Ideal type. It has to be specifically pointed out here that the concepts of "region" and "area" are also not sociologically well-defined. Attempts towards defining these concepts will facilitate proper examination of the issue of representativeness. Once good research data from Rural India are accumulated for comparative purposes, the ground will be prepared for thinking in terms of Indian Village as a concept.

Social Setup

The social structure of Indian village communities, list some of the important factors of change, and attempt a broad analysis of the major trends of change.

For an understanding of the structure and problems of Indian village society we have to view the village both as a distinct isolable entity, and as a link in the chain of a wider inter-village organization. An individual village derives some of the characteristic features of its organization from the great national tradition of India, while the traditions of the region or the culture area in which it is located also contribute substantially toward shaping its value-orientation, ethos, and general pattern of life. Notwithstanding these national and regional influences, there is much that is individual to the village; its pattern of inter-group adjustment gives a certain degree of distinctiveness to the village. The Indian village is thus sufficiently isolable, but it is not an isolate, and has therefore to be viewed as a community within a larger community.

The interplay of several different kinds of solidarities determines the structure and organization of Indian village communities. Kinship, caste, and territorial affinities are the major determinants that shape the social structure of these communities. An individual belongs to a family-nuclear, compound or joint; and the family belongs to a lineage as well as to a large group of relatives having kin or affinal ties with it. These units belong to an endogamous sub-caste or caste; in some instances we find a number of endogamous sub-castes grouped together as a caste. Non-Hindu religious groups in villages tend to function as separate castes. Most of the Hindu castes are fitted into one of the four major divisions of Hindu society, called varna. Solidarities provided by kin and caste tend to merge, but those of territorial affinity belong to a different level. An individual and his family belong also to a village, which is often multi-caste in its composition. The village itself is a part of a network of neigh-bouring villages, the region, and the nation. The structural model of Indian peasant communities can be presented in the following diagram:

In the following diagram dotted circles show the comparatively less effective units of social structure. Non-Hindu groups also fit this scheme. In Diagram A, rather than being described as a "sub-caste" or "caste", they should be called "religious group", and of course they are outside the varna organization of Hindu society.

Structural Setup

Caste is perhaps the most important single organizing principle in these communities, and it governs to a very considerable degree the organization of kinship and territorial units. In this system of segmentary division of society the different segments are kept apart by complex observances emerging from an all-pervading concept of ritual pollution. The caste divisions are regarded as divinely ordained and are hierarchically graded. The difference between the different segments is defined by tradition and is regarded as permanent. In inter-group relations the caste structure works according to a set pattern of principles: hierarchy and social distance manifest and express themselves in rules and regulations that are calculated to avoid ritual pollution and maintain ritual purity. Marriage, commensality, and physical contacts particularly are governed by strict rules. It has been pointed out earlier that castes are endogamous. Matrimonial alliances outside the caste are viewed with disapproval and are forbidden by tradition.

Complex rules of commensality specify the castes from which a particular caste may accept different kinds of food. Foods are classified into several categories, depending on the degree to which they are susceptible to pollution. Everyday interaction between the different castes is also governed by caste rules: persons from some castes should never be touched, while physical contact with some others should be avoided under special conditions, such as a state of ritual purity. Caste largely determines occupational choice: with the exception of a few "open" occupations which may be pursued by anyone irrespective of caste, a large number of crafts and occupations are caste monopolies and can be practised only by certain castes. In its functioning an individual caste generally illustrates a distinctive way of life, for different castes have different sets of prescribed norms of conduct and expectations regarding standards of behaviour. These norms and expected standards of behaviour cover such aspects of life as observance of rules of purity especially those of bathing and washing (at appropriate hours) public conduct, and even dress and speech. Another important feature of caste may also be noted in this connection. In new situations demanding group decisions and group action in recent years, caste has shown its dormant strength and has proved itself a cohesive force. Most local, and even some state and national elections were fought along caste lines, and in these the contestants depended to a great extent on the support of their caste fellows. Within a village the caste system manifests itself as a vertical structure in which individual castes are hierarchically graded and kept permanently apart and at the same time are linked and kept together by some well-defined expectations and obligations which integrate them into the village social system. The horizontal ties of a caste, too, are important, for a village caste group has strong links with its counterparts in other villages, and in several spheres of life they tend to act together. In order to be able to discharge the control functions implied in the complex norms associated with the system, castes have local and regional organizations and associations which have the authority to enforce the rules and customs of the caste.

The great diversity of forms in the family and kinship organisation of Indian peasant communities makes the task of presenting a general account of them somewhat difficult. Contrary to common belief the basic unit of social organization in these communities is not the large joint family, but the nuclear family and the smaller joint family in which only a part of those who should have constituted the ideal larger joint family live together, and even the latter generally breaks up when minors attain maturity and a degree of economic self-sufficiency. Recent village studies have shown that large joint families are relatively few in number and they too are largely confined to the upper, i.e., the priestly, trading, and agricultural castes. In some parts of north Indian plains it has been observed that a house is shared by a number of people having close lineal ties, who live not as one family, but as distinct nuclear families organized as separate hearths or chulhas. However, very special ties are recognized between a family and the local group of near kin, i.e., all other families lineally related to it up to the third generation. The solidarity between this cluster of families expresses itself on ceremonial occasions and in times of stress and calamity. In the hour of need they must support each other, and mutual consultations among them in regard to all major decisions are regarded as desirable. Informally the local group of near kin functions as an effective agency of social control. The larger circle of relations has more or less the same functions, though physical distance between the different constituent units naturally makes its functioning less effective. The outlook of the people has been distinctly kin-oriented, and in an hour of need or stress they almost instinctively look to their kin for sympathy and support.

The village as a unit of social structure cuts across the boundaries of kin and caste and unites a number of unrelated families within an integrated multicaste community. Structurally the village communities can be divided into three main groups: the "single settlement" village, in which the community shares a common and compact settlement site, the "nucleated" village which has a central settlement as the nucleus around which there are a number of smaller satellite settlements, and the "dispersed" village community, in which the community consists of a series of dispersed homesteads having well-defined ties with one another.

Both have a number of common features. They are stable populations generally, with a common past and a number of shared values. They recognize and emphasise their individual identity, and in certain situations act as one unit. Their economy is built largely around agriculture; economically and socially the agricultural castes are the most important, while the non-agricultural occupations are subsidiary to agriculture. Land is greatly loved and valued, and the community as a whole shares some common problems and acculturative influences. Being largely caste-structured, the community finds itself integrated in terms of traditional patterns that define the interactions between the different segments of the community in the fields of economy, socio-religious life, and village administration. Operating under traditional arrangements, artisan and other occupational castes render services to the agriculturist in their respective fields of specialization; in return the agriculturist gives them a stipulated share of the crops when they are harvested. Socio-religious life, especially ceremonials and rituals connected with birth, puberty, marriage and death, are so organized that they require participation by a large number of castes at various stages. As the rites progress, at different points small fees have to be paid to the castes that are assisting. For these purposes there are established patron-client relationships under which families of occupational castes are affiliated with families of agriculturists; for services-in the socio-religious field even non-agriculturists are covered by these traditional arrangements. Among the occupational castes themselves there is often a barter of their traditional services. A similar integration of various castes and their functions is seen in the organization of village administration and village rituals, in both of which the different castes often have well-defined position and functions. A common organized authority of the village gives it a still greater unity, and besides maintaining law and order tries effectively to secure observance of village norms. This invariably consists of influential and responsible members of different castes living in the village.

17

Social Revolution

Like all other phenomena the rural society too has been changing since its emergence. Its technology, economy and social institutions, its ideology, art and religion, have undergone a ceaseless change. This change has sometimes been imperceptibly slow, sometimes strikingly rapid, and at some moments even qualitative in character resulting into the transformation of one type of rural society into another type.

To discern change in a system, to recognize its direction, to understand the objective and subjective forces which bring it about and, further, to consciously accelerate the process of change by helping the progressive trends within the changing system— this constitutes a scientific approach to and active creative intervention in the life of a system.

Social Elements

We will now refer to the forces and factors, conscious or unconscious, which bring about change in rural society.

Close investigators of rural society have enumerated a number of these forces and factors, the following being the principal among them.

The Background

Natural forces such as floods, earthquakes, famines and others affect the territorial zone in which the rural people live. They have a disastrous effect on the flora and the fauna of the zone which often considerably influences the economic life of the people, and, in the case of earthquakes of dangerous intensity, even sometimes results in large-scale loss of human life and material devastation. The rural collectivity lives in the midst of a specific geographical and geological milieu and manipulates them through agriculture, mining and other operations. Hence a profound change in earth structures modifies or sometimes even convulses its life processes.

These are the natural forces which bring about change in rural society.

There are human factors, too, which operate to alter that society.

Industrial Boom

As observed earlier, man carries on his struggle against the environment by means of tools. He has, therefore, been ceaselessly engaged in improving the old tools and inventing new ones. Though the inventors create new tools consciously, they are unable to prognosticate the social consequences of their inventions which are sometimes far-reaching. The invention of new tools, new means of transport and communications, and the discovery of new materials such as iron, new chemical substances and others, result in the change in the life of the rural people, in their economy and even in the structures of their social and political relations. The far-reaching economic, social and political outcomes of outstanding inventions like the plough, the steam engine and others, were not and could not be predicted by their inventors.

As Prof. Ogburn observes, the invention of radio led to about 150 major changes in social life.

The invention of steam-driven machinery in England resulted in the evolution of modern industries, which, at a certain stage of their development, needed foreign market. This led to the political and the economic expansion of Britain and the rise and growth of the British Empire. Once the power-driven technique was invented, it was adopted by other nations also. Western nations, in steady succession, developed modern industries and, due to the need of foreign market for their industrial products, conquered other countries and built up empires. This changed the economic and political life of those nations as well as of those who were subjected to them. The societies of the countries of both the dominant as well as the subject nations were either completely transformed or appreciably modified.

What is true of the national societies is also true of the rural society since it is an integral part of the national society.

Next we will survey the methods and devices adopted by social groups and organizations to consciously bring about the alteration or transformation of the rural world.

Eminent sociologists like Sims and others have collected and mentioned various techniques and methods used by these groups and organizations. The following are the chief among them

Persuasive Method: The protagonists of this method seek to convince the rural population of the necessity of effecting changes in the rural society in various spheres, technical, economic, social and others, through organized propaganda campaign. They endeavour to popularise among them various rural reforms or rural reconstruction programmes and exhort them to implement these programmes.

The distinguishing characteristic of this method lies in the fact that its proponents restrict their effort only to the propaganda of their programmes. They do not themselves initiate or participate in implementing the programmes. They leave this to the rural people themselves.

This is because the exponents of this method have almost limitless faith in the force of argument. They hold the view that it is possible by means of a suitable argument to convince the rural people of the need for change in the rural social structure, to kindle in them the urge for such a change, to popularise among them an appropriate programme of rural reform or reconstruction and, through this, to rouse them to practical activity for the accomplishment, of that programme.

Demonstrative Method: This method is also known as the method of propaganda through example or by deed. The exponents of this method endeavour to popularise their programme of rural reconstruction or specific reform by themselves implementing it on a miniature scale. They declare that the rural population would be more easily convinced of the advantages of a programme of rural change if the advantages of such a programme are demonstrated in action. They consider this method more effective than that of mere oral and written propaganda.

For instance, they organize demonstration farms to convince the farmers of the superiority of a new technique and new and better methods of agricultural production. They start model agricultural colonies based on the co-operative principle to rouse the farmers to the recognition of the economic advantages of co-operative farming so that they themselves, on their own initiative, may combine or integrate their individual uneconomic or semi-economic holdings and embark on the road to co-operative or collective agriculture. They establish a few educational and health centres so that the rural population may recognize the benefits of education and hygiene and, thereafter, themselves start schools and health centres in the entire rural area.

"Compulsory" Method: The state itself often intervenes and, through legislation, brings about changes in the rural life or the rural social structure. It is not the will and the initiative of the rural people but of the state that determine and accomplish those changes. During the War, "To rural America, along with the rest, coercive measures were applied. Among other things, production was made compulsory, prices were fixed, the disposal of food stuffs prescribed and time of labour regulated by law."

In India, a number of states have recently enacted anti-zamindari laws to alter land relations in the rural areas.

Such "compulsory" intervention of the state in the life of the rural people has been increasing in modern times.

Method of Social Pressure: This method is adopted by a rural individual, a group or a class to achieve a desired change in the life of the rural people or in the rural social or economic structure. The means resorted to vary widely. They may include petitioning, passive resistance, individual and group satyagraha, processions and marches, strikes and demonstrations, even individual terrorism (for instance killing of moneylenders or landlords by farmers or tenants), mass revolts, revolutions and others.

These forms of pressure and struggle have been growing more and more prevalent in modern times.

The rural sociologist has to carefully analyse and study these forms of struggle since they have been playing a significant role in transforming rural societies of various countries in the contemporary epoch.

Contact Method: "It is generally recognized that one of the most effective means of social change is found in contact of cultures where peoples of different cultures come in touch with one another, cross-fertilization takes place. "

In the medieval age, the town and the village lived almost independent social, economic and cultural existence. This separatism was increasingly undermined as a result of the extension and wider and wider ramification of modern means of transport and communication all over the country and resultant closer and closer contact of urban and rural populations. Further, the village economy was transformed and became an integral part of the national and even international economy. This created and multiplied the points of contact between the rural and urban societies and their populations. This increasingly led to the changes in the socio-economic structure of the rural society and the life of the rural people.

The historical tendency is towards a growing urbanization of the rural society due to the stronger impact of the urban forces on the latter.

Educational Method: The increasing spread of modern education among the rural people through the establishment of schools and other educational institutions has been one of the very effective means to bring about changes in the rural life and the rural social structure. The village people, when they are initiated in scientific knowledge of life and the world, would find it easy to break with superstition which affects their consciousness and keeps them conservative.

A group of social thinkers invest the educational method with decisive importance in bringing about the rural change.

We have referred above to some of the principal methods observed by some of the eminent rural sociologists, which have been operating to bring about the rural change.

These methods should be carefully studied by those who desire to evolve a programme of rural reform or reconstruction. They should assess the value of these methods and assign them a proportional significance while elaborating such a programme.

Social Change in Effect

The main changes are noticed in the caste, the joint family system and village administration through Panchayats which together formed the base of the old social edifice. The rise of internal markets, assisted by the extension of railways and roads, and the expansion in foreign trade of agricultural commodities transformed the old self-sufficient economy of the village based on barter into a market economy, based on cash. With the gradual urbanisation of the village, the rigidity of the division of labour among the community softened. The old caste barriers to economic mobility have been slowly giving way. The expansion of towns, the diversification of employment opportunities in trade and services and the glamour and attractions of city life have created a steady drift towards the city. This has been responsible for loosening the hold of the joint family system on the members. There has also been continuous drain on the intelligentsia among the rural population. The two World Wars drew from the village population into military service hundreds of thousands who imbibed a new outlook on life. After their return from the distant theatres of war they have added a new ferment to the social urges of the rural community, already seething with discontent under the pressure of poverty. The advent of freedom with a new promise and hope, the acceleration of economic and social reform measures, resulting in the abolition of large landed estates and the protection of the rights of the tenants and labourers, the political enfranchisement of the vast population under adult suffrage, have all widened the horizon of economic standards in the village and have further complicated the problems of adjustment and of devising a new social order for the villages.

The Traditions

The significant among the factors of change in the social order have been the rise in the age of marriage, the improved status of women, the lesser vogue of caste despotism and of purdah, the removal of the disabilities of sections of population under caste hierarchy and in general, the realignment of family relations. But it must however be said that while glimpses of change in outlook are noticed among the educated in the village community, in respect of social disabilities, the old order is kept intact in the observances of the privileges. Untouchability, access to places of public convenience as wells, etc., and public worship were the three crucial barriers and all the three have given way under legislative compulsion and educative propaganda. The inner change of heart, which is the result of enlightened education, is yet far from achievement. In one respect no change is visible. The tanner and sweeper still live on the outermost fringe of the village, often on opposite sides, though the Brahmin is losing his halo and the untouchable, the stigma. The two tests of free association in a modern society are food and marriage. In the village, they are still as strong a barrier as they were and education has done nothing to weaken them. The cow is more the object of veneration, than a problem in economic improvement.

Style of Life

In objective terms a standard of living consists of three main elements: (1) the level of consumption or the composition of goods and services of a specific quantity and quality consumed by an individual, family or group within a given period; (2) social services and free services, particularly those which relate to health, education and recreation, and (3) working conditions which affect not only the worker's health and earning capacity but also the size and regularity of his income. As a dynamic concept, it implies in the first place the eradication of poverty, among the rural community and in the second, improving the content of living of all categories of workers with regard to consumption, social and free services and conditions of work.

Examined on the basis of the above terms, it would be difficult to answer the question whether there has been an improvement in the standard of living of the rural community. While the view is often held that the rise in prices during the war period ushered in a period of prosperity, evidence is lacking as to the category of the population which was actually benefited and the extent of increase in prosperity. While a relative improvement in the stan-dard of living of the strata of economic land-holders may be accepted, the available data indicate that there has been a deterioration in the other sections of the agricultural population who form the majority.

Aesthetic culture is an integral part of the total culture of a society. It expresses, in art terms; the ideals, the aspirations, the dreams, the values, and the attitudes of its people, just as its intellectual culture reveals its knowledge of the natural and social worlds which surround them.

A systematic study of the aesthetic culture of the Indian rural society, in its historical movement of the dissolution of old types and the emergence of new ones, is vital for the study of the changing pattern of the cultural life of the rural people. Further, since art reflects social life and its changes, such a study will help the rural sociologist to comprehend the movement of the rural society itself as it progressed from its past shape to its present one. It will also reveal the changes in the psychological structures of the rural people and its sub-groups.

Eminent sociologists have enumerated the following principal arts comprising the aesthetic culture of rural society:

(1) Graphic Arts such as Drawing, Painting, Engraving and others which have two dimensional forms.

(2) Plastic Arts which "involve the manipulations of materials to yield three dimensional forms — that is to say — carving and modelling in high and low relief and in the round."

(3) Folklore comprised of "myths, tales, proverbs, riddles, verse together with music."

(4) Dance and drama which combine the three forms mentioned above and therefore are "synthetic" arts.

Outstanding rural sociologists like Herskovief, Sorokin, Zimmerman, Galpin, and others have also located a number of specific characteristics of the aesthetic culture of the rural people living in society based on subsistence economy. The following are the important among them:

Art was fused with life. As Sorokin remarks, "The arts were not sharply differentiated from religion, magic, intellectual pursuits, and other activities. Aesthetic elements penetrated to practically all daily occupations including agricultural work and they were an inseparable part of religious and other cultural activities."

The people as a whole took part in artistic activities. This is in contrast to the situation in the present society where the people are divided into artists who perform art and the audience which enjoys it. This antithesis was not known to earlier society.

A social group, a family, or the village people as a whole, did not break itself into actors and spectators when they engaged themselves in artistic activity. Men, women, and children of the group, all participated in it; "they were both the actors and the audience." There were very few professional artists in that society. In the social division of labour artistic work was not still separated from the total social work so as to create a special body of social workers like artists.

Art was predominantly familistic. The pre-modern society, the life of the rural aggregate had familistic character. Consequently, the rural art, which was fused with the life of the rural people, also bore the impress of familism. "The significance, the manifestations, the content and the symbolism of rural aesthetic activities were permeated with familism. Births, marriages, deaths and sickness of members of the family were the main subjects of rural art."

The technique of art was simple. This was due to comparatively low level of general technique of the period, on which the technique of art depends. The instruments of rural art were the products of the village artisan industry. Often the family itself made some of these in the home. This is in contrast to the instruments of modern art which are the products of modern industries and are therefore complex, highly specialised, varied and multifold. A simple drum

(Dhol Nagara, Dholak, Duff, Khanjri, Nobati); a flute made out of simple reeds or handy wood; a few stringed instruments not complicated in structure (Ektar, Ravanhatha); some metal instruments of simple design like gongs, bells, Mantras, some wooden instruments like Kartal; ordinary metal vessels of domestic use like Thali, Gagar, Lota or drinking pot, tongs; such natural objects as branches of trees, feathers of birds, shells, conches; these constituted the technical prerequisites of art in the pre-modern Indian rural society. Further, art performances were organized not in theatres and concert halls as in modern times but either in domestic premises or in open village spaces. The village drama was enacted not on any imposing stage equipped with colourful curtains, spotlights, and rich scenery in the background. Much of the realism was achieved not by suggestive or symbolic artifice but was created by histrionics.

Art had agrarian life processes as its main content. Since art was fused with life, it depicted the life of the rural people in its various aspects, economic, social and religious. For instance, "The most common of the work songs of non-urbanized agricultural peoples were those that accompanied collective agricultural occupations, hunting and fishing, grain grinding and milling, flax-thrashing, corn-thrashing, ploughing and seeding, fruit-picking and so forth...... Some of their religious and magical songs were concerned with love, death, mourning, health and fertility, others dealt with agricultural activities and were sung as a part of the religious and magical rites connected with spring, summer fall and winter festivities, still others honoured the grove, wood, field and corn deities ...... Both work songs and religious songs were inseparably connected with daily life and with the religion and magic that centred in agriculture." Even a cursory survey of the songs of the Indian rural people corroborates the above view. Agricultural work processes like sowing, reaping, and harvesting; or other work processes like the fetching of water from the well by women; or sentiments of gratitude to gods for successful agricultural operations or plaintive appeal to them for their fruition, form the main thematic content of those songs. Dance, another form of art, had also, for its predominant content the real agrarian life processes. Similarly, the folklore composed of legends, myths and stories, mostly dealt with the same theme either in a direct or symbolic form. Ornamental and decorative rural arts also bore the impress of the rural environmental and social milieu. The specific flora and fauna found in the rural area provided material for design. Rural artistic creations in these and other spheres "are based on rural environment and occupation; trees, flowers and plants, horses, cattle and other animals, birds and, fish and peasant houses." Further, geometrical designs characterizing those arts had a magical meaning bearing on various agrarian life processes. The rural sociologists have also observed that "Agricultural characteristics are most clearly manifest in songs, music, dances, stories, proverbs, riddles, literature, pantomimes, festivals, dramatic performances, and similar forms of the arts; they are less conspicuous in designs, ornamentations, architecture and sculpture, but even here if properly interpreted, the agricultural stamp is noticeable."

Art creations were predominantly collective creations, collective inspirit. This is one of the most striking features of the rural art. While in the urban area, songs, stories, dramas, and such other art pieces, have been the products of individual artists, practically the entire folklore of the rural people, comprising rural songs and tales as well as rural dramas, has been the collective creation of generations of rural artists. Their authorship cannot be traced to individual artists since no individual artists created them. They remain, therefore, almost always anonymous in origin. As a result of this, the rural art has been overwhelmingly collective in spirit. It has expressed the fears, joys, aspirations, and dreams of the collectivity even more than most of the social art of the urban society. Further, it has been marked with profound natural-dreams of the collectivity even more than most of social art of the urban society. Further, it has been marked with profound naturalness, sincerity, and spontaneity. This is in contrast to the urban art which is either commercialized and, therefore, caters largely to the emotions of its potential buyers or is super-individualistic (ivory tower art) and embodies the individualistic caprices and momentary emotions of the artist. Further, rural art has expressed the sentiments and life experiences of countless generations. It has been, therefore, also more organic and durable than most of the urban art.

Rural art was non-commercial. In agrarian societies based on self-sufficient economies, products have not the character of commodities. Thinkers and artists create their intellectual and artistic products not for the market but for the direct consumption of the village rural aggregate that looks after their needs. Rural art, hence, is not commercialized. Since the rural artist is not motivated by the urge to make profit through his art creations, his artistic activity is urged on only by the artistic aim. The urban artist, in contrast to this, is torn between two urges; one, the urge for artistic self-expression and the other, the need to make livelihood in a competitive economic environs by producing for the market and hence by adapting his art to the tastes of those who can buy it. This dualism disrupts his artistic personality and tends to distort his art. The rural artist does not suffer from these contradictory motives and his art is, therefore "harmonious." Here we must strictly guard ourselves against the danger of idealizing rural art and the self-sufficient society which generates that art. In such a society, the individual is not still differentiated from the collectivity, be it the joint family, the caste, or the village community. The individual is subordinated to these groups. The structure and environment of such a society do not, therefore, provide freedom for the development of the creative individuality of its members or scope for them to strike out new unconventional paths of thought and craftsmanship. This puts a limitation on the rural art though its collective spirit should be properly noted and valued. The competitive socio-economic environs of the modern society, on the other hand, while differentiating and liberating the individual from the pressure of the collectivity on his free development, tends to weaken his social urges. Most of the urban art is, therefore, individualistic. It mostly portrays the struggles of the individual against the stifling forces of the unplanned competitive society. Excepting for a growing minority art current which mirrors the dream of, and struggle for a higher co-operative society, the existing urban art is, largely, socially sterile, morbid or escapist.

Artistic craftsmanship and culture were transmitted from generation to generation orally. This was due to the fact that there existed no printing press which would produce literature on art.

Further, there did not exist any schools or academies of art in self-sufficient societies. Hence, they were mainly the family elders who trained the youngsters in the knowledge and execution of arts like folk songs, folk dances and others.

We have referred elsewhere to the process of the transformation of the old rural society into the new modern society.

The Departure

We will briefly summarize the most striking features of this transformation in the sphere of rural aesthetic culture. Art gradually became a specialized activity of the artist. The village population increasingly became differentiated into artists and the rest. Individual artist or a group of artists sang and danced on festive occasions, the rest of the village people constituting the audience. The technique of art also slowly altered, became more complex, thanks to the ability of modern industry to produce complex art instruments. Above all, since commodity production extended to the village also, art itself became a commodity and the artist, a seller of the artistic goods. Pecuniary gain became the main motif of artistic creation.

Art, moreover, became gradually separated from life. Its thematic content changed. It began to draw its themes and imagery from new sources such as the travails of the individual struggling against the pressures of a competitive socio-economic environment. Formerly, it dealt with the vicissitudes of the life of the village collectivity; now it concerned itself with the fate of the individual. Thus art increasingly ceased to be a collective activity of the village group as a whole dealing with its collective life processes and became the individual activity of the artist dealing with the problems of the individual struggling in a competitive world. Further, the traditional practice of handing down art from generation to generation also began to decline since the printing press made it possible to perpetuate art techniques and art creations like folk songs and village tales in the printed form.

The modern cinema with its film songs and film stories, the gramophone with its song records, together with the radio, slowly began to penetrate the rural zone and became new means of aesthetic delight for the rural population.

These developments led to the increasing urbanization of the rural aesthetic culture. Thus under the impact of the technical and economic forces of modern society, not only did the socio-economic structure of the rural society undergo a single transfor-mation but its aesthetic culture with its specific characteristics also suffered an increasing change.

The Indian rural society, for the last one hundred and fifty years, has been experiencing a historical change. The change has not, however, advanced to the same extent as in some other countries since a foreign power which ruled India during this period retarded the process of rapid industrialization and resultant modernization of our country. In West European countries and the U. S. A. the urbanization of the old rural society and its aesthetic culture have advanced to a far greater degree than in India. It must, however, be noted that even in those advanced countries the aesthetic culture of the rural society possesses a number of specific characteristics which distinguish it from the aesthetic culture of the urban society.

It is essential for the Indian rural sociologist to study the aesthetic culture of the contemporary rural Indian people and the transformation it is undergoing. Such a study will enable him to comprehend the transformation of the life of the rural people and their struggles, dreams and aspirations. Art reveals life through more subtle nuances and often provides a more authentic picture of life than what even history books can give. The French society of Balzac's period is more vividly and truthfully laid bare when viewed through the prism of his great realistic novels than as revealed by the French historians in their works.

"To a superlative degree the arts express the qualities which an age prizes, the human actions which it cherishes, and the ideals which it ennobles..... In the aesthetic attitude, a culture can be captured and held, not as a set of bare facts to be statistically tabulated, but as a function of the travail of human minds."

The aesthetic culture of the rural people should be next studied from the standpoint of (1) its content and (2) its form.

True Culture

The rural aesthetic culture, a rich complex of myths, legends, folk songs, folk tales, riddles and proverbs, dances, dramas and pantomimes, and graphic and plastic arts, transmitted from generation to generation, embodies directly or symbolically the world outlook, social conceptions and ethical norms of the rural people as they emerged and changed across ages. It can serve as a very valuable source material for a rural sociologist of imagination and insight to build up a concrete vivid picture of the technical, economic, social, religious, moral and cultural life of the rural aggregate in various periods. Since the rural aesthetic culture was always anchored in the life of the rural people, was fused with it and, further, artistically mirrored it, it would reveal what technique they employed in material production in a particular period, what weapons they used in warfare, what ornaments and costumes they wore, what houses they built and lived in, what socio-economic system prevailed during that period, what social classes comprised it, what social conflicts rent it, what type of family and other social institutions then existed, what customs ruled the people, what views and attitudes they held on diverse problems, what norms and criteria determined their social conduct. It will thus not only lay bare the social structure and life of the people in a past period but will also disclose their social, ethical and religious conceptions as well as their material and ideal aspirations and aims. It will also reveal the story of their brave social endeavour, also of their reverses and victories.

The enormous rich material comprising the rural aesthetic culture has to be first assembled, analysed and classified. The next task for the rural sociologist is to interpret it with deep historical imagination and sociological insight. This alone will help him to achieve a living objective picture of the rural society and the rural life as they existed in the past. This is specially necessary because no detailed written history is available.

The Indian rural society is divided into a number of regional rural societies.

A comparative study of the contents of the aesthetic cultures of these units will disclose elements common to them such as a number of common, folk songs, folk tales, myths, proverbs, riddles and other, though generally to be found with regional variations.

Such a discovery will help to comprehend the process of the diffusion of culture which had taken place in various rural zones of India in the past. It will also help to get an adequate picture of the historical process of the contacts and collisions, amalgamation or even assimilation, among numerous tribes and communities which lived in India in past epochs. A veritable past history of the Indian rural society and the Indian rural humanity can be composed through such a comparative study of the various rural aesthetic cultures of the various rural zones today.

Such a history of the Indian rural society is indispensable for evolving the history of the Indian society as a whole.

There are various means of deciphering the past history of the Indian people. The study of the variegated and massive content of the aesthetic cultures of the regional agrarian groups and its evaluation will serve as perhaps one of its most fruitful means for that purpose. Nevertheless, all the varied means should be utilised in mutual co-ordination.

After studying the content of the rural aesthetic culture, it is necessary to study the specific forms in which this culture is expressed.

There exists an organic relationship between the content and the form of art. It consists in the unity of its form and content, the content determining the form.

The specific content of the rural aesthetic culture outlined previously determines the specific forms of that culture. It determines the styles of painting, engraving, sculpture and architecture; the designs of costumes and ornaments; the tunes of folk songs and the rhythms of folk poetry; the structures of folk tales, dances and dramas. Further, a good proportion of that culture is marked with symbolism and it is the task of the rural sociologist to penetrate through the symbols and uncover the hidden significant ideas conveyed in an art work.

The Indian rural aesthetic culture comprising various regional rural cultures exhibits a variety of styles, patterns and modes. For instance, we have such varied forms as Sorathas, Dohas, Chaupais, and Chhappas, Kirtans, Bhajans, Abhangas, Pavadas, Deshis, Horis, Kajaris, Kawalis and others in the domain of poetry and song; Rasas, Garbas and others in the sphere of dance; and Bhavais, Ramlilas, Tamasas and other in the field of drama. Similarly the words of other rural arts also reveal a rich diversity of forms.

The study of different forms of the art cultures of different regional rural communities will help us to distinguish them as distinct cultural units. Further, since the agrarian life possesses certain common characteristics, though with local and regional variations, such a study will also reveal how basically the same life content has been variously handled in the sphere of art by different agrarian communities.

A considerable amount of specialization is found in the agrarian arts mainly because the art is fused with concrete activities like sowing, reaping, harvesting and others or with such articles of utility as ornaments and earthenware. Again, since the art creations maintain a thematic continuity, the arts dealing with them are enriched from generation to generation. There is this continuous improvement of agrarian arts, their forms, styles and patterns.

A study of the forms of various regional aesthetic cultures discloses the significant fact that a number of them are essentially the same with regional variations only. This would assist the rural sociologist to resolve the problem of the diffusion of art forms, and of the migrations of a number of rural arts.

The Indian rural people have a long and rich history of aesthetic culture. Musical concerts and dramas were a feature of the rural life during the Maurya period and have been, as A. S. Altekar states, described as "Preksha," by Chanakya and "Samaja" by Ashoka. They were an integral part of the celebrations of religious festival such as Ram-Navmi, Gokul-Ashtami, Dushera, Ganesh Chaturthi, and Holi. They were also organised at village and inter-village fairs which were great social occasions in pre-modern times.

Since the advent of the British in India, as previously seen, a process of the fundamental alteration of Indian society began. As a result of this the psychology of the rural people also changed. The old aesthetic culture began to decline. The process is still continuing. The old arts have been gradually declining though the new modern ones have not been replacing them with the same tempo.

The rural sociologist is confronted with the problem of a renaissance of the rural aesthetic culture. He has to resolve a number of problems germane to a programme of such a renaissance. What will be the nature of the new aesthetic culture? What will be its content and form? Will the new rural arts be fused with the new rural life? Will the organic unity of art and life, the basic characteristic of the old aesthetic culture, be preserved in the new art? Will the new rural art retain the sincerity and the spontaneity of the old one or will it be sophisticated as a good section of the modern urban art is? What will be the ideology informing it? Will it be a mass art in which the people participate or will it be a distinct domain of the professional artists? Will it be a commercialized art produced by artists who subordinate their self-expression to the needs of the market or an ivory tower art where the artists create solely for their own satisfaction, or an art which is social and still provides free self-expression for the artists? These are some of the vital problems which the rural sociologist has to investigate.

Further, modern humanity has at its disposal an advanced technology which can create a complex and multifold technique of art. The material means and resources available today for such arts as painting, music, drama architecture and others are simply astounding. They can serve as the material prerequisite for the creation of a rich and variegated artistic mass culture which can express profound social ideas and portray individual and mass emotions in all their complexity and variety. The new art by means of the material technique accessible to it can work up not merely a few simple collective ideas and emotions as the old rural art did, but also the multifold and complex collective as well as indivi-dualized ideas and emotions which the modern rural humanity even today conceives and feels under the impact of a changing agrarian world. With the steady transformation of the rural society, the social relations are being constantly recast engendering new conceptions and feelings, new social passions, dreams and aspirations.

The existing rural aesthetic culture is in a state of increasing disorganization. This, in the final analysis, is the result of the increasing disorganization of the rural society itself of which it is the aesthetic reflex. The crisis of culture is the product of the crisis of society.

The problem arises whether the process of increasing disorganization and dissolution which the present rural aesthetic culture is undergoing will culminate into the emergence of a new historically higher aesthetic culture.

It depends on how the crisis of the present rural society is resolved. If the present rural society is replaced by one materially and culturally more advanced and based on co-operative social relations; a higher aesthetic culture will spring as a beautiful flower on the tree of such a higher type of society.

As mentioned before, the rural aesthetic culture has been declining and some of the rural arts even disappearing. From the standpoint of the history of the evolution of the Indian art, it is necessary to preserve the knowledge of the present rural aesthetic culture. Further, this is also necessary because, in absence of the written history of the early phase of the Indian society and insufficiently recorded history of subsequent phase, the rural aesthetic culture with its myths and legends, folk tales and folk songs, dances and dramas, paintings, engravings and statues, can provide a clue to the life of the Indian people in past epochs.

Modern technical means such as printing press, gramo-phone, camera, film and others can be made use of for preserving the rural songs and stories, statuary and architecture, fables and legends, through printing, recording and photographing. For all these reasons a careful study of the rural aesthetic culture is indispensable for the student of the rural society.

Additional Reading

Bhaskara Rao, Digumarti (1994). *Scientific Aptitude*, New Delhi: Ashish Publishing House. ISBN 81-7024-658-X.

Bhaskara Rao, Digumarti (1995). *Animal Kingdom*. New Delhi: Discovery Publishing House. ISBN 81-7141-274-2.

Bhaskara Rao, Digumarti (1995). *Batracology*. New Delhi: Discovery Publishing House. ISBN 81-7141-279-3.

Bhaskara Ṛao, Digumarti (1997), *Scientific Attitude*. New Delhi: Discovery Publishing House. ISBN 81-7141-308-0.

Bhaskara Rao, Digumarti (1996). *Scientific Attitude vis-à-vis Scientific Aptitude*. New Delhi: Discovery Publishing House. ISBN 81-7141-308-0.

Bhaskara Rao, Digumarti, Editor (1996). *Encyclopaedia of Education for All*, 5 Volumes. New Delhi: APH Publishing Corporation. ISBN 81-7024-759-4 (set).

Vol. I *Education for All: The World Conference*. ISBN 81-7024-760-8.

Vol. II *Education for All: The EPA-9 Summit*. ISBN 81-7024-761-6.

Vol. III *Education for All: Quality Education for All*. ISBN 81-7024-762-6.

Vol. IV *Education for All: Planning and Monitoring*. ISBN 81-7024-763-4.

Vol. V *Education for All: The Indian Scenario*. ISBN 81-7024-764-0.

Bhaskara Rao, Digumarti, Editor (1996). *Global Perceptions on Peace Education*, 3 Volumes. New Delhi: Discovery Publishing House. ISBN 81-7141-319-6.

Bhaskara Rao, Digumarti, Editor (1996). *National Policy on Education*. 2 Volumes. New Delhi: Anmol Publications Pvt. Ltd. ISBN 81-7488-323-1.

Bhaskara Rao, Digumarti, Editor (1997). *Care the Child*, 2 Volumes. New Delhi: Discovery Publishing House. ISBN 81-7141-394-3.

Bhaskara Rao, Digumarti, Editor (1997). *Education for the 21st Century*. New Delhi: Discovery Publishing House. ISBN 81-7141-389-7.

Bhaskara Rao, Digumarti, Editor (1997). *Reflections on Scientific Attitude*. New Delhi: Discovery Publishing House, ISBN 81-7141-319-6.

Bhaskara Rao, Digumarti, Editor (1997). *Success Story of a Primary Education Project*. New Delhi: APH Publishing Corporation. ISBN 81-7024-850-7.

Bhaskara Rao, Digumarti, Editor (1997). *World Food Summit*. New Delhi: Discovery Publishing House. ISBN 81-7141-386-2.

Bhaskara Rao, Digumarti, Editor (1998). *Adolescence Education*. New Delhi: Discovery Publishing House. ISBN 81-7141-432-X.

Bhaskara Rao, Digumarti, Editor (1998). *Community and School Nutrition Education*. New Delhi: Discovery Publishing House. ISBN 81-7141-435-4.

Bhaskara Rao, Digumarti, Editor (1998). *District Primary Education Programme*. New Delhi: Discovery Publishing House. ISBN 81-7141-396-X.

Bhaskara Rao, Digumarti, Editor (1998). *Earth Summit*, 2 Volumes. New Delhi: Discovery Publishing House. ISBN 81-7141-435-4.

Bhaskara Rao, Digumarti, Editor (1998). *National Policy on Education: Towards an Enlightened and Humane Society*, New Delhi: Discovery Publishing House. ISBN 81-7141-426-5.

Bhaskara Rao, Digumarti, Editor (1998). *Reforming School Education*. New Delhi: Discovery Publishing House. ISBN 81-7141-403-6.

Bhaskara Rao, Digumarti, Editor (1998). *Teacher Education in India*. New Delhi: Discovery Publishing House. ISBN 81-7141-406-0.

Bhaskara Rao, Digumarti, Editor (1998). *World Summit for Social Development*. New Delhi: Discovery Publishing House. ISBN 81-7141-420-6.

Bhaskara Rao, Digumarti, Editor (2000). *Education for All: Achieving the Goal*, 3 Volumes, New Delhi: APH Publishing Corporation. ISBN 81-7648-152-1.

Vol. I *The Global Consensus*. ISBN 81-7648-155-6.

Vol. II *Mid-Decade Review Reports of Regional Seminars*. ISBN 81-7648-154-8.

Vol. III *Issues and Trends*. ISBN 81-7648-155-6.

Bhaskara Rao, Digumarti, Editor (2000), *International Encyclopaedia of AIDS*, 11 Volumes in 13 Parts. New Delhi: Discovery Publishing House. ISBN 81-7141-6 (Set).

Vol. 1 *Introduction to HIV/AIDS*. ISBN 81-7141-523-7.

Vol. 2 *HIV/AIDS—Issues and Challenges*, 2 Parts. ISBN 81-7141-524-5.

Vol. 3 *HIV/AIDS—Socio Economic Realities*. ISBN 81-7141-524-3.

Vol. 4 *HIV/AIDS—Law Ethics and Human Rights*, 2 Parts. ISBN 81-7141-526-1.

Vol. 5 *AIDS and NGOs*. ISBN 81-7141-527-X.

Vol. 6 *AIDS and Home Care*. ISBN 81-7141-528-8.

Vol. 7 *STD Case Management*. ISBN 81-7141-529-6.

Vol. 8 *HIV/AIDS Prevention and Care—Teaching Modules for Nurses and Midwives*. ISBN 81-7141-530-X.

Vol. 9 *HIV Prevention Education for Education for Educational Institutions*. ISBN 81-7141-531-8.

Vol. 10 *Instructional Modules for AIDS Education*. ISBN 81-7141-532-6.

Vol. 11 *School Health Education to Prevent AIDS and STD—A Package for Curriculum Planners*. ISBN 81-7141-5338-4.

Bhaskara Rao, Digumarti, Editor (2000). *International Encyclopaedia of Science and Technology Education*, 11 Volumes. New Delhi: Discovery Publishing House. ISBN 81-7141-548-2 (Set).

Vol. 1 *Science and Technology Education*. ISBN 81-7141-568-7.

Vol. 2 *Science Education in Developing Countries*. ISBN 81-7141-570-9.

Vol. 3 *Organisational Structure of Science*. ISBN 81-7141-570-9.

Vol. 4 *Science Education in Asia and the Pacific*. ISBN 81-7141-571-7.

Vol. 5 *Science and Technology Education for All*. ISBN 81-7141-572-5.

Vol. 6 *Values, Ethics, Talent and Girls in Science and Technology Education*. ISBN 81-7141-573-3.

Vol. 7 *Popularization of Science and Technology Education*. ISBN 81-7141-574-1.

Vol. 8 *Science, Power and Society*. ISBN 81-7141-575-X.

Vol. 9 *Information Technology*. ISBN 81-7141-576-8.

Vol. 10 *Teacher Training in Science and Technology Education*. ISBN 81-7141-577-6.

Vol. 11 *Teacher Training in Science and Technology: A Curriculum Framework*. ISBN 81-7141-578-4.

Bhaskara Rao, Digumarti, Editor (2001). *Distance Education in Different Countries*. New Delhi: APH Publishing Corporation. ISBN 81-7648-229-3.

Bhaskara Rao, Digumarti, Editor (2001). *Decentralised Management of Education (Management of Education in Panchayati Raj and Municipal Bodies)*. New Delhi: Discovery Publishing House. ISBN 81-7141-617-9.

Bhaskara Rao, Digumarti, Editor (2001). *Electrochemistry for Environmental Protection*. New Delhi: Discovery Publishing House. ISBN 81-7141-619-5.

Bhaskara Rao, Digumarti, Editor (2001). *Global Educational Studies*. New Delhi: Discovery Publishing House. ISBN 81-7141-616-0.

Bhaskara Rao, Digumarti, Editor (2001). *Global Synthesis of Educational Assessment*. New Delhi: Discovery Publishing House. ISBN 81-7141-613-6.

Bhaskara Rao, Digumarti, Editor (2000). *International Encyclopaedia of Human Rights*. 7 Volumes in 13 Parts. New Delhi: Discovery Publishing House. (Royal Size). ISBN 81-7141-567-9 (Set).

Vol. 1 *International Instruments of Human Rights*, 2 Parts. ISBN 81-7141-595-4.

Vol. 2 *Regional Instruments of Human Rights*. ISBN 81-7141-604-7.

Vol. 3 *Human Rights and the United Nations*, 2 Parts. ISBN 81-7141-605-5.

Vol. 4 *Fact Files of Human Rights*, 3 Parts. ISBN 81-7141-605-3.

Vol. 5 *Study Stories of Human Rights*, 3 Parts. ISBN 81-7141-607-3.

Vol. 6 *International Meetings on Human Rights*, 2 Parts. ISBN 81-7141-608-X.

Vol. 7 *Professional Training in Human Rights*. ISBN 81-7141-609-8.

Bhaskara Rao, Digumarti, Editor (2001). *Jomtein Decade of Education*. New Delhi: Discovery Publishing House. ISBN 81-7141-618-7.

Bhaskara Rao, Digumarti, Editor (2001). *Nuclear Materials: Issues and Concerns*, 2 Volumes. New Delhi: Discovery Publishing House. ISBN 81-7141-611-X.

Bhaskara Rao, Digumarti, Editor (2001). *World Conference on Education for All*. New Delhi: APH Publishing Corporation. ISBN 81-7141-274-9.

Bhaskara Rao, Digumarti, Editor (2001). *World Conference on Higher Education*, New Delhi: Discovery Publishing House. ISBN 81-7141-610-1.

Bhaskara Rao, Digumarti, Editor (2001). *World Conference on Science*. New Delhi: Discovery Publishing House. ISBN 81-7141-612-8.

Bhaskara Rao, Digumarti, Editor (2003). *Inspiring Experience in Teacher Education*. New Delhi: Discovery Publishing House. ISBN 81-7141-656-X.

Bhaskara Rao, Digumarti, Editor (2003). *International Studies in Education*, 3 Volumes, New Delhi: Discovery Publishing House. ISBN 81-7141-647-0.

Bhaskara Rao, Digumarti, Editor (2003). *Military Conversion: Impact on Science and Technology*, New Delhi: Discovery Publishing House. ISBN 81-7141-578-4.

Bhaskara Rao, Digumarti, Editor (2003). *United Nations Millennium Summit*. New Delhi: Discovery Publishing House. ISBN 81-7141-632-2.

Bhaskara Rao, Digumarti, Editor (2003). *World Assembly on Aging*. New Delhi: Discovery Publishing House. ISBN 81-7141-637-3.

Bhaskara Rao, Digumarti, Editor (2004). *World Conference on Human Rights*. New Delhi: Discovery Publishing House. ISBN 81-7141-661-6.

Bhaskara Rao, Digumarti, Editor (2003). *World Education Forum*. New Delhi: Discovery Publishing House. ISBN 81-7141-639-X.

Bhaskara Rao, Digumarti, Editor (2004). *Education Employment and Human Resource Development*. New Delhi: Discovery Publishing House. ISBN 81-7141-681-0.

Bhaskara Rao, Digumarti, Editor (2004). *Successfully Schooling*. New Delhi: Discovery Publishing House. ISBN 81-7141-677-2.

Bhaskara Rao, Digumarti, Editor (2004). *European Education and Teachers*. New Delhi: Discovery Publishing House. ISBN 81-7141-702-7.

Bhaskara Rao, Digumarti, Editor (2004). *Teachers in a Changing World*. New Delhi: Discovery Publishing House. ISBN 81-7141-694-2.

Bhaskara Rao, Digumarti, Editor (2004). *Learning to Live Together*, 4 Volumes. New Delhi: Discovery Publishing House.

Vol. 1 *International Conference on Learning to Live Together.*

Vol. 2 *Globalisation and Living Together.*

Vol. 3 *Curriculum for Learning to Live Together.*

Vol. 4 *Science Education for the Contemporary Society.*

Bhaskara Rao, Digumarti (2004). *International Guidelines on Open and Distance Education*, New Delhi: Discovery Publishing House.

Bhaskara Rao, Digumarti, Editor (2004). *Adult Learning in the 21st Century*. New Delhi: Discovery Publishing House.

Bhaskara Rao, Digumarti, Editor (2004). *Educational Practices: Research and Recommendations*. New Delhi: Discovery Publishing House.

Bhaskara Rao, Digumarti, Editor (2004). *Chernobyl: Never Again*. New Delhi: APH Publishing Corporation.

Bhaskara Rao, Digumarti, Editor (2004). *Virology and Immunology*. New Delhi: APH Publishing Corporation.

Bhaskara Rao, Digumarti, C.A.P. Swami and B.S.V. Dutt (1997). *Self-Evaluation in Student Teaching*. New Delhi: Discovery Publishing House. ISBN 81-7141-374-9.

Bhaskara Rao, Digumarti and B.S.V. Dutt, Editors (2003). *Education: Programmes and Policies*. New Delhi: APH Publishing Corporation. ISBN 81-7648-470-9.

Bhaskara Rao, Digumarti and D. Naresh Kumar (2004). *School Teacher Effectiveness*. New Delhi: Discovery Publishing House.

Bhaskara Rao, Digumarti and D. Sridhar (2002). *Job Satisfaction of School Teachers*. New Delhi: Discovery Publishing House. ISBN 81-7141-652-7.

Bhaskara Rao, Digumarti and Digumarti Pushpa Latha (1994). *Achievement in Biology*. New Delhi: Discovery Publishing House. ISBN 81-7141-264-5.

Bhaskara Rao, Digumarti, C. Sridevi and K. Vijaya (1995). *Achievement in Social Studies*. New Delhi: Discovery Publishing House. ISBN 81-7141-281-5.

Bhaskara Rao, Digumarti and Digumarti Pushpa Latha (1995). *Achievement in English*. New Delhi: Discovery Publishing House. ISBN 81-7141-283-1.

Bhaskara Rao, Digumarti and Digumarti Pushpa Latha (1994). *Achievement in Science*. New Delhi: Discovery Publishing House. ISBN 81-7141-280-70.

Bhaskara Rao, Digumarti and Digumarti Pushpa Latha (1995). *Achievement in Mathematics*. New Delhi: Discovery Publishing House. ISBN 81-7141-278-5.

Bhaskara Rao, Digumarti and Digumarti Pushpa Latha, Editors (1998). *International Encyclopaedia of Women*. 5 Volumes. New Delhi: Discovery Publishing House. ISBN 81-7141-410-9.

Vol. 1 *Status of World's Women*. ISBN 81-7141-494-X.

Vol. 2 *Women, Education and Empowerment*. ISBN 81-7141-498-1.

Vol. 3 *Women Challenges and Advancement*. ISBN 81-7141-497-4.

Vol. 4 *Women and Family Health*. ISBN 81-7141-497-4.

Vol. 5 *Women and International Action*. ISBN 81-7141-498-2.

Bhaskara Rao, Digumarti, Digumarti Pushpa Latha and Digumarti Harshitha, Editors (2001). *Biological Warfare*. New Delhi: Discovery Publishing House. ISBN 81-7141-597-0.

Bhaskara Rao, Digumarti, Digumarti Pushpa Latha and Digumarti Harshitha, Editors (2001). *Women as Educators*. New Delhi: Discovery Publishing House. ISBN 81-7141-602-0.

Bhaskara Rao, Digumarti and Digumarti Harshitha, Editors (2001). *Education in India*. New Delhi: APH Publishing Corporation. ISBN 81-7141-207-2.

Bhaskara Rao, Digumarti, Digumarti Pushpa Latha and Digumarti Harshitha, Editors (2001). *Assessing Learning Achievement*. New Delhi: Discovery Publishing House. ISBN 81-7141-601-2.

Bhaskara Rao, Digumarti, Digumarti Pushpa Latha and Digumarti Harshitha, Editors (2001). *Energy Security*. New Delhi: Discovery Publishing House. ISBN 81-7141-598-9.

Bhaskara Rao, Digumarti, Digumarti Harshitha and K.R.S.S. Rao, Editors (1999). *Advanced Biotechnology*. New Delhi: Discovery Publishing House. ISBN 81-7141-516-4.

Bhaskara Rao, Digumarti and K.R.S. Sambhasiva Rao, Editors (1996). *Current Trends in Indian Education*. New Delhi: Discovery Publishing House. ISBN 81-7141-311-0.

Bhaskara Rao, Digumarti and K. Vijaya (1995). *A Text Book of Evaluation*. Ambala Cantt: The Associated Publishers.

Bhaskara Rao, Digumarti and N.V.M. Mohana Rao (2002). *Problems of Mentally Handicapped Children*. New Delhi: Discovery Publishing House. ISBN 81-7141-645-4.

Bhaskara Rao, Digumarti and S. Chandra Mohan (2002). *Sports Management*. New Delhi: APH Publishing Corporation. ISBN 81-7648-467-9.

Bhaskara Rao, Digumarti and Sk. Johni Basha (2004). *Teachers' Population Education Awareness*. New Delhi: APH Publishing Corporation.

Bhaskara Rao, Digumarti, V.V. Rao, V.V. Lakshmi and V.V. Krishna, Editors (1999). *Status and Advancement of Women*. New Delhi: APH Publishing Corporation. ISBN 81-7648-169-6.

Babu, P.C., Author and Digumarti Bhaskara Rao, Editor (2004). *Flowers of Wisdom*. New Delhi: Discovery Publishing House. ISBN 81-7141-695-0.

Bhagya Lakshmi, Lingineni, Author and Digumarti Bhaskara Rao, Editor (2000). *Reading and Comprehension*. New Delhi: Discovery Publishing House. ISBN 81-7141-543-1.

Bhuvaneswara Lakshmi, Gadde, Author and Digumarti Bhaskara Rao, Editor (2000). *Attitude Towards Science*. New Delhi: Discovery Publishing House. ISBN 81-7141-541-6.

Devraj, T.A.S., Author and Digumarti Bhaskara Rao, Editor (1997). *Trace Analysis of Uranium and Thorium*. New Delhi: Discovery Publishing House. ISBN 81-7141-375-7.

Durga Rani, K., Author and Digumarti Bhaskara Rao, Editor (2000). *Educational Aspirations and Scientific Attitudes*. New Delhi: Discovery Publishing House. ISBN 81-7141-555-55.

Dutt, B.S.V. and Digumarti Bhaskara Rao (2001). *Empowering Primary Teachers*. New Delhi: Discovery Publishing House. ISBN 81-7141-615.2.

Ediger, Marlow and Digumarti Bhaskara Rao (1996). *Science Curriculum*. New Delhi: Discovery Publishing House. ISBN 81-7141-321-8.

Ediger, Marlow and Digumarti Bhaskara Rao (2000). *Teaching Mathematics Successfully*. New Delhi: Discovery Publishing House. ISBN 81-7141-552-0.

Ediger, Marlow and Digumarti Bhaskara Rao (2001). *Teaching Science Successfully*. New Delhi: Discovery Publishing House. ISBN 81-7141-600-4.

Ediger, Marlow and Digumarti Bhaskara Rao (2001). *Teaching Social Studies Successfully*. New Delhi: Discovery Publishing House. ISBN 81-7141-596-2.

Ediger, Marlow and Digumarti Bhaskara Rao (2002). *Philosophy and Curriculum*. New Delhi: Discovery Publishing House. ISBN 81-7141-631-4.

Ediger, Marlow and Digumarti Bhaskara Rao (2002). *Improving School Administration*. New Delhi: Discovery Publishing House. ISBN 81-7141-633-0.

Ediger, Marlow and Digumarti Bhaskara Rao (2002). *Elementary Curriculum*. New Delhi: Discovery Publishing House. ISBN 81-7141-658-6.

Ediger, Marlow and Digumarti Bhaskara Rao (2003). *Language Arts Curriculum*. New Delhi: Discovery Publishing House. ISBN 81-7141-657-8.

Ediger, Marlow and Digumarti Bhaskara Rao (2004). *Teaching Language Arts Successfully*. New Delhi: Discovery Publishing House. ISBN 81-7141-678-0.

Ediger, Marlow and Digumarti Bhaskara Rao (2004). *Teaching Mathematics in Elementary Schools*. New Delhi: Discovery Publishing House. ISBN 81-7141-687-X.

Ediger, Marlow and Digumarti Bhaskara Rao (2004). *Teaching Science in Elementary Schools*. New Delhi: Discovery Publishing House. ISBN 81-7141-709-4.

Ediger, Marlow and Digumarti Bhaskara Rao (2004). *School Curriculum and Administration*. New Delhi: Discovery Publishing House. ISBN 81-7141-709-4.

Ediger, Marlow and Digumarti Bhaskara Rao (2004). *Modern Elementary School*. New Delhi: Discovery Publishing House.

Ediger, Marlow and Digumarti Bhaskara Rao (2004): *Relevancy in Elementary Curriculum*. New Delhi: Discovery Publishing House. ISBN 81-7141-751-5.

Ediger, Marlow and Digumarti Bhaskara Rao, (2004). *Teaching Social Studies in Elementary Schools*. New Delhi: Discovery Publishing House.

Ediger Marlow, B.S.V. Dutt and Digumarti Bhaskara Rao (2004). *Teaching English Successfully*. New Delhi: Discovery Publishing House. ISBN 81-7141-707-8.

Harshitha, Digumarti and Digumarti Bhaskara Rao, Editors (2004). *Educational Innovations*. New Delhi: Discovery Publishing House.

Indira Devi, Author and J. Prasanth Kumar and Digumarti Bhaskara Rao, Editors (2004). *Values in Language Text Books*. New Delhi: Discovery Publishing House.

Jayasree, Kandi, Author and Digumarti Bhaskara Rao, Editor (1999). *Correlates of Socialisation*. New Delhi: Discovery Publishing House. ISBN 81-7141-517-2.

John Babu, Chikati, Author and T.J.R. Prasad, G.M. Madhukar and Digumarti Bhaskara Rao, Editors (1996). *Problem Solving in Mathematics*. New Delhi: APH Publishing Corporation. ISBN 81-7648-273-0.

Lalitha, T., Author and K.S. Prabhakaram, D.S.N. Sastry and Digumarti Bhaskara Rao, Editors (2004). *Educational Philosophic Beliefs*. New Delhi: Discovery Publishing House. ISBN 81-7141-765-5.

Madhu Bala, Jampala, Author and Digumarti Bhaskara Rao, Editor (2004). *Adjustment Problems of Hearing Impaired*. New Delhi: Discovery Publishing House.

Marja, Talvi and Digumarti Bhaskara Rao, Editors (1996). *Educational Leadership and Social Changes*. New Delhi: Discovery Publishing House. ISBN 81-7141-320-X.

Nirmala Jyothi, M., Author and Digumarti Bhaskara Rao, Editor (2003). *Non-detention Systems in School Education*. New Delhi: Discovery Publishing House. ISBN 81-7141-654-3.

Prabhakaram, K.S., Author and Digumarti Bhaskara Rao, Editor (1998). *Concept Attainment Model in Mathematics Teaching*. New Delhi: Discovery Publishing House. ISBN 81-7141-424-9.

Prasanth Kumar, J., Author and Digumarti Bhaskara Rao, Editor (1998). *Effectiveness of Distance Education System*. New Delhi: Discovery Publishing House. ISBN 81-7141-437-0.

Prasanth Kumar, J., Author and G. Sundara Rao and Digumarti Bhaskara Rao, Editors (2000). *Open University Student Support Services*. New Delhi: Discovery Publishing House. ISBN 81-7141-550-4.

Ramatulasamma, K., Author and Digumarti Bhaskara Rao, Editor (2002). *Job Satisfaction of Teacher Educators*, New Delhi: Discovery Publishing House. ISBN 81-7141-655-1.

Rama Krishnaiah, D., Author and Digumarti Bhaskara Rao, Editor (1998). *Job Satisfaction of College Teachers*, New Delhi: Discovery Publishing House. ISBN 81-7141-438-9.

Rama Kumar Ratnam, M., Author and Digumarti Bhaskara Rao, Editor (1998). *Dukka: Suffering in Early Buddhism*. New Delhi: Discovery Publishing House. ISBN 81-7141-653-5.

Rathaiah, Lavu and Digumarti Bhaskara Rao, Editors (1996). *International Innovations in Education*. New Delhi: Discovery Publishing House. ISBN 81-7141-359-5.

Ramesh, Ganta and Digumarti Bhaskara Rao, Editors (1998). *Environmental Education: Problems and Prospects*. New Delhi: Discovery Publishing House. ISBN 81-7141-423-0.

Rathaiah, Lavu and Digumarti Bhaskara Rao (1997). *Achievement Correlates*. New Delhi: Discovery Publishing House. ISBN 81-7141-385-4.

Reddy, Sudhakar Y., Author, and Digumarti Bhaskara Rao, Editor (2003). *Creativity in Adolescents*. New Delhi: Discovery Publishing House. ISBN 81-7141-659-4.

Reddy, M.S., Author and Digumarti Bhaskara Rao, Editor (2004). *Creativity in College Students*. New Delhi: Discovery Publishing House. ISBN 81-7141-697-7.

Radramamba, B., Author and Digumarti Bhaskara Rao, Editor (2003). *Problems of Teaching*. New Delhi: APH Publishing Corporation. ISBN 81-7648-462-8.

Sanjeeva Rao, P.C., Author and Digumarti Bhaskara Rao, Editor (1996). *A Text Book of Geology*. New Delhi: Discovery Publishing House. ISBN 81-7141-313-7.

Satya Narayana V., Author and Digumarti Bhaskara Rao, Editor (2001). *Physical Education, Social Attitudes and Leadership Qualities*. New Delhi: Discovery Publishing House. ISBN 81-7141-593-8.

Srinivasulu Reddy, M., and K.R.S. Sambasiva Rao, Authors and Digumarti Bhaskara Rao, Editor (1999). *A Text Book of Aquaculture*. New Delhi: Discovery Publishing House. ISBN 81-7141-482-6.

Srinivasa Rao, Mandalapu, Author and Digumarti Bhaskara Rao, Editor (2004). *Achievement Motivation and Achievement in Mathematics*. New Delhi: Discovery Publishing House. ISBN 81-7141-674-8.

Vanaja, M. Author and Digumarti Bhaskara Rao, Editor (1999). *Inquiry Training Model*. New Delhi: Discovery Publishing House. ISBN 81-7141-515-6.

Vanaja. M. and N. Sneha Latha, Authors and Digumarti Bhaskara Rao, Editor (2004). *Student Shyness*. New Delhi: APH Publishing Corporation.

Valeri V. Koustiouk, Author and Digumarti Bhaskara Rao, Editor (2002). *A Text Book of Cryogenics*. New Delhi: Discovery Publishing House. ISBN 81-7141-642-X.

Valeri V. Koustiouk, Author and Digumarti Bhaskara Rao, Editor (2004). *Refrigeration and Environment*. New Delhi: APH Publishing Corporation.

Veena Kumari, Balusu and Digumarti Bhaskara Rao (1996). *Operation Black Board*. New Delhi: Ashish Publishing Corporation. ISBN 81-7024-711-X.

Veena Kumari, Balusu, Author and Digumarti Bhaskara Rao, Editor (2000). *Psycho-Social Correlates of Achievement*, New Delhi: Discovery Publishing House. ISBN 81-7141-547-4.

Vanaja, M., Author and Digumarti Bhaskara Rao, Editor (1999). *Inquiry Training Model*. New Delhi: Discovery Publishing House. ISBN 81-7141-515-6.

Venkata Rao, P. and Digumarti Bhaskara Rao (1989). *A Text Book of Zoology—Junior Intermediate*. Guntur: Vignan Publishers.

Venkata Rao, P. and Digumarti Bhaskara Rao (1989). *A Text Book of Zoology—Senior Intermediate*. Guntur: Vignan Publishers.

Venugopala Rao, K., Author and Digumarti Bhaskara Rao, Editor (2000). *Teacher Morale in Secondary Schools*. New Delhi: Discovery Publishing House. ISBN 81-7141-551-2.

Vidya, C., Author and Digumarti Bhaskara Rao. Editor (1996). *A Text Book of Nutrition*. New Delhi: Discovery Publishing House. ISBN 81-7141-309-9.

Vidya Bharathi, D., Author and Digumarti Bhaskara Rao, Editor (2000). *Educational Philosophies of Swami Vivekananda and John Dewey*. New Delhi: APH Publishing Corporation. ISBN 81-7648-309-9.

Books in Telugu Language

Bhaskara Rao, Digumarti (1986). *Dhrushya Sravana Bodhanapakaranalu* (Audio Visual Teaching Aids). Guntur: Nagarjuna Publishers.

Bhaskara Rao, Digumarti (1993). *Jeevasashtra Bodhana* (Teaching of Biology). Guntur: Nagarjuna Publishers.

Bhaskara Rao, Digumarti (1995). *Vignanasasthra Bodhana* (Teaching of Science) Guntur: Nagarjuna Publishers.

Bhaskara Rao, Digumarti (1997). *Vidya Manovignana Seshtram* (Educational Psychology). Guntur: Creative Press.

Bhaskara Rao, Digumarti (1998). *DSC Study Material*. Guntur: Nagarjuna Publishers.

Bhaskara Rao, Digumarti (1998). *Upadhyayudu Vidya*. (Teacher and Education). Guntur: Nagarjuna Publishers.

Bhaskara Rao, Digumarti (1998). *Vidya Drukpadalu* (Prespectives of Education). Guntur: Nagarjuna Publishers.

Bhaskara Rao, Digumarti (1999). *EdCET Teaching Aptitude*. Guntur: Nagarjuna Publishers.

Bhaskara Rao, Digumarti (2001). *Bharata Samajamulo Upadyayudu Vidya* (Teacher and Education in Emerging Indian Society). Guntur: Nagarjuna Publishers.

Bhaskara Rao, Digumarti (2001). *Bhoutika Sastra Bodhana Paddathulu* (Methods of Teaching Physical Science). Guntur: Nagarjuna Publishers.

Bhaskara Rao, Digumarti (2001). *Jeeva Sastra Bodhana Padhathulu* (Methods of Teaching Biology). Guntur: Nagarjuna Publishers.

Bhaskara Rao, Digumarti (2001). *Vidya Manovignana Sastram* (Educational Psychology). Guntur: Nagarjuna Publishers.

Bhaskara Rao, Digumarti (2003). *Patsala Yajamanyam/Paripalana* (School Management and Administration). Guntur: Nagarjuna Publishers.

Bhaskara Rao, Digumarti (2004). *Vidya Sanketika Sastram mariyu Computer Vidya* (Educational Technology and Computer Education). Guntur: Nagarjuna Publishers.